"Jarvis Williams has made a significa... contribution with this work on the Holy Spirit in Galatians. He situates his study in the Second Temple Jewish context of Paul's day and also enters the conversation with contemporary scholarship on the role of the Spirit. At the same time, he offers a robust exegetical defense of his own reading. Williams shows the danger of false polarities and thus reads Galatians as both apocalyptic and salvation-historical, as cosmic and individual. Along the same lines, he doesn't divide theology from ethics, showing that the work of the Spirit transforms individual lives and communities."

Thomas R. Schreiner, James Buchanan Harrison Professor of New Testament Interpretation at The Southern Baptist Theological Seminary

"For many years theologians have debated salvation issues in Galatians, such as justification and what Paul meant by works of the law. These conversations are important, but Williams widens the perspective to look at how the Spirit plays a crucial role in vertical, horizontal, and cosmic dimensions of the gospel. This carefully argued book demonstrates that Paul was passionate about human transformation by the living God in Christ Jesus through the Spirit."

Nijay K. Gupta, professor of New Testament at Northern Seminary

"Paul's Letter to the Galatians—a classic source for our understanding of salvation by God's grace in Christ apart from works—reaches its climax with that faith expressing itself in action. Thanks to Christ's Spirit, those in Christ are simply a different sort of people! We are grateful to Professor Williams for tracing God's energizing power through these pages."

A. Andrew Das, Niebuhr Distinguished Chair at Elmhurst University

"In *The Spirit, Ethics, and Eternal Life,* Jarvis Williams provides us with a carefully researched investigation of a crucially important set of related themes in Paul's letter to the Galatians. Painstaking scholarship is applied to topics of incredible relevance for Christian theology and living in this and any age: the intersecting themes of God's Spirit, eternal life, and Christian ethics. This book will help many gain a much better grasp of Paul's life-transforming theology and ethics, for the good of the church!"

Roy E. Ciampa, Armstrong Chair of Religion and chair of the Department of Biblical and Religious Studies at Samford University

"With his customary exegetical precision, Jarvis Williams joins his voice to a growing chorus advocating the modest but still controversial proposal: how we live actually matters to God. Williams shows that the key to holding together God's initiating grace, Christ's salvific death, and our walking in newness of life is itself a gift from God—the Holy Spirit, the promised gift that would make righteous those who trust in Christ for righteousness. He articulates a gospel that makes room for all Paul has to say about God's gracious initiatives *and* our responsibility not to receive this grace in vain."

David A. deSilva, Trustees' Distinguished Professor of New Testament and Greek at Ashland Theological Seminary

THE SPIRIT, ETHICS, AND ETERNAL LIFE

PAUL'S VISION FOR THE CHRISTIAN LIFE IN GALATIANS

JARVIS J. WILLIAMS

ivp
Academic
An imprint of InterVarsity Press
Downers Grove, Illinois

InterVarsity Press
P.O. Box 1400 | Downers Grove, IL 60515-1426
ivpress.com | email@ivpress.com

InterVarsity Press® is the publishing division of InterVarsity Christian Fellowship/USA®. For more information, visit
intervarsity.org.

All Scripture quotations, unless otherwise indicated, are translated by the author.

The publisher cannot verify the accuracy or functionality of website URLs used in this book beyond the date
of publication.

Cover design and image composite: David Fassett
Interior design: Jeanna Wiggins

ISBN 978-1-5140-0232-2 (print) | ISBN 978-1-5140-0233-9 (digital)

Printed in the United States of America ∞

Library of Congress Cataloging-in-Publication Data
A catalog record for this book is available from the Library of Congress.

30   29   28   27   26   25   24   23 | 8   7   6   5   4   3   2   1

To our beloved son,

Jordan Andrew Williams

(deceased August 24, 2020),

whom I, along with his mother and brother,

eagerly await to see and hold

on the day of resurrection

CONTENTS

ACKNOWLEDGMENTS

THIS BOOK IS THE RESULT of several years of my ongoing research on Paul's soteriology in his Second Temple Jewish context. As with previous publications, I have many people to thank for the completion and publication of this book, but space allows me only to thank a few. First and foremost, I owe thanks to my wife of twenty years, Ana, and my beloved teenage son, Jaden. They are the joys of my life! They are two of the reasons I enjoy life and my work. They keep me focused on the things that are the most important in life. And, while they always support me and my work, they thankfully often remind me that there are many more important things to life than writing books. They are absolutely right!

I thank InterVarsity Press, especially to my previous editor at IVP Academic, Ms. Anna Moseley Gissing. I am thankful to Anna for her invitation to me to submit a book proposal to IVP. She graciously expressed interest in my writing, and she worked hard to support it. She promptly responded to my emails and guided me through the proposal process. She has offered much encouragement throughout the writing process. I'm especially thankful for Anna's work and efforts to support, promote, encourage, and recruit voices of color at IVP. Many thanks to David McNutt, my current editor at IVP, for his careful work on my manuscript during the editorial process and for making the transition smooth from one editor to another.

I thank the board of trustees at The Southern Baptist Theological Seminary for granting me a research and writing sabbatical for the spring

2021 academic semester. I owe thanks to the many students at Southern Seminary who interacted with some of the content in this book through class lectures at the MDiv level and through discussions in PhD seminars. I owe many thanks to Dr. Roy Ciampa, the chair and S. Louis and Ann W. Armstrong Professor of Biblical and Religious Studies in the Howard College of Arts and Sciences at Samford University, for his kind and gracious invitation to me to deliver the September 2021 Holley-Hull lecture and for the family in whose name and honor the lecture series was established. Portions of that lecture were related to this book. I'm also thankful for the conversations I had with Roy, students, other faculty, and staff at both Samford University and Beeson Divinity School during my time at Samford. I'm especially grateful for their kind hospitality and appreciation of me and my work during my short time on campus. I'm thankful to my good friend, Dr. Ryan Lister, while a professor of Theology at Western Seminary in Portland, for his kind invitation to give lectures there related to this book. I'm thankful for both his and the seminary's kind hospitality during my time there. I'm thankful for the critical engagement of material in this book and for the interest that students and faculty showed in material related to this book. I'm thankful to Dr. Bill Hathaway, professor of psychology and executive vice president for academic affairs at Regent University in Virginia Beach for his kind invitation to lecture on material related to this book. I'm particularly grateful for the kind and gracious hospitality that the Regent University campus community showed me during my visit there, and I'm very grateful for the critical engagement of the material related to this book and the dialogue with the divinity faculty. I thank *Christianity Today* and Lexham Press for letting me publish here material that I previously published with them.

Finally, I dedicate this book to my deceased son, Jordan Andrew Williams. He was conceived on June 16, 2020. However, because of complications with the pregnancy, he died August 24, 2020, the morning the doctors told my wife and me she was pregnant. His mother, brother, and I never had the chance to see Jordan—to hold him, to kiss him, or to see him grow up—but we love him immensely nevertheless. To this day, our hearts still ache with great pain as we look forward with great joy and anticipation to the day of resurrection when we will see Jordan face to face and hold him for the first time. With intense sorrow because of the pain of his death and with intense joy that surrounds our sorrow because of our hope of resurrection in Christ, I dedicate this book to my beloved son, Jordan Andrew Williams (deceased August 24, 2020).

Introduction

Thesis, Arguments, and Contribution

In W. D. Davies's famous monograph on Paul's theology, *Paul and Rabbinic Judaism*, he boldly states, "No interpretation of Paul's doctrine of the Spirit can be accepted which does not regard it as integral to the whole of his thought."[1] Not every Pauline scholar agrees with Davies's statement, as many scholars focus their work on justification, union with Christ, or on another important part of Paul's soteriology.[2] However, the enormous history of scholarship on the Spirit in Paul shows many concur the Spirit is important to his theology.[3] The Spirit's

---

[1]W. D. Davies, *Paul and Rabbinic Judaism: Some Rabbinic Elements in Pauline Theology*, 4th ed. (Philadelphia: Fortress, 1980), 202.

[2]For example, see the numerous Pauline theologies that argue for a different center of Paul's theological thought besides the Spirit.

[3]Gordon Fee, *God's Empowering Presence: The Holy Spirit in the Letters of Paul*, 2nd ed. (Grand Rapids, MI: Baker, 2011) argues the Spirit is central to Paul's theology. I say more about this in the history of research below. For a few additional examples of the scholarship on the Spirit in Paul's theology, see bibliographies cited in Fee and in Hermann Gunkel, *The Influence of the Holy Spirit: The Popular View of the Apostolic Age and the Teaching of the Apostle Paul* (Philadelphia: Fortress, 2008); originally published in German as *Die Wirkungen des heiligen Geistes nach der populären Anschauungen der apostolischen Zeit und der Lehre des Apostels Paulus* (Göttingen: Vandenhoeck & Ruprecht, 1888); David John Lull, *The Spirit in Galatians: Paul's Interpretation of Pneuma as Divine Power*, SBLDS 49 (Chico: Scholars Press, 1980); John Yates, *The Spirit and Creation in Paul*, WUNT 2:251 (Tübingen: Mohr Siebeck, 2008); Volker Rabens, *The Holy Spirit and Ethics in Paul: Transformation and Empowering for Religious-Ethical Life*, 2nd ed. (Minneapolis: Fortress, 2014); Rodrigo J. Morales, *The Spirit and the Restoration of Israel: New Creation and New Exodus Motifs in Galatians*, WUNT 282 (Tübingen: Mohr Siebeck, 2010); C. C. Lee, *The Blessing of Abraham, the Spirit, and Justification in Galatians: Their Relationship and Significance for Understanding Paul's Theology* (Eugene, OR: Pickwick, 2013). See also the citations, appendix, and bibliography in Rabens, *The Holy Spirit and Ethics in Paul*. I use the shorthand *Spirit* throughout the book to refer to the Holy Spirit.

significance in Paul's theology in Galatians is evident by the numerous times he refers to the Spirit and to the important theological concepts he connects to the Spirit in the central section of the letter in Galatians 3:1–6:10.[4] As the title of my book suggests, my monograph focuses on only one aspect of the Spirit in Paul's letter to the Galatians: namely, the relationship between the Spirit, personal agency, ethical transformation, and eternal life.[5]

Paul explicitly mentions the Spirit numerous times in Galatians (Gal 3:2-3, 5, 14; 4:6, 29; 5:5, 16-18, 22, 25; 6:1, 8, 18).[6] In Galatians 3:2-3 and 3:5, Paul reminds the Galatians with a series of questions that they received the Spirit by faith and not by works of law. In Galatians 3:13-14, he states Jesus died so that they would receive the Spirit, which he also identifies as the blessing of Abraham (Gal 3:14). In Galatians 4:4-6, he says Jesus was born into the world as a Jewish man under the law to redeem those under the law and to give them adoption into God's family as sons. The result is that God sent forth Jesus' Spirit into the hearts of those adopted as sons attesting to the fact that God is now their Father.

In Galatians 5:16, Paul commands the Galatians to "walk in the Spirit." In Galatians 5:16-26, he argues the Galatians must walk in the Spirit to

---

[4]E.g., Jesus' representative and substitutionary death (Gal 3:13-14); Jesus' death, the Spirit, and sonship (Gal 4:6); the Spirit and justification (Gal 5:5); walking in the Spirit and eternal life (Gal 5:16, 18, 21; 6:8-9). Paul often refers to the Holy Spirit in his letters: Rom 1:4, 9; 2:29; 5:5; 7:6; 8:2, 4-6, 9-11, 13-16, 23, 26-27; 9:1; 11:8; 12:11; 14:17; 15:13, 16, 19, 30; 1 Cor 2:4, 10-14; 3:16; 4:21; 5:3-5; 6:11, 17, 19; 7:34, 40; 12:3-4, 7-11, 13; 14:2, 12, 14-16, 32; 15:45; 16:18; 2 Cor 1:22; 2:13; 3:3, 6, 8, 17-18; 4:13; 5:5; 6:6; 7:1, 13; 11:4; 12:18; 13:13; Gal 3:2-3, 5, 14; 4:6, 29; 5:5, 16-18, 22, 25; 6:1, 8, 18; Eph 1:13, 17; 2:2, 18, 22; 3:5, 16; 4:3-4, 23, 30; 5:18; 6:17-18; Phil 1:19, 27; 2:1; 3:3; 4:23; Col 1:8; 2:5; 1 Thess 1:5-6; 4:8; 5:19, 23; 2 Thess 2:2, 8, 13; 1 Tim 3:16-4:1; 2 Tim 1:7, 14; 4:22; Titus 3:5.

[5]My book primarily focuses on Galatians, but Richard Hays was correct years ago when he said, "Of all the New Testament writers, Paul offers the most extensive and explicit wrestling with ethical issues." Richard B. Hays, *The Moral Vision of the New Testament: A Contemporary Introduction to New Testament Ethics* (New York: HarperCollins, 1996), 14.

[6]He also discusses multiple theological concepts related to the Spirit in the letter without using the term Spirit (e.g., the revelation of Christ "in" Paul [Gal 1:15-16], justification by faith [Gal 2:16-17; 3:11; 5:5], walking in the truth of the gospel [Gal 2:14], co-crucifixion with Christ [Gal 2:19], living by faith in the Son of God [Gal 2:20; 3:6-9], not nullifying Jesus' death [Gal 2:21], eternal life [Gal 2:20; 3:12, 21], seed of Abraham, heirs of the promise, children of the free woman [Gal 3:29; 4:7; 4:21-31; 5:1], enslavement to love one another [Gal 5:13], doing good toward all [Gal 6:10], boasting in the cross [Gal 6:14], the recognition that neither social boundaries nor ethnic marks of distinction determine status among the people of God [Gal 3:28; 5:6; 6:15], and new creation [Gal 6:15]).

inherit the kingdom of God. In Galatians 5:18, he mentions being led by the Spirit. In Galatians 5:25, he refers to receiving life by the Spirit and conducting one's daily life by the Spirit. In Galatians 6:8-9, he states the Galatians must sow in the Spirit to inherit eternal life. Each of these statements suggests the Galatians *can* and *must* walk in step with the Spirit to inherit the kingdom of God and eternal life because of God's saving action *in* Christ *for* Jews and Gentiles and *for* the world (Gal 3:2-14; cf. 1:4). The Galatians' walk in the Spirit, that is, their ethical transformation, proves they have already begun to participate in eternal life now in this present evil age in anticipation of their inheritance of the kingdom of God in the age to come *because* of God's saving action in Christ *for* Jews and Gentiles and *for* the world (Gal 1:1, 4; 3:1–6:15). Furthermore, Paul suggests the Galatians' obedient walk in the Spirit is also *necessary to, while not the foundation upon which* they would inherit the kingdom of God and reap eternal life because of God's work in them to give them eternal life so that they would walk in the Spirit. That is, they received eternal life only by faith in Christ by the Spirit apart from works of the law, and they must walk in the Spirit so that they would inherit the kingdom of God because they received life in Christ by faith by means of the Spirit (Gal 5:5, 25). Their transformed, God-given ability to conduct themselves in obedience by the Spirit was part of God's saving action in Christ and provided the proof that God in Christ has given them life by the Spirit by faith in Christ alone (Gal 3:14; 4:5-6; 5:16-26; 6:8-9).

The "other" gospel of the opponents in Galatia, which focused not on God's saving action in Christ for Jews and Gentiles but on the human action of obedience to the law, would cause the Galatians to remain enslaved under the law's curse and to the present evil age; would only lead the Galatians to an eschatological anathema; and would cause them to return again to a life of idolatry (Gal 1:8-9; 4:8-31). Subscribing to works of the law would have never granted them freedom from the law's slavery under the power of sin to walk in obedience and freedom in the power of the Spirit as the liberated ones commanded now to love one another as themselves. To the contrary, the opponents nullified God's saving action in Christ, part of which is the distribution of the liberating Spirit into the hearts of those who have been justified by faith (Gal 1:8-9; 2:21; 3:1-14; 4:5-6; 6:8). However, Paul's gospel focuses on God's saving action in the crucified and resurrected Christ alone. One very important aspect of his gospel message to the Galatians was the work of the Spirit in their midst to free them from bondage to sin and the cosmic forces of evil, and to lead them to life now and in the age to come (Gal 1:4; 3:1–5:26).

THESIS: THE MULTIPLE DIMENSIONS OF GOD'S SAVING ACTION IN CHRIST

My thesis is twofold: first, Paul describes God's saving action in Christ for Jews and Gentiles and for the world in Galatians as vertical (justification by faith [Gal 2:16]), horizontal (love one another [Gal 2:11-14; 5:14–6:10]), and cosmic ("deliverance from the present evil age"; [Gal 1:4]); deliverance from the elementary principles of the world (Gal 4:3-11); and new creation (Gal 6:15). Second, God's vertical, horizontal, and cosmic saving action in Christ is *the* reason Paul commands the Galatians to walk in the Spirit, the reason they *can* walk in the Spirit, the reason they have life in the Spirit, and the reason they *must* walk in the Spirit to participate in eternal life now in the present evil age and to inherit the kingdom of God in the age to come.

To support my thesis, I offer the following six arguments. First, God revealed in Paul that Jesus is the good news to be preached "among the Gentiles" (Gal 1:15-16). God's revelation of his Son in Paul was both a visual and audible revelation (cf. Acts 9:1-22; 22:6-21). The Spirit was active in Paul through this revelation about the exalted Christ, compelling and convincing him by his indwelling presence and power in Paul that Jesus is the Son of God (Acts 9:1-22; 22:6-21). Paul's remarks about God sending his Son in the fullness of time to redeem us and to make us adopted members into his family supports this point about Paul's experience of the Spirit on the Damascus Road and after Ananias laid hands on him (Gal 4:4-6; cf. 1:15-16; Acts 9:1-22; 22:6-21). Prior to Damascus, Paul vigorously persecuted the church of

God (cf. Acts 7:58–8:3; 9:1-22; Gal 1:13-14). After God revealed the Son to Paul on the Damascus Road, he immediately preached that Jesus is the Son of God (Gal 1:15–2:10; cf. Acts 9:1-22).

God's sending of his Son to redeem those under the curse of the law resulted in God sending forth the "Spirit of his Son" to dwell "in our hearts" (Gal 4:6).[7] God's revelation of his Son in Paul was a revelation that indwelled him (filled) (Gal 1:15-16; cf. 3:2-3, 14; 4:6), enabled (helped) him (Gal 2:19), energized (created life in) him (Gal 2:20),[8] transformed him (Gal 1:15-23), and empowered (strengthened) him (Gal 2:8-9) to live in obedience to the gospel of Jesus Christ and to be faithful to his mission as an apostle to the Gentiles (Gal 3:14; 4:6; cf. 1:15-16). Paul realized that by this revelation of Christ in him by the Spirit, God's saving action in Christ was the moment when God invaded the present evil age to inaugurate new creation in Christ, and the moment he became crucified to the world (= to the present evil age), and the world to him (Gal 1:15-16; 2:19-20; 6:15).

Second, through Christ's death and resurrection (Gal 1:1, 4), God delivers Jewish and Gentile sinners "from the present evil age" and "from the curse of the law" by faith (Gal 1:1, 4; 3:13). Paul explicitly refers to Jesus' resurrection only once in the letter in Galatians 1:1. Each time, however, he refers to the cross in the letter, he assumes the resurrection. Because Jesus is alive, God gives life through Christ, not by the law (cf. Gal 3:21). Paul states Jesus' death delivers us "from the present evil age" (Gal 1:4), redeems "us from the curse of the law" (Gal 3:13), distributes the Spirit to Jews and Gentiles who have faith in Christ (Gal 3:1-5, 14), and gives life (Gal 3:21; 5:25) to Jews and Gentiles by faith (Gal 3:2-5, 14). Paul fronts the letter with a reference to Jesus' resurrection (Gal 1:1), and he accentuates "God revealed his Son in me" so that he would preach Jesus as good news among the

---

[7] Unless otherwise indicated, all translations of New Testament texts are mine.

[8] I borrow the language of "energism" from John M. G. Barclay, *Paul and the Gift* (Grand Rapids, MI: Eerdmans, 2015), 441-42. I apply it to the work of the Spirit in believers. This energizing work of the Spirit in believers is grounded in God's saving action in Christ for Jews and Gentiles and for the cosmos.

Gentiles (Gal 1:1, 15-16). This revelation of Christ in Paul refers to both Jesus' resurrection and exaltation (cf. Acts 9:1-22).

In Galatians, Paul highlights the cross and resurrection as the moment God acted in Christ to deliver Jewish and Gentile sinners and the cosmos from slavery to the present evil age (Gal 1:1, 4, 15, 19-20; 3:15–4:11). Paul frames the letter with references to the cross (Gal 1:4; 6:17). He either directly or indirectly refers to the cross multiple times throughout the letter.[9] He refers to the cross by mentioning Jesus' death (Gal 1:4; 2:20-21), his act of redemption (Gal 3:13; 4:5), his cross or the crucifixion (Gal 3:1, 13; 5:11; 6:12, 14), his co-crucifixion with Christ (Gal 2:19), humans crucifying the sinful passions of the flesh (Gal 5:24), or the marks of Jesus in his own body (Gal 6:17).

Third, Paul states that Jesus died on the cross to "deliver us from the present evil age" and to "redeem us from the law's curse," with the result that we receive the Abrahamic blessing of the Spirit by faith (Gal 3:13-14). God's saving action for Jews and Gentiles through Christ's death and the Galatians' experience of this salvation by faith in Christ alone was also the moment when the Galatians were adopted into God's family as sons in salvation history (Gal 4:5). God "sent the Spirit of his Son" into the hearts of Christ-following Jews and Gentiles (Gal 4:6). His Son's Spirit cries out to God as Father on behalf of those whom the Son has redeemed (Gal 4:6). The Spirit's work in them through Christ's redemption for them proves Jews and Gentiles, once enslaved to the law and to the present evil age (Gal 3:15–4:11), are now free sons and heirs of Abraham's inheritance through God (Gal 4:7–5:1, 13). The Spirit's work in Jews and Gentiles through Christ, then, proves God's deliverance of the entire creation has now broken into this present evil age in Christ (Gal 3:13-14). The distribution of the Spirit to Jews and Gentiles, who are justified by faith alone in Christ alone and who attest to their justification by faith by walking in the Spirit, proves they have received the blessing of

---

[9]For my brief discussion of the cross and the Spirit in Galatians, see Jarvis J. Williams, *Galatians*, NCCS (Eugene, OR: Cascade, 2020), 4-7; *Christ Redeemed "Us" from the Curse of the Law: A Jewish Martyrological Reading of Galatians 3.13*, LNTS 524 (New York: T&T Clark, 2019), 2-3.

Abraham, which is the Spirit (Gal 2:16; 3:6-14; 5:2-5).[10] Those who walk in the Spirit are signposts that God's saving action in Christ has begun now to renew the cosmos in this present evil age (Gal 6:15).

Fourth, the Spirit indwells (fills) (cf. Gal 3:2, 5, 14; 4:6), transforms (Gal 3:3), energizes (creates/gives life) (Gal 3:21; 5:25; 6:8; cf. 6:15), and enables, empowers, strengthens, and helps (Gal 5:5, 18, 22, 25; 6:1) Christ-following Jews and Gentiles in the assemblies of Galatia to walk in the Spirit and to live contrary to the flesh and the present evil age. Through Christ's redemption of the Galatians from the curse of the law by his death and resurrection (Gal 1:1, 4; 3:13-14), the Spirit frees the Galatians to choose actively to live by the Spirit in the present evil age (Gal 5:1, 16-26) as he gives them the fruit of the Spirit upon their participation in Christ by faith (Gal 5:22). As a result, those in Christ by the power of the Spirit triumphantly (not perfectly!) oppose the flesh and the present evil age as they walk in step with the Spirit, even while living in the present evil age (Gal 5:16-26). Because of God's saving action in Christ, the Galatians had already both conquered the flesh's power and the present evil age (Gal 1:1, 4, 15-16; 2:11–6:10), and they had already begun to participate in the renewal of creation and the hope of righteousness (Gal 5:5; 6:15).

Fifth, those in Christ have the Spirit living in them by faith (Gal 3:2-14; 4:5-7). They can and must walk in step with the Spirit to inherit eternal life (Gal 5:21) because God has definitively acted in Christ "to deliver us" and the cosmos from the present evil age (Gal 1:4; 6:15) so that we would participate in eternal life now by faith in Christ in this present evil age and in the age to come (Gal 2:16–3:29). The age to come has already broken into the present evil age by the indwelling presence and power of the Spirit (Gal 1:4; 3:14; 4:5-6; 5:16-26). The evidence of the breaking-in of the age to come now is those who participate in Christ in faith by walking in the Spirit, and they prove by their obedience that God in Christ has already begun the process of cosmic renewal (Gal 3:1–6:15).

---

[10]I argue for this reading of the genitive in the exegetical sections.

Those in Christ must walk in the Spirit to inherit eternal life, because walking in the Spirit is a manifestation of the life God has already given to all who are justified by faith in Christ and who await the "hope of righteousness by faith by the Spirit" (Gal 2:16–3:14; 5:5–6:10). The future certainty of eternal life is realized and manifested now in part through Jewish and Gentile Christ followers as they walk a path of obedience in the power of the Spirit in community with one another in the assemblies of Christ and in their daily rhythms in society because of the freedom they have in Christ by faith in the power of the Spirit (Gal 5:13–6:10).

Sixth, Paul warns the Galatians their failure to walk in the Spirit in obedience to the gospel would result in their falling short of inheriting the kingdom of God and eternal life (Gal 5:16, 21; 6:8-10). He asserts we await future righteousness (= justification) by faith "by the Spirit" (Gal 5:6). On the contrary, those who walk in accordance with circumcised flesh and the Mosaic covenant will not benefit from Christ's death in the judgment, will sever themselves from Christ, will obligate themselves to keep the entire law to gain life, will subject themselves to an apostolic curse and to the curse of the law, and will not inherit eternal life (Gal 1:8-9; 3:10; 5:2-5; 6:8-9). In Paul's view in Galatians, Christ-following Jews and Gentiles can, must, and will walk in freedom as slaves of love toward one another in obedience to the gospel in the power of the Spirit because of God's saving action *for* and *in* them through Christ and because of his liberation of creation from the present evil age. Thus, their walk of obedience in the power of the Spirit is the proof of God's saving action for them and for the cosmos through Christ and is necessary for those justified by faith alone in Christ alone to inherit the kingdom of God (Gal 5:19-21).

To be clear, according to Paul, the Galatians' obedience to the gospel in step with the Spirit is neither the fundamental *ground* of their inheritance of the kingdom of God and eternal life nor the *result of* their inheritance of the kingdom of God or eternal life. Both of these preceding ideas are contrary to Paul's argument and to his soteriology in

Galatians.[11] Rather, because of God's vertical, horizontal, and cosmic saving action in Christ for Jews and Gentiles and for the world through Christ, an obedient walk in the power of the Spirit is both the *necessary proof* that Jews and Gentiles have already begun to participate now in eternal life and necessary for anyone who participates in Christ in faith to inherit the kingdom of God and eternal life (Gal 5:21; 6:8-10). Walking in the Spirit is evidence of eternal life to be received by faith by the Spirit, and life in the Spirit is one aspect of God's saving action in Christ for Jews and Gentiles in Galatians (Gal 3:13-14; 4:5-6; 5:16–6:10), for God's saving action in Christ in Galatians is vertical, horizontal, and cosmic.

The Galatians' walk of obedience in the Spirit is one expression of the eternal life Jews and Gentiles receive by faith alone in Christ alone because of God's saving action in Christ. Jesus died for their sins to deliver them from the present evil age (Gal 1:4) and to give them the Spirit by faith, which is the blessing of Abraham (Gal 3:13-14; 4:6). Because of God's saving action in Christ, those with faith in Christ experience eternal life by the Spirit: in Galatians 5:25, Paul says "since we have life by the Spirit, let us conduct our daily lives by the Spirit." Consequently, the Galatians can, must, and will walk in the Spirit so that they will inherit the kingdom of God in the age to come. They can, must, and will sow in the Spirit so that they will reap eternal life (Gal 6:8-9). They already received eternal life in this present evil age by faith alone in Christ alone, and God in Christ had already given them life by faith by the Spirit. Jesus died to deliver them from the present evil age and to give them the Spirit by faith (Gal 1:4; 3:13-14; 4:5-6).

CONTRIBUTION

As the history of research will show, scholars have written much on the Spirit in Paul's theology. However, critical scholars have wrongly

---

[11] For a similar point, see Victor Paul Furnish, *Theology and Ethics in Paul* (Louisville: Westminster John Knox, 2009), 226. I cite the 2009 6th edition in this monograph. However, I nuance some things differently from Furnish in my discussion of the Spirit, ethical transformation, and eternal life. Furnish's comment occurs in a discussion of the indicative and the imperative in Paul's theology, not in a discussion about the Spirit.

drawn a hard and fast distinction between Paul's ethics and theology. For example, Martin Dibelius claimed in the 1960s the New Testament authors (and more specifically Paul in Gal 5–6 and Rom 12–15) created their ethical parenesis piecemeal by reproducing the moral instruction present within the general Hellenistic society in which they lived. Paul's ethical exhortations, so the argument goes, were not connected to his gospel.[12] In his famous Galatians commentary, H. D. Betz asserted Galatians 5:1–6:10 is not a uniquely Pauline Christian ethic, but Paul's ethics are simply his reflections on and conformity to the ethics of his Hellenistic contemporaries.[13]

My analysis of the relevant texts in Galatians, the concepts related to the Spirit; personal agency, ethical transformation, and eternal life in Galatians; and my analysis of selected Jewish texts will argue that Paul's ethical exhortations in Galatians are grounded in and are part of his message of God's saving action in Christ for Jews, Gentiles, and the world. A specific point I make throughout the book is that Paul's ethics are part of his soteriology in Galatians.[14] That is, God's salvation in Christ includes ethical transformation by faith and by the power of the Spirit.

With other scholars, I agree that the term *soteriology* has its limitations in New Testament studies when considering ancient texts, because the term is a modern Christian theological creation. Paul's soteriology is also complex in both Christian and Jewish New Testament scholarship. In this monograph, however, I use the term to refer to God's saving action in Christ for Jews and Gentiles and for the world. Indeed, my efforts to highlight the soteriological nature of Paul's ethics in Galatians is one of my contributions in this monograph.

---

[12]For example, see Martin Dibelius and Heinrich Greeven, *James*, trans. Michael A. Williams, Hermeneia (Philadelphia: Fortress, 1976), 5. Hays, *Moral Vision of the New Testament*, 17, pointed me to this observation.

[13]H. D. Betz, *Galatians*, Hermeneia (Philadelphia: Fortress, 1979), 292. Original citation in Hays, *Moral Vision of the New Testament*, 17.

[14]For a collection of essays on soteriology in selected texts in Second Temple Judaism, see Daniel M. Gurtner, ed., *This World and the World to Come: Soteriology in Early Judaism*, LSTS (New York: Bloomsbury, 2011).

According to Volker Rabens, Kurt Stalder is the primary scholar who focused an entire monograph on the Spirit and ethics in Paul's theology.[15] However, to my knowledge, there is not a single monograph in English-speaking scholarship on Galatians that focuses exclusively on the relationship between the Spirit, personal agency, ethical transformation, and eternal life in Galatians with an emphasis on the Spirit for the purpose of shining a fresh ray of light onto Paul's soteriology in Galatians. I also set Paul's remarks about the Spirit, personal agency, ethical transformation, and eternal life in Galatians in conversation with his comments about love of neighbor (Gal 5:13-14; 6:2) and ethnic conciliation (Gal 2:11-14; 3:28; 6:16). A third contribution comes in the conclusion, where I offer some practical suggestions regarding ways in which understanding the relationship between Paul's presentation of God's saving action in Christ, personal agency, ethical transformation, and eternal life in Galatians could shape and inform a Christian contribution to ethnic and racial discourse in the public square and a Christian ethic of social engagement, as I attempt to provide an exegetical and theological starting place from Galatians for Christians to develop a sustainable, contemporary Pauline theological ethic grounded in Paul's message of God's saving action in Christ for a rapidly changing society.

My contribution fills a void by arguing that in Galatians, Paul prioritized God's saving action in and through Christ for Jews and Gentiles and for the cosmos as the cause of and the reason for the Galatians' personal agency and ethical transformation. Ethical transformation is part of God's saving action in Christ; an obedient walk in the Spirit in the Christian community of faith and in society with real people in this present evil age is one aspect of God's saving action in Christ, and an obedient walk in the Spirt is necessary for the Galatians' future inheritance of the kingdom of God (Gal 5:21) and eternal life in the age to come (Gal 6:8-9). An obedient walk in the Spirit proves the Galatians have been justified by faith and have already begun to participate in life in the

---

[15]Kurt Stalder, *Das Werk des Geistes in der Heiligung bei Paulus* (Zurich: EVZ-Verlag, 1962). My comments about Stalder are dependent upon Rabens, *Holy Spirit and Ethics in Paul,* 253.

age to come by faith alone in Christ alone as they live now in this present evil age by walking in step with the Spirit (Gal 5:16-26). To be clear, an obedient walk in the Spirit does not justify anyone. Paul emphatically says Jews and Gentiles are justified by faith alone in Christ alone. Rather, an obedient walk in the Spirit proves that one is justified; yet obedience is necessary so that justified Jews and Gentiles will inherit the kingdom of God (Gal 5:21). Obedience is the proof, given by God's saving action in Christ to be received by faith, that God's verdict of justification is indeed true for all who have trusted by faith alone in Jesus Christ alone.

To elaborate on the above point, God's saving action in Christ is the foundational reason the Galatians initially received the Spirit by faith in Christ, participated in eternal life by faith in Christ in the present evil age, and will participate in the age to come, and the foundational reason they must obey, can obey, and will obey in step with the Spirit so that they will inherit the kingdom of God and eternal life (Gal 5:16–6:10). In Galatians, salvation is entirely about what God has done for Jews and Gentiles in Christ. As several New Testament scholars have observed, Paul, in this sense, talks about God's saving action in Christ and the soteriological benefits it accomplishes for those who receive the gift of salvation by faith in an already-not-yet tension (not contradiction!). God's saving action in Christ is the foundational reason Jews and Gentiles are justified by faith in Christ alone and are liberated from their transgressions (Gal 1:4; 3:10-13, 19) and their enslavement to sin's power (Gal 3:22-24; 4:1-9); the reason the creation is liberated from enslavement to sin and to the present evil age (Gal 1:4; 6:15); and the reason the Galatians are liberated from the power of sin in order to walk in obedience to the gospel in step with the Spirit and in love for one another (Gal 1:4; 5:1–6:10). Yet the Galatians must walk in step with the Spirit to inherit the kingdom of God (Gal 5:16-25), and they must sow in the Spirit to reap eternal life and to avoid sowing in the flesh and reaping eschatological corruption (Gal 6:8-9).

Paul's opponents preach the "other" and "distorted" gospel of works of the law in Galatia. Their gospel focuses on circumcision and the precondition of Gentiles performing human works of law to participate in eternal life now and to inherit eternal life in the age to come instead of focusing on God's saving action through the gospel of Jesus Christ alone, through whom the Galatians received the Spirit by faith alone in Christ alone (Gal 3:14; 4:5-6; cf. Gal 1:1, 4; 3:1–4:21). Human works of the law are not within the realm of God's saving action in Christ because they have no relationship with either Christ or the life-giving power of the Spirit, whom God gives to Jews and Gentiles by faith alone in Christ alone because he died for their sins to deliver them from the present evil age (Gal 1:4) and to redeem them from the curse of the law so that they would receive the Spirit as sons of God (Gal 3:13-14; 4:5-6).

Not human works of the law, but only a complete embrace of Paul's gospel by faith, leads to eternal life because Paul's gospel, and his gospel alone, focuses on God's saving action in and through Christ for Jews and Gentiles and for the world. It emphasizes a complete rejection of the opponents' gospel, which focuses on a human agency that is enslaved to the present evil age and on human works of law that enslave to the present evil age (Gal 3:15–5:1). Stated another way, only accepting Paul's gospel of God's saving action in Christ by faith alone leads to the reception of the Spirit and grants the Galatians life in the Spirit by faith, and only an obedient walk in the Spirit results in those spiritual ones (those who walk in the Spirit) inheriting the kingdom of God (Gal 5:21) and sowing in the Spirit so that they will reap eternal life and escape eschatological destruction (Gal 6:8-9). Faith in Jesus Christ alone gives the Galatians the Spirit who transforms, fills, energizes, and empowers them to participate in eternal life now in the present evil age as they experience a liberated personal agency and ethical transformation because of God's saving action in Christ (Gal 5:21). In Christ by the Spirit, the Galatians were able to make a conscious (and free!) choice to walk in step with the Spirit because they had already participated in God's saving action in Christ and received life from the Spirit (Gal 1:15–6:10).

Walking in the Spirit and ethical transformation are on the side of God's saving action in Christ, not fundamentally on the side of human action, although the Galatians must daily make a free and conscious choice to walk in step with the Spirit because of their participation in God's saving action in Christ by faith. That is, walking in the Spirit and ethical transformation are not human-generated works of obedience that serve as means by which the Galatians will inherit the kingdom of God and eternal life. Instead, an obedient walk in the Spirit is an important aspect of God's saving action in Christ (Gal 1:4; 3:1–6:15). Only those who receive God's saving action in Christ as a gift by faith are the ones in whom the Spirit dwells and are the ones who live in step with the Spirit (Gal 3:13-14; 4:5-6; 5:16-26). Furthermore, Paul's exhortations in Galatians 5:13–6:10 to walk in the Spirit are neither detached from Paul's soteriology in the letter nor from his purpose of writing Galatians.[16] Instead, Paul's exhortations to the Galatians to pursue an obedient walk in the Spirit are exhortations about the necessity and reality of personal agency and ethical transformation because of God's saving action for them in Christ. God's saving action in Christ for Jews and Gentiles creates personal agency and ethical transformation in them, and both these are part of God's saving action in Christ for Jews and Gentiles; both are part of the good news that Paul preached (Gal 1:6–6:10; esp. 3:1; 5:20-21). Both are important to his soteriology in Galatians (cf. Gal 5:13–6:10), for ethical transformation is both a direct result of the transforming power of the Spirit and necessary for inheriting the kingdom of God (Gal 5:20-21; cf. 5:16-26).

OUTLINE OF THE PROJECT

I support my thesis by an exegetical analysis of the relevant texts in Galatians. Where appropriate for my argument, I also set Paul's discussion of the relationship between the Spirit, personal agency, ethical transformation, and eternal life in Galatians in conversation both with selected Old Testament texts and Second Temple Jewish texts. I discuss

---

[16]For an early important monograph on the relationship between Gal 5:13-6:10 and the rest of the letter, see John M. G. Barclay, *Obeying the Truth: A Study of Paul's Ethics in Galatians* (Edinburgh: T&T Clark, 1988).

these Jewish texts to compare their remarks throughout the exegetical chapters about the relationship between the law, personal agency, ethical transformation, and life with Paul's statements about the relationship between the Spirit, personal agency, ethical transformation, and eternal life in Galatians.[17]

The following chapter presents a history of research on selected scholarship on the Spirit and ethics in Paul, with an emphasis on Galatians, to show my distinct contribution to the relationship between the Spirit, personal agency, ethical transformation, and eternal life in Paul's soteriology in Galatians. Chapter three discusses the relationship between God's revelation of the resurrected and crucified Christ in Galatians. I argue Paul frames his revelation of God in Christ in the language of apocalyptic and with forensic and salvation-historical language. The chapter further argues Paul connects the arrival of the Spirit amid the Galatians with God's apocalyptic invasion of the world in Christ's cross and resurrection. This chapter engages the key texts in Galatians and a few of the scholars who have highlighted apocalyptic soteriology in Galatians. The chapter further argues the flesh and the Spirit represent two different and opposing ages in Galatians. The flesh represents the old age, and the Spirit represents the new age inaugurated by Christ's cross and resurrection. As a result of these two opposing ages, Paul argues the Galatians are not free to do whatever they want (Gal 5:17). They are free to be slaves of one another in love (Gal 5:13-14).

Chapter four argues those justified by faith in Christ alone can, will, and must walk in step with the Spirit to inherit the kingdom of God. Galatians 5:21 is Paul's only explicit reference to the kingdom of God in the letter. This chapter sets my argument in the context of Paul's remarks about the Spirit, the cross, the resurrection, and the authority of his gospel in the letter. God's saving action in Christ for Jews and Gentiles and for the world was an invasive and disruptive act of sending his Son

---

[17]For a recent book on law and life in Judaism and Paul, see Preston M. Sprinkle, *Law and Life: The Interpretation of Leviticus 18:5 in Early Judaism and in Paul*, WUNT 2/1 (Tübingen: Mohr Siebeck, 2008).

to deliver Jews and Gentiles from the present evil age. His saving action in Christ granted to those justified by faith with Spirit-energized, Spirit-empowered, Spirit-transformed, and Spirit-enabling personal agency and ethical transformation in Christ. This personal agency and ethical transformation prove Jews and Gentiles have been justified by faith right now in this present evil age and guarantees they will be justified by faith on the day of judgment and participate in the future inheritance of the kingdom of God in the age to come. They have already begun to participate in it right now by faith and by the power of the Spirit.

Chapter five brings together the arguments in chapters three and four. Here I discuss Paul's comments about the Spirit, personal agency, ethical transformation, and eternal life in the context of his argument in the letter that he is anxious and deeply concerned about the Galatians' situation because they are contemplating a turn away from his gospel, which gives to them the Spirit and life by faith. Their embrace of the law, which leads to a curse, keeps them enslaved and does not give them life in the Spirit (Gal 3:1–6:10). This chapter offers a reading of the letter that gives the Spirit a more prominent role in Paul's argument than some of the other readings in the history of scholarship. If my arguments in chapters three and four are correct, then Paul's anxiety over the Galatians and his forceful arguments to persuade them from turning away from his gospel arise in part because he fears they do not have the Spirit, which he says is the blessing of Abraham. Therefore, he fears they will not inherit the kingdom of God. If they lack the Spirit, then they certainly do not have any of the soteriological blessings for which Jesus died and was resurrected since both the Spirit dwelling in the Galatians and a walk in step with the Spirit are the emblems and the signposts that they have already begun to participate in God's vertical, horizontal, and cosmic saving action in Christ for Jews and Gentiles and for the cosmos right now in this present evil age.

Chapter six reflects on the relationship between the Spirit and ethical transformation in Paul's soteriology in Galatians. This chapter makes the point that it is wrong to separate soteriology and ethics in Galatians into two separate realms. In fact, Paul would say ethics are soteriological in nature since Christians experience personal agency, ethical transformation, and eternal life because of God's saving action for them and for the cosmos in Christ. The soteriological gift of the Spirit received by faith and given because of Jesus' death for our sins and because of his resurrection from the dead liberates Jewish and Gentile Christians from the present evil age, enables them to choose life in the Spirit, and creates in them the fruit of the Spirit. This chapter also offers practical reflections related to spiritual formation and ethical transformation in daily Christian living. These reflections include setting Paul's remarks about the Spirit and ethical transformation in Galatians in conversation with his comments about love of neighbor to provide a biblical and theological foundation, grounded in Paul's theology of God's saving action in Christ for Jews, Gentiles, and the world, to develop a contemporary Christian ethic of social engagement in the public square.

2

A Selected History of Interpretation of the Spirit and Ethics in Galatians

As I stated in chapter one, work on the Spirit in Paul's theology is plentiful. However, my history of research focuses on selected scholarship on the relationship between the Spirit, personal agency, ethical transformation, and eternal life in Galatians. I discuss the scholars below in chronological order under the specific concepts into which I categorize them based on their view of the relationship between the Spirit, personal agency, ethical transformation, and eternal life.[1]

The Spirit and Ethical Power: Hermann Gunkel

In his short but classic book on the Spirit, Hermann Gunkel suggests the Spirit's activities were important to the early Christian communities.[2] He claims the presence of the Spirit in Acts and the Pauline literature supports this. Gunkel's primary concern is to study the kind of experiences both Paul and the early Christian communities thought to be derivative from the Spirit and the reason this is so. This line of

---

[1]For further discussion that covers 140 years of research "on the sanctifying work of the Spirit" and ethics in Pauline theology, see Volker Rabens, *The Holy Spirit and Ethics in Paul: Transformation and Empowering for Religious-Ethical Life*, 2nd ed. (Minneapolis: Fortress, 2014), 253-306.

[2]Hermann Gunkel, *The Influence of the Holy Spirit: The Popular View of the Apostolic Age and the Teaching of the Apostle Paul* (Philadelphia: Fortress, 2008); originally published in German as *Die Wirkungen des heiligen Geistes nach der populären Anschauungen der apostolischen Zeit und der Lehre des Apostels Paulus* (Göttingen: Vandenhoeck & Ruprecht, 1888). Source cited in this monograph is the English translation.

investigation, Gunkel claims, helps him "define" the nature of "an activity of the Spirit and thus that of the Spirit himself" and aids in revealing the connection between the Spirit and related ideas.[3] Gunkel points out Paul has a positive disposition for the gifts of the Spirit, for he too, as other Christians, experienced them,[4] while agreeing Paul had some experiences of the Spirit unique to him.[5]

Gunkel's remarks about the Spirit in Galatians are most pertinent for my work. He argues that in Galatians, the Spirit's presence and work in the cosmos "are a divine guarantee of the Christian faith."[6] Gunkel says Paul recalls to the Galatians' memory God provided conclusive evidence of validity and origins of his gospel by reminding them that he worked miracles in their midst by the Spirit (Gal 3:1-5).[7] The Spirit "is the content of that promise" given to Abraham (Gal 3:14).[8] Paul associates the inheritance of the kingdom with the promise (Gal 3:18, 29; 5:21). Thus, according to Gunkel, the Galatians' "possession of the Spirit and the future possession of the kingdom are so mutually related that they can be interchanged."[9] Since Paul speaks elsewhere of the Spirit as the seal of a future inheritance, each believer shares the destiny of inheriting the kingdom of God: "So for Paul there must be an inner connection between the concepts πνεῦμα and βασιλεία θεοῦ."[10]

The Spirit and the inheritance of the kingdom of God are not to be equated. "They belong together," but Christians receive the Spirit in this age and the inheritance of the kingdom in the future.[11] When speaking about spiritual gifts elsewhere in Paul's writings, Gunkel says they have ethical significance,[12] but he thinks the Spirit's activities are present in many "Christian functions." Paul views these functions as miraculous

---

[3]Gunkel, *Influence of the Holy Spirit*, 9-10.
[4]Gunkel, *Influence of the Holy Spirit*, 76-90.
[5]Gunkel, *Influence of the Holy Spirit*, 91-97.
[6]Gunkel, *Influence of the Holy Spirit*, 81.
[7]Gunkel, *Influence of the Holy Spirit*, 81.
[8]Gunkel, *Influence of the Holy Spirit*, 81.
[9]Gunkel, *Influence of the Holy Spirit*, 82.
[10]Gunkel, *Influence of the Holy Spirit*, 82-83.
[11]Gunkel, *Influence of the Holy Spirit*, 83.
[12]Gunkel, *Influence of the Holy Spirit*, 89.

whereas Gunkel states neither Judaism nor the early Christians regarded these functions as "a supernatural power."[13]

The Spirit should guide Christians (the spiritual ones) in every area of their lives because they can be led by the Spirit's power.[14] Gunkel further says Paul never asserts that becoming a Christian is "a work of the Spirit." He claims Paul understands Christian conversion as God's work in humanity.[15] Rather, Gunkel says, "faith is the presupposition for the reception of the Spirit (this is particularly clear in Gal 3:14)."[16]

Gunkel states Paul has conflicting views regarding the time when Christians receive the Spirit (at baptism [1 Cor 12:13]) and when they believed (Gal 3:2).[17] But the supernatural activities of the Spirit occurred at baptism.[18] However, the Spirit and power are connected in the Christian life, and the power of the Spirit is a normal rhythm of the Christian life. Christians experience both the power of the Spirit and the Spirit's activities (cf. Gal 3:4).[19] The Spirit leads Christians (Gal 5:18), but Paul "does not conceive this power energizing the Christian as something alien, something external to him and summoning him."[20] Instead, says Gunkel, Paul suggests the power of the Spirit takes hold of the believer and changes his pattern of life.[21] The Spirit is a power that "rules the Christian," and this power is "superhuman," so that the believer would not do whatever he wants (Gal 5:17).[22]

The Spirit's power is a transcendent power that performs the miracle of the Christian life when he comes upon those who have faith "in God through Christ, and in them he works God's will." One example of this, says Gunkel, is Paul identifies the Christian life as "a new creation" (Gal 6:15).[23]

---

[13]Gunkel, *Influence of the Holy Spirit*, 91.
[14]Gunkel, *Influence of the Holy Spirit*, 91.
[15]Gunkel, *Influence of the Holy Spirit*, 91.
[16]Gunkel, *Influence of the Holy Spirit*, 91.
[17]Gunkel, *Influence of the Holy Spirit*, 91.
[18]Gunkel, *Influence of the Holy Spirit*, 92
[19]Gunkel, *Influence of the Holy Spirit*, 93.
[20]Gunkel, *Influence of the Holy Spirit*, 93.
[21]Gunkel, *Influence of the Holy Spirit*, 93.
[22]Gunkel, *Influence of the Holy Spirit*, 93-94.
[23]Gunkel, *Influence of the Holy Spirit*, 94-95.

The new existence of the Christian by the Spirit is the state of one who has been "begotten of the Spirit" to become "a child of the Jerusalem above" (Gal 4:26).[24] The Spirit supernaturally intervenes in the lives of those with faith to create a break between the old creation and the new creation.[25] Paul's own experience of the Spirit in his personal transformation shows that "man can do nothing by his own natural powers" but by "him who strengthens him."[26] Paul views "the entire life of the Christian [as] an activity of the πνεῦμα." The Christian's life demonstrates "a powerful, transcendent, divine power."[27] The Spirit also does inexplicable activities. Every action of the Spirit is a miracle.[28]

The Spirit's divine activities in the lives of believers have ethical significance.[29] Christian obedience and eternal life are two different activities of the Spirit, but they "stand in organic connection with each other."[30] Gunkel asserts, according to Paul, "the result of walking in the Spirit is eternal life, just as surely and naturally as fruit results from the seed."[31] The life given to Christians by the Spirit is eternal life that has already begun right now.[32] This life given by the Spirit is both realized in the future in a heavenly existence and presently realized in moral transformation (Gal 5:25).[33]

THE SPIRIT AND CHRIST-MYSTICISM: ALBERT SCHWEITZER

In his famous book on mysticism in Paul, Albert Schweitzer discusses the role of the Spirit in Paul's soteriology under the category of "Pauline mysticism."[34] By Pauline mysticism, Schweitzer means we enter into a relationship with God only in "Christ-mysticism."[35] Paul

---

[24]Gunkel, *Influence of the Holy Spirit*, 95.
[25]Gunkel, *Influence of the Holy Spirit*, 95.
[26]Gunkel, *Influence of the Holy Spirit*, 95.
[27]Gunkel, *Influence of the Holy Spirit*, 95.
[28]Gunkel, *Influence of the Holy Spirit*, 95.
[29]Gunkel, *Influence of the Holy Spirit*, 106.
[30]Gunkel, *Influence of the Holy Spirit*, 107.
[31]Gunkel, *Influence of the Holy Spirit*, 107.
[32]Gunkel, *Influence of the Holy Spirit*, 107.
[33]Gunkel, *Influence of the Holy Spirit*, 108.
[34]Albert Schweitzer, *Mysticism of Paul the Apostle*, 3rd ed. (Baltimore, MD: Johns Hopkins University, 1998).
[35]Schweitzer, *Mysticism of Paul the Apostle*, 3.

was "in Christ."[36] In Christ, Paul knew he experienced a resurrection above this evil and fading world that we experience by the senses, and he already belonged to Christ in his bodily existence as he lived in this world.[37] In Christ, Paul was certain of future resurrection.[38] In Christ, Paul believed he was God's child.[39]

Schweizer's comments about the Spirit are interconnected to his understanding of "Christ-mysticism." According to Schweizer, the Spirit is the believer's proof of his participation in the resurrection.[40] However, Paul teaches something here that is "self-evident," while, says Schweizer, it "was not foreseen in the thought of the traditional eschatology, the teaching of Jesus, or the belief of the primitive Christian community."[41] As the Davidic Messiah, God endows Jesus with the Spirit.[42] Because he has the Spirit, Jesus is able to bring "the Kingdom of Peace."[43] The Spirit is the believer's "life-principle of His Messianic personality and of the state of existence characteristic of His Messianic Kingdom."[44] Believers partake in Jesus' Spirit because they are "predestined sharers in the glory of the Messiah."[45] The Spirit in believers "proves" to them that God has delivered them from "the natural state of existence" and placed them into the supernatural realm.[46] They are "in the Spirit," that is, not "in the flesh."[47] The believer's position "of being in the Spirit is only a form of manifestation of the being-in-Christ."[48] Both of these, however, describe "one and the same state," which is mystical union with Christ.[49] Because believers are in the Spirit, God raises them above every aspect of the

---

[36]Schweizer, *Mysticism of Paul the Apostle*, 3.
[37]Schweizer, *Mysticism of Paul the Apostle*, 3.
[38]Schweizer, *Mysticism of Paul the Apostle*, 3.
[39]Schweizer, *Mysticism of Paul the Apostle*, 3.
[40]Schweizer, *Mysticism of Paul the Apostle*, 160.
[41]Schweizer, *Mysticism of Paul the Apostle*, 160.
[42]Schweizer, *Mysticism of Paul the Apostle*, 160.
[43]Schweizer, *Mysticism of Paul the Apostle*, 160.
[44]Schweizer, *Mysticism of Paul the Apostle*, 165.
[45]Schweizer, *Mysticism of Paul the Apostle*, 165.
[46]Schweizer, *Mysticism of Paul the Apostle*, 167.
[47]Schweizer, *Mysticism of Paul the Apostle*, 167.
[48]Schweizer, *Mysticism of Paul the Apostle*, 167.
[49]Schweizer, *Mysticism of Paul the Apostle*, 167.

flesh.[50] They experience circumcision of the heart by the Spirit because
the Spirit gives them life and assures them they are God's justified children.[51] However, the believer must choose whether he will faithfully live
in step with the Spirit.[52] Otherwise, he gives up "the being-in-the-Spirit
and the resurrection state of existence, of which this is the pledge"
(Gal 5:16-17, 25; 6:7-8).[53]

Regarding the Spirit and ethical transformation, Schweitzer argues
Paul teaches ethics are a fruit of the Spirit, not a fruit of repentance
(Gal 5:22).[54] He suggests that for John the Baptist, Jesus, and "the
Primitive-Christian community," the entirety of ethics is under the category of repentance.[55] They preached the need to have a change of
attitude about past sins. This change consisted of repentance for sins
committed in the past and a resolve to live differently going forward, as
the repentant experienced liberation from earthly things and anticipated
the kingdom of the Messiah (cf. Mt 3:2; 4:17; Acts 2:38).[56] However,
according to Paul, says Schweitzer, "ethics is no longer repentance."[57]
Paul never uses the word "repentance" in an ethical context (cf. 2 Cor 7:9-10;
12:21; Rom 2:4).[58]

For Paul, repentance "is only the ethical act leading up to baptism; the
freedom from earthliness and sinfulness, which the baptized man is to
maintain, is more than repentance,"[59] for ethical living is a way of life
interconnected to Paul's concept of mystically being in Christ.[60] Because
of the believer's mystical union with the death and resurrection of Christ,
"the ethic of expectation directed towards the Kingdom of God, which
was based on belief in the Messiahship of Jesus, was transformed into

---

[50]Schweitzer, *Mysticism of Paul the Apostle*, 167.
[51]Schweitzer, *Mysticism of Paul the Apostle*, 167.
[52]Schweitzer, *Mysticism of Paul the Apostle*, 168.
[53]Schweitzer, *Mysticism of Paul the Apostle*, 169.
[54]Schweitzer, *Mysticism of Paul the Apostle*, 294.
[55]Schweitzer, *Mysticism of Paul the Apostle*, 293.
[56]Schweitzer, *Mysticism of Paul the Apostle*, 293.
[57]Schweitzer, *Mysticism of Paul the Apostle*, 293.
[58]Schweitzer, *Mysticism of Paul the Apostle*, 293.
[59]Schweitzer, *Mysticism of Paul the Apostle*, 293.
[60]Schweitzer, *Mysticism of Paul the Apostle*, 294.

the Christian ethic."[61] That is, the Christian ethic is the specific ethic that Christ produces in all who unite themselves to him by faith.[62]

According to Schweitzer, Joel's prophecy about the Spirit influenced primitive Christianity. It perceived the Spirit in terms of power that would come upon Christians because of a promise that God would work a miracle on all flesh.[63] This primitive Christian understanding, says Schweitzer, conceives of the Spirit as coming upon believers so that they can communicate with the "super earthly world" as they both receive and announce divine revelations.[64] Paul, however, connects the Spirit with mystically being in Christ. By virtue of being united with the death and resurrection of Christ via mystical union, believers receive the glorified Christ's Spirit "as the life-principle of the super-natural state of existence on which he has now entered." Consequently, ethical living "is nothing else than the Spirit's working." According to Schweitzer, Paul's view ends the "impoverishment" of Joel's view of the Spirit. He instead points his readers back to what the earlier prophets said about the Spirit: namely, "the Spirit bestows upon man a new mind and a new heart."[65]

Schweitzer says Paul can discuss ethics only by means of his mystical doctrine of being in Christ, not when he discusses his doctrine of justification by faith.[66] Paul never derives ethics from justification by faith.[67] In fact, Schweitzer says Paul affirms an "inherently irrational" position that faith neither needs nor desires works in order to reject sufficiently the importance of works.[68] As a result, Schweitzer says, Paul makes it "impossible to give ethics any real foundation."[69] Paul constructs "an ethic independent of faith-righteousness."[70] Justification, or

---

[61]Schweitzer, *Mysticism of Paul the Apostle*, 294.
[62]Schweitzer, *Mysticism of Paul the Apostle*, 294.
[63]Schweitzer, *Mysticism of Paul the Apostle*, 294.
[64]Schweitzer, *Mysticism of Paul the Apostle*, 294.
[65]Schweitzer, *Mysticism of Paul the Apostle*, 294.
[66]Schweitzer, *Mysticism of Paul the Apostle*, 294.
[67]Schweitzer, *Mysticism of Paul the Apostle*, 294.
[68]Schweitzer, *Mysticism of Paul the Apostle*, 294.
[69]Schweitzer, *Mysticism of Paul the Apostle*, 294.
[70]Schweitzer, *Mysticism of Paul the Apostle*, 294.

"faith-righteousness," makes sinners right with God; it does not transform them to live an ethical life.[71]

In Paul's theology, justification does not intersect with ethics and redemption.[72] Paul's mysticism provided him with "a concept of redemption from which ethics directly results as a natural function of the redeemed state."[73] Mysticism provides a "logical foundation for the paradox" of faith and ethics: prior to redemption, humans could not do good works, but after redemption humans can and must produce good works since Christ "brings them forth."[74] Paul's ethics are "wholly supernatural, without thereby becoming unnatural."[75] His ethics are simply "the mysticism of being-in-Christ, conceived from the point of view of will."[76] Jesus' ethics begin with an appeal to submit one's will to God. Paul, however, believes humans (prior to participation in Christ) are incapable of submitting to God's will. Paul's ethics, therefore, assume "the new creation" of the Spirit, "who has come into existence in the dying and rising again with Christ."[77]

The struggle between the flesh and the inward person in Romans 7 is a pre-baptism struggle, not a post-baptism struggle.[78] Those "in Christ" are "lord over the flesh" because they have died and risen again with Christ and because they have the Spirit.[79] They have "crucified the flesh with its passions and lusts (Gal 5:24)."[80] As a result, those in Christ are able now to "walk in the Spirit" (Gal 5:25).[81] Paul does not tell us how the new and old relate to one another (Rom 7:22).[82] He just tells us that the new is daily renewed in the midst of suffering (2 Cor 4:16),[83] and the

---

[71]Schweitzer, *Mysticism of Paul the Apostle*, 295.
[72]Schweitzer, *Mysticism of Paul the Apostle*, 295.
[73]Schweitzer, *Mysticism of Paul the Apostle*, 295.
[74]Schweitzer, *Mysticism of Paul the Apostle*, 295.
[75]Schweitzer, *Mysticism of Paul the Apostle*, 296.
[76]Schweitzer, *Mysticism of Paul the Apostle*, 296.
[77]Schweitzer, *Mysticism of Paul the Apostle*, 296.
[78]Schweitzer, *Mysticism of Paul the Apostle*, 296.
[79]Schweitzer, *Mysticism of Paul the Apostle*, 296.
[80]Schweitzer, *Mysticism of Paul the Apostle*, 296.
[81]Schweitzer, *Mysticism of Paul the Apostle*, 296.
[82]Schweitzer, *Mysticism of Paul the Apostle*, 296.
[83]Schweitzer, *Mysticism of Paul the Apostle*, 296.

new person has become a reality "through the dying and rising again with Christ."[84] The Spirit has taken hold of those in Christ;[85] they have the mind of Christ,[86] and the old, natural way of thinking no longer applies to them.[87] The Spirit enables those in Christ to do good through Jesus' death and resurrection.[88]

Paul's ethics derive "solely from the character of the new state of existence which results from the dying and rising again with Christ and the bestowal of the Spirit."[89] Believers are not perfect, but "the powers of death and resurrection are at work in them" because they have died and risen with Christ and are in union with him.[90] By the believer's will, the believer "should progressively make into a reality his death to the flesh and sin, and his being ruled in his thinking and acting by the new life-principles of the Spirit."[91] Believers demonstrate by their ethical behavior to what degree the powers of death and resurrection with Christ have worked in them.[92] At least on one occasion in Galatians (5:13–6:10), Paul describes his ethics "as the putting into operation of the dying and rising again with Christ."[93] Here he discusses the works of the flesh and the Spirit, and he commands the Galatians to walk in a manner appropriate "to their deadness of the flesh and their life in the Spirit."[94]

Schweitzer says Paul expounds his mysticism and ethics together in more detail in Romans 5:1–8:17.[95] There Paul shows unity between an "active" and "passive" ethic.[96] The only "keen" ethic is one that ethically evaluates all of our actions and experiences in life.[97] Before we can truly

---

[84]Schweitzer, *Mysticism of Paul the Apostle*, 296-97.
[85]Schweitzer, *Mysticism of Paul the Apostle*, 297.
[86]Schweitzer, *Mysticism of Paul the Apostle*, 297.
[87]Schweitzer, *Mysticism of Paul the Apostle*, 297.
[88]Schweitzer, *Mysticism of Paul the Apostle*, 297.
[89]Schweitzer, *Mysticism of Paul the Apostle*, 297.
[90]Schweitzer, *Mysticism of Paul the Apostle*, 297.
[91]Schweitzer, *Mysticism of Paul the Apostle*, 301.
[92]Schweitzer, *Mysticism of Paul the Apostle*, 301.
[93]Schweitzer, *Mysticism of Paul the Apostle*, 301.
[94]Schweitzer, *Mysticism of Paul the Apostle*, 301.
[95]Schweitzer, *Mysticism of Paul the Apostle*, 302.
[96]Schweitzer, *Mysticism of Paul the Apostle*, 302.
[97]Schweitzer, *Mysticism of Paul the Apostle*, 302.

experience ethical action, we must be "purified and liberated from the world" by our endurance of life's experiences.[98] "In the ethic of the dying and rising again with Christ passive and active ethics are interwoven as in no other."[99] Schweitzer continues. "The being 'not as the world' in action is the expression of the being made free from the world, through suffering and dying with Christ."[100] This, says Schweitzer, forms the "greatness and originality of Paul's ethics."[101] Schweitzer thinks Romans 5–8 are some of the most important chapters written about ethics.[102]

Elsewhere in his letters, Paul formulates the essence of his ethics, arising out of mystical dying and rising with Christ, in the language of "sanctification, giving up the service of sin, living for God, bringing forth fruit for God, serving the Spirit" (cf. 1 Thess 4:3; Rom 6:6, 11, 13; 8:5, 12-14; 12:1).[103] Paul's comments about righteousness/justification by faith may cause some to object to his ethical exhortations, but his mystical union with Christ explains that believers must live in obedience (Rom 6:1-2).[104] Liberation from the curse of the law does not lead to freedom to sin because the Spirit "immediately" places the liberated under Christ's new and perfect law of love (Gal 5:13-14, 18; 6:2; Rom 8:2, 4).[105] Love is the "highest manifestation" of mystical union in Christ.[106] Consequently, love is "the essence of faith."[107] Only those who have the Spirit can fulfill the law's ethics.[108] For Paul, love is the greatest expression of the Spirit.[109]

---

[98]Schweitzer, *Mysticism of Paul the Apostle*, 302.
[99]Schweitzer, *Mysticism of Paul the Apostle*, 302.
[100]Schweitzer, *Mysticism of Paul the Apostle*, 302.
[101]Schweitzer, *Mysticism of Paul the Apostle*, 302.
[102]Schweitzer, *Mysticism of Paul the Apostle*, 302.
[103]Schweitzer, *Mysticism of Paul the Apostle*, 302.
[104]Schweitzer, *Mysticism of Paul the Apostle*, 303.
[105]Schweitzer, *Mysticism of Paul the Apostle*, 303.
[106]Schweitzer, *Mysticism of Paul the Apostle*, 307.
[107]Schweitzer, *Mysticism of Paul the Apostle*, 307.
[108]Schweitzer, *Mysticism of Paul the Apostle*, 303.
[109]Schweitzer, *Mysticism of Paul the Apostle*, 309.

THE SPIRIT AND THE ETHICAL DECISION TO OBEY:
RUDOLF BULTMANN

In a significant 1924 article, Rudolf Bultmann argued Paul's command
to obey flows from his indicative of justification.[110] As scholars know
well, Martin Heidegger's existential theory influenced Bultmann's
reading of Paul.[111] Bultmann argued God frees the sinner from sin
through justification by faith. Because sin died through justification,
Paul admonishes the justified to fight against sin.[112] Bultmann acknowledges that the indicative-imperative language in Paul at first appears to
be an antinomy.[113] Paul articulates an eschatological salvation. Paul
derives the imperative from the indicative of justification.[114] For
Bultmann, however, justification is a decisive ethical act.[115]

In his *New Testament Theology*, translated in English in 1951 and in
1955 in two volumes, he explains more clearly the relationship between
his existentialist view of justification, the Spirit, and the indicative and
imperative.[116] He defines faith as "obedient submission to God's 'grace,'
the acceptance of the cross of Christ . . . the surrender of man's understanding of himself, in which he lives 'unto himself,' tries to achieve life
by his own strength, and by that very fact falls victim to the powers of
sin and death and loses himself."[117] Faith/the obedience of faith in Bultmann's view "is also released from these powers."[118] Faith bestows "the
new self-understanding," which is "freedom."[119] The believer receives life
and "his own self" by this freedom.[120] The believer experiences this
freedom because he is "ransomed" and "no longer belongs to himself

---

[110]Rudolf Bultmann, "Das Problem der Ethik bei Paulus," *ZNW* 23 (1924): 123-40.

[111]However, scholars point out Heidegger did not self-identify as an existentialist.

[112]Bultmann, "Das Problem der Ethik bei Paulus," 123.

[113]Bultmann, "Das Problem der Ethik bei Paulus," 123.

[114]Bultmann, "Das Problem der Ethik bei Paulus," 126.

[115]Bultmann, "Das Problem der Ethik bei Paulus," 129.

[116]Insight from Rabens, *Holy Spirit and Ethics in Paul*, 274.

[117]Rudolf Bultmann, *Theology of the New Testament*, 2 vols., trans. Kendrick Grobel (Waco, TX:
Baylor University Press, 2007), 1:330.

[118]Bultmann, *Theology of the New Testament*, 1:331.

[119]Bultmann, *Theology of the New Testament*, 1:331.

[120]Bultmann, *Theology of the New Testament*, 1:331.

(1 Cor 6:19)."[121] The believer entrusts himself to God as he yields "entirely to the grace of God."[122] Because of faith, the believer acknowledges he belongs to God and must live for him (Rom 14:7; cf. 7:4; Gal 2:19; 2 Cor 5:14).[123] Bultmann says the "mightiest" articulation of freedom occurs in 1 Corinthians 3:21-23: "For all things are yours . . . whether the world or life or death or the present or the future, all are yours . . . and you are Christ's; and Christ is God's."[124]

Believers' freedom in Christ liberates them from death's power to strive and will to live according to the Spirit, while being faced with the possibility of choosing to walk according to the flesh.[125] The person of faith has the freedom to make one of two choices. Yet, they are set free not to live in accordance with the flesh but in accordance with the Spirit as they serve God and Christ (Gal 5:13; cf. Rom 7:6; 14:18; 16:18).[126] The believer's freedom is not a "mysterious emancipation from sin and death considered as powers of nature."[127] This freedom from sin is the "possibility, once flung away, of realizing the commandment's intent to bestow life."[128] God required the good (life) of believers both prior to and subsequent to their deliverance.[129] According to Bultmann, therefore, freedom from the power of death means one possesses a "genuine future."[130] Contrary to the believer's former existence under death's power, now the believer has a future.[131] Consequently, infers Bultmann, Paul's command to walk in the Spirit derives from the indicative of justification by faith without contradicting it.[132]

Paul exhorts his audience to be what they are by constantly appropriating God's grace by means of faith.[133] This means by "concrete

---

[121]Bultmann, *Theology of the New Testament*, 1:331.
[122]Bultmann, *Theology of the New Testament*, 1:331.
[123]Bultmann, *Theology of the New Testament*, 1:331.
[124]Bultmann, *Theology of the New Testament*, 1:331.
[125]Bultmann, *Theology of the New Testament*, 1:331.
[126]Bultmann, *Theology of the New Testament*, 1:331-32.
[127]Bultmann, *Theology of the New Testament*, 1:332.
[128]Bultmann, *Theology of the New Testament*, 1:332.
[129]Bultmann, *Theology of the New Testament*, 1:332.
[130]Bultmann, *Theology of the New Testament*, 1:332.
[131]Bultmann, *Theology of the New Testament*, 1:332.
[132]Bultmann, *Theology of the New Testament*, 1:332.
[133]Bultmann, *Theology of the New Testament*, 1:332-33.

obedience," which is a real possibility for the believer as he walks in the Spirit since sin no longer has dominance over him (Rom 6:14).[134] Bultmann contradicts the idealistic view of moral progress by which the so-called perfect man is progressively realized in an "endless progress."[135] According to Bultmann's understanding, the state of sin-lessness (= freedom from sin's power) is currently realized by those with faith by means of God's righteousness.[136] "Its transcendence is that of the divine verdict, and man's relation to it is that of obedience of faith."[137]

The indicatives are the motivation for the imperatives.[138] An example of this is the command to "live by the Spirit" because we "walk by the Spirit" (Gal 5:25). This statement intends to avoid the "misunderstanding that there must first be a walking by the Spirit, which would then establish this living by the Spirit."[139] However, Paul's meaning, says Bultmann, "is clear": faith bestows the possibility to live by the Spirit, and faith "must be explicitly laid hold of by walking in the Spirit" since Paul's indicatives are the basis of his imperatives.[140]

Important for Bultmann's understanding of the Spirit and ethics is his understanding of baptism. Bultmann says believers receive the Spirit at baptism. Their reception of the Spirit at baptism means they are free "from the power of sin and death."[141] The conferral of the Spirit upon believers at baptism and the belief that the Spirit is "a miraculous, divine power" are general Christian views with which Paul agrees (1 Cor 6:11; 12:13; 2 Cor 1:22; cf. Rom 15:19; 1 Cor 2:4).[142] Paul uses supernatural and fluid language when he discusses the Spirit.[143] This suggests Paul is not concerned with speculation about the "idea of the Spirit."[144] Paul

---

[134]Bultmann, *Theology of the New Testament*, 1:332-33.
[135]Bultmann, *Theology of the New Testament*, 1:332.
[136]Bultmann, *Theology of the New Testament*, 1:332.
[137]Bultmann, *Theology of the New Testament*, 1:332.
[138]Bultmann, *Theology of the New Testament*, 1:333.
[139]Bultmann, *Theology of the New Testament*, 1:333.
[140]Bultmann, *Theology of the New Testament*, 1:333.
[141]Bultmann, *Theology of the New Testament*, 1:333.
[142]Bultmann, *Theology of the New Testament*, 1:333.
[143]Bultmann, *Theology of the New Testament*, 1:333.
[144]Bultmann, *Theology of the New Testament*, 1:334.

understands the Spirit as "something" that resides in a believer (Rom 8:9, 11; 1 Cor 6:19) and that is bound to a specific location.[145] However, Bultmann says, the "locution" of the Spirit should not "be taken strictly" since "locution" can also refer to the assembly of faith (1 Cor 3:16), "in which case a conception strictly corresponding to the literal wording is inconceivable."[146] Since Paul refers to the "spiritual body" (1 Cor 15:44), he "strongly suggests," says Bultmann, that the Spirit is material similar to how the concept "glory" is material.[147] But Paul's sporadic reference to the Spirit as a substance does not determine his understanding of the Spirit.[148]

The Spirit is contrary to the flesh (Gal 5:16; 6:8; Rom 8:4).[149] "Flesh is the quintessence" of the present evil age, which controls the one who lives in accordance with the flesh.[150] The Spirit is the "quintessence" of the new, unseen, independent, eternal realm, "which becomes the controlling power for and in him who orients his life 'according to the Spirit.'"[151] The flesh's power binds one to death, but the Spirit is revealed in that he "gives the believer freedom, opens up the future, the eternal, life."[152] For Paul, Bultmann asserts, freedom is the believer's openness "for the genuine future, letting one's self be determined by the future."[153] The Spirit, therefore, could be labeled "the power of futurity."[154] The believer's future determines the present; the Spirit comes to the believer at baptism and is the one by whom believers are "rightwised" (justified) at baptism (1 Cor 6:11) and become part of Christ's body (1 Cor 12:3; cf. Gal 3:27).[155] The believer's "eschatological existence" is labeled both a "being in Christ" and a "being in the Spirit" (Rom 8:9).[156] Thus, the believers can be said to

---

145 Bultmann, *Theology of the New Testament*, 1:334.
146 Bultmann, *Theology of the New Testament*, 1:334.
147 Bultmann, *Theology of the New Testament*, 1:334.
148 Bultmann, *Theology of the New Testament*, 1:334.
149 Bultmann, *Theology of the New Testament*, 1:334.
150 Bultmann, *Theology of the New Testament*, 1:334.
151 Bultmann, *Theology of the New Testament*, 1:334.
152 Bultmann, *Theology of the New Testament*, 1:334.
153 Bultmann, *Theology of the New Testament*, 1:335.
154 Bultmann, *Theology of the New Testament*, 1:335.
155 Bultmann, *Theology of the New Testament*, 1:335.
156 Bultmann, *Theology of the New Testament*, 1:335.

have Christ's Spirit, of whom it could also be said that Christ is "in you" without any difference in message.[157]

Bultmann admits that a "peculiar double meaning" exists with the word "Spirit." The Spirit can communicate the idea of the miraculous granted upon those with faith, the source of newness of life, and can also refer to the believer's daily walk on earth in step with the Spirit.[158] When Paul says to the Galatians "if we live by the Spirit, let us walk by the Spirit" (Gal 5:25), Bultmann asserts the first reference to the Spirit is to "power," and the second is another way of referring to the phrase "according to the Spirit" (as in 5:16).[159] Paul's primary concept here is "the miraculous power of God" since the Spirit has the power to liberate "from the power of sin and death" (Rom 8:2).[160] The Spirit "grants freedom of action and opens up the possibility of 'reaping eternal life'" (Gal 6:8).[161] The Spirit is also "the norm for walking."[162] The believer's "newly opened possibility" to take hold of "life" inherently has within it the idea of the ethical imperative.[163] According to Bultmann, "freedom and demand constitute a unity: Freedom is the reason for the demand, and the demand actualizes the freedom."[164]

Interpreters of Paul understand Paul's conception of the Spirit only when they grasp the unity between "freedom and demand."[165] This means that "when the Spirit is conceived of not as a mysterious power working with magical compulsion but as the new possibility of genuine, human life which opens up to him who has surrendered his old understanding of himself, letting himself be crucified with Christ, in order to experience the 'power of his resurrection' (Phil 3:10)."[166] To be led by the Spirit, thus, does not mean to be "dragged along by the

---

[157]Bultmann, *Theology of the New Testament*, 1:335.
[158]Bultmann, *Theology of the New Testament*, 1:335-36.
[159]Bultmann, *Theology of the New Testament*, 1:336.
[160]Bultmann, *Theology of the New Testament*, 1:336.
[161]Bultmann, *Theology of the New Testament*, 1:336.
[162]Bultmann, *Theology of the New Testament*, 1:336.
[163]Bultmann, *Theology of the New Testament*, 1:336.
[164]Bultmann, *Theology of the New Testament*, 1:336.
[165]Bultmann, *Theology of the New Testament*, 1:336.
[166]Bultmann, *Theology of the New Testament*, 1:336.

Spirit will-nilly," but assumes a "decision" to choose either the "flesh" or the "Spirit" (Rom 8:12-14; Gal 5:16-18; 1 Cor 12:12).[167] This unity between the concepts of "power and demand" is found within the so-called "seemingly mythological expressions" like "the mind of the Spirit" (Rom 8:6, 27) and the "desires of the Spirit" (Gal 5:17).[168] These expressions suggest the Spirit establishes a "new will," the origin of which is "within the salvation-deed of God."[169] This new will has a specific telos, liberated from the power of the flesh, now able to do battle against it, and led by God's commands.[170] Bultmann infers that herein is the "solution of the contradiction" that believers receive the Spirit at baptism and that the Spirit manifests "its operation in special deeds."[171] Both faith and "eschatological existence" come to all believers, but "this possibility must actualize itself in the concrete deed from case to case."[172]

For Paul, says Bultmann, the Spirit is responsible for ethical behavior (Rom 8:4-9).[173] The Spirit fights against the flesh (Gal 5:17).[174] The virtue list is the Spirit's fruit (Gal 5:22; cf. Rom 14:17).[175] According to Bultmann, "this is no spiritualizing, ethicizing, re-interpretation of the "Spirit" concept."[176] Instead, Paul believes that "free, ethical obedience can have its origin only in miracle."[177] God himself must free us from the chains of sin and the flesh so that we would obey him.[178] However, for Bultmann, Paul does not attribute faith as "inspired" by the Spirit.[179] Rather, he asserts, "The Spirit is the gift which faith receives (Gal 3:2, 5, 14) and in which the grace of God appropriated by faith becomes effective in

---

[167]Bultmann, *Theology of the New Testament*, 1:336.
[168]Bultmann, *Theology of the New Testament*, 1:336.
[169]Bultmann, *Theology of the New Testament*, 1:336.
[170]Bultmann, *Theology of the New Testament*, 1:336.
[171]Bultmann, *Theology of the New Testament*, 1:336-37.
[172]Bultmann, *Theology of the New Testament*, 1:337.
[173]Bultmann, *Theology of the New Testament*, 1:337.
[174]Bultmann, *Theology of the New Testament*, 1:337.
[175]Bultmann, *Theology of the New Testament*, 1:337.
[176]Bultmann, *Theology of the New Testament*, 1:337.
[177]Bultmann, *Theology of the New Testament*, 1:337.
[178]Bultmann, *Theology of the New Testament*, 1:337-40.
[179]Bultmann, *Theology of the New Testament*, 1:330.

concrete living."[180] Virtues are a fruit of the Spirit, and faith works in the realm of these virtues.[181] For example, the act of circumcision is irrelevant in Christ, but "faith working through love or a new creation" matters (cf. Gal 5:6; 6:15).[182]

NEW LIFE IN THE SPIRIT AND ETHICS: VICTOR P. FURNISH

In his *Theology and Ethics in Paul*, Victor P. Furnish discusses the sources behind Paul's theology and ethics.[183] His thesis is that the Old Testament is "a source for his ethical teaching in that it provides him with a perspective from which he interprets the whole event of God's act in Christ, and the concomitant and consequent claim God makes on the believer."[184] Paul gives specific "concrete and relevant" ethical exhortations in his letters to demonstrate to his churches their ethical responsibilities.[185] Paul recognized Christians live in a real world and their ethical responsibilities are not divorced from their critical engagement in it.[186]

Furnish argues Paul's ethical exhortations are also "inclusive." That is, Paul endeavors to avoid suggesting there are limitations to the "good" Christians must do or to the "evil" they could possibly do (cf. Phil 4:6).[187] One example to which Furnish points is Philippians 4:8, where, he suggests, Paul exhorts the Philippians to pursue all things that are virtuous.[188] "Paul's exhortations are *inclusive* at the same time

---

[180]Bultmann, *Theology of the New Testament*, 1:330.

[181]Bultmann, *Theology of the New Testament*, 1:330.

[182]Bultmann, *Theology of the New Testament*, 1:330. See also 1:314-30 for Bultmann's discussion on faith.

[183]Victor P. Furnish, *Theology and Ethics in Paul*, 6th ed. (Louisville: Westminster John Knox, 2009).

[184]Furnish, *Theology and Ethics in Paul*, 42-43. However, Furnish adds three qualifications of this thesis. First, the Old Testament and ethics in Judaism inform Paul's ethics, but "the specific collection, collation, and casuistic application of ethical rules, wisdom, and maxims seem not to be part of his purpose." Second, interpreters of Paul, therefore, must not point to the similarities between Old Testament and Jewish texts and Paul's ethics as proof that his ethical teaching is the same "in character, function, and objective with Jewish materials." Third, Jewish presence in Paul's ethics does not dismiss Hellenistic influences on him. See Furnish, *Theology and Ethics in Paul*, 43.

[185]Furnish, *Theology and Ethics in Paul*, 72-75.

[186]Furnish, *Theology and Ethics in Paul*, 74-75.

[187]Furnish, *Theology and Ethics in Paul*, 75-77.

[188]Furnish, *Theology and Ethics in Paul*, 76.

that they are concrete. . . . Paul's ethic is by no means provincial."[189] He commands his congregations "to espouse every conceivable moral excellence, to be open to every possible good and closed to every possible evil."[190]

Paul's ethical exhortations sought to persuade his churches to live an ethical life.[191] He does not appeal to a "new morality" to compel his churches to ethical responsibility.[192] Instead, he willingly uses the concepts and ideas found in the ethical norms of the culture in addition to using Scripture to persuade his audience to ethical responsibility.[193] He also appeals to them to accept what was generally viewed as a morally right and ethically proper way of life.[194]

In certain places in Furnish's monograph, he talks about the relationship between the Spirit and ethical transformation. Paul, in Galatians 5:22-23, speaks of behavioral qualities "as the fruit of the Spirit."[195] He neither describes this fruit as works nor as the believer's character traits.[196] They are instead "manifestations of the gift of God."[197] This is exactly why Paul identifies them as "fruit of the Spirit."[198] Paul neither describes the fruit in Galatians 5:22-23 as "moral duties," as one might find in pagan Hellenistic literature.[199] Rather, he describes this fruit as part of the believer's "new life in the Spirit."[200] Unlike the Hellenistic virtue tradition, Paul commands his congregations to live in accordance with the Spirit, not in accordance with their natural disposition, and he emphasizes that believers can walk in the Spirit because of God's saving action in Christ.[201]

---

[189]Furnish, *Theology and Ethics in Paul*, 77.
[190]Furnish, *Theology and Ethics in Paul*, 77.
[191]Furnish, *Theology and Ethics in Paul*, 77-81.
[192]Furnish, *Theology and Ethics in Paul*, 77-81.
[193]Furnish, *Theology and Ethics in Paul*, 77-81.
[194]Furnish, *Theology and Ethics in Paul*, 77-81.
[195]Furnish, *Theology and Ethics in Paul*, 87.
[196]Furnish, *Theology and Ethics in Paul*, 87.
[197]Furnish, *Theology and Ethics in Paul*, 87.
[198]Furnish, *Theology and Ethics in Paul*, 87.
[199]Furnish, *Theology and Ethics in Paul*, 87.
[200]Furnish, *Theology and Ethics in Paul*, 87.
[201]Furnish, *Theology and Ethics in Paul*, 89.

The powers of the present evil age seek to destroy the people of God and to cause death to reign supremely over the entire creation.[202] God's sovereign power creates life even as there is opposition between the flesh and the Spirit.[203] God himself will annihilate these forces of opposition between flesh and Spirit in the future in the age to come.[204] God's power is not "this-worldly." Instead, his power is "transcendent of this age and will have its full effect only in the age to come when the present powers are finally subdued and abolished."[205] God will likewise on this day of judgment retributively pay each human in accordance with their works in this life,[206] because "God wills the good and is aggressively opposed to what is evil."[207]

Furnish further argues Paul's doctrine of retribution is grounded in his belief that humans are responsible moral agents,[208] who by virtue of their obedience enter God's kingdom.[209] However, says Furnish, Paul affirms the reason they participate in eternal life is because of God's gift of grace (Rom 6:23).[210] God's power is "creative and redemptive," and this creative power is exercised through the gospel.[211] God's saving power causes a "new creation," which is in an entirely new relationship with its Creator (Gal 6:15).[212] God's saving power is already here and not yet realized.[213] God's not yet future saving power is already currently at work now in those in Christ, and those in Christ are "a new creation."[214]

Furnish argues that Paul asserts those in Christ have a guaranteed hope now and that they would inherit the promises God made to Abraham.[215]

---

[202]Furnish, *Theology and Ethics in Paul*, 118.
[203]Furnish, *Theology and Ethics in Paul*, 118.
[204]Furnish, *Theology and Ethics in Paul*, 118.
[205]Furnish, *Theology and Ethics in Paul*, 118.
[206]Furnish, *Theology and Ethics in Paul*, 119.
[207]Furnish, *Theology and Ethics in Paul*, 120.
[208]Furnish, *Theology and Ethics in Paul*, 120.
[209]Furnish, *Theology and Ethics in Paul*, 121.
[210]Furnish, *Theology and Ethics in Paul*, 121.
[211]Furnish, *Theology and Ethics in Paul*, 121.
[212]Furnish, *Theology and Ethics in Paul*, 125.
[213]Furnish, *Theology and Ethics in Paul*, 126.
[214]Furnish, *Theology and Ethics in Paul*, 126.
[215]Furnish, *Theology and Ethics in Paul*, 127-29.

"Paul's view of the Spirit," says Furnish, "is closely related to all these themes."[216] Paul calls the promise "the promise of the Spirit" (Gal 3:14).[217] The recipients of God's promise are children of God and likewise receive "the Spirit of [God's] Son" (Gal 4:6).[218] The Spirit testifies to the children of God that they are in fact children of God (cf. Rom 8:14, 16).[219] According to Furnish, Paul does not "equate God's Spirit with his power."[220] Still, he affirms that the Spirit "works with divine power" in the children of God.[221] Both the Spirit and divine power are "closely allied in the apostle's thinking" (cf. 1 Thess 1:5; 1 Cor 2:4).[222] The Spirit is "powerfully operative," the sign of the eschatological promise in Joel 2:28-29 with accompanying signs and wonders, and signifies for Paul the inauguration of the new age.[223]

Furnish claims that for Paul, the Spirit signifies the coming of the eschaton into the present evil age.[224] He asserts, "One might say the Spirit is the operative presence of God's love with men" (Rom 5:5).[225] The Spirit comes into the hearts of believers by faith, and thereby those in Christ are "encountered and claimed by God's love which makes him a son, thus an heir to the promise of salvation" (Gal 4:6-7).[226] The Spirit works effectively in "eschatological power" in the present evil age.[227] This, Furnish argues, Paul makes clear when he refers to the "Spirit's *life-giving* power" (cf. 2 Cor 3:6).[228] The "life-giving power of the Spirit" is the life that comes in Christ since the Spirit breaks into the present evil age because of Jesus' death and resurrection.[229]

---

[216]Furnish, *Theology and Ethics in Paul*, 129.
[217]Furnish, *Theology and Ethics in Paul*, 129.
[218]Furnish, *Theology and Ethics in Paul*, 129.
[219]Furnish, *Theology and Ethics in Paul*, 129.
[220]Furnish, *Theology and Ethics in Paul*, 129.
[221]Furnish, *Theology and Ethics in Paul*, 129.
[222]Furnish, *Theology and Ethics in Paul*, 129-30.
[223]Furnish, *Theology and Ethics in Paul*, 130.
[224]Furnish, *Theology and Ethics in Paul*, 130.
[225]Furnish, *Theology and Ethics in Paul*, 130.
[226]Furnish, *Theology and Ethics in Paul*, 130.
[227]Furnish, *Theology and Ethics in Paul*, 130.
[228]Furnish, *Theology and Ethics in Paul*, 130.
[229]Furnish, *Theology and Ethics in Paul*, 130-31.

Both the Spirit and power of God are connected with Jesus' cross and resurrection (Rom 1:3-4).[230] "In Paul's thinking . . . the work of the Spirit does not stand apart from the total 'eschatological event' of Christ's death and resurrection."[231] The Spirit's outpouring attests that God's saving power "is already operative and effective in its mission to give 'life.'"[232]

Furnish, however, makes clear that Paul suggests "the Spirit is a harbinger" and "the ground" of future hope.[233] The Spirit's power is already giving life in the present evil age (2 Cor 3:6) and will give life in the future (Rom 8:11), because he is both an actively working power and is "the ground of hope."[234] The Spirit makes a present reality the completion of salvation in Christ that is yet to come.[235] The tension between the already and not yet "finds its focal point in Paul's concept of the Spirit."[236] The Spirit's operative power brings into the present the power of the future age to come without dissolving the future age into the present evil age.[237] In Christ, believers are free to obey God.[238] In fact, Furnish asserts that Paul's view is God's redemption in Christ includes both deliverance from enslavement to the powers of the present evil age and emancipation to obey God.[239] "For Paul, obedience is neither preliminary to the new life (as its condition) nor secondary to it (as its result and eventual fulfillment). Obedience is *constitutive* of new life."[240] Paul does not, says Furnish, assume the believer's obedience spontaneously as an "expression of new life" in Christ.[241] Paul's imperatives and indicatives are integral to his theology.[242] His imperatives attempt to compel those

---

[230]Furnish, *Theology and Ethics in Paul*, 131.

[231]Furnish, *Theology and Ethics in Paul*, 131.

[232]Furnish, *Theology and Ethics in Paul*, 131.

[233]Furnish, *Theology and Ethics in Paul*, 131.

[234]Furnish, *Theology and Ethics in Paul*, 131-32.

[235]Furnish, *Theology and Ethics in Paul*, 132.

[236]Furnish, *Theology and Ethics in Paul*, 132-33.

[237]Furnish, *Theology and Ethics in Paul*, 133-35.

[238]Furnish, *Theology and Ethics in Paul*, 225.

[239]Furnish, *Theology and Ethics in Paul*, 225.

[240]Furnish, *Theology and Ethics in Paul*, 225.

[241]Furnish, *Theology and Ethics in Paul*, 227.

[242]Furnish, *Theology and Ethics in Paul*, 227.

in Christ to a "deliberate response to God's claim without which faith forfeits its distinctive character as obedience."[243] Quoting Tannehill, Furnish states, "The believer is not simply dragged along by the Spirit as if he had no choice. The believer is actively enlisted in the struggle. He is *exhorted* to not let sin reign in his body, and this exhortation is a serious matter, for by sinning the believer can fall back into the old slavery to sin."[244]

When Paul speaks of being led by the Spirit (Rom 8:14; Gal 5:18), he speaks with reference to the power of the flesh being broken, the flesh's deeds being put to death (Rom 8:12-14), and the contrast between a life led by the Spirit and a living under the law's power (Gal 5:18).[245] His remarks about the Spirit here neither speak to specific behavioral patterns nor guidance toward specific ethical actions.[246] The Spirit helps believers understand God's whole redemption in Christ to those who are mature in Christ (cf. 1 Cor 3).[247] However, Paul does not say the Spirit enables individual Christians to understand his will so as to know the difference between right and wrong.[248] In fact, Paul never, says Furnish, expounds upon a theory of how one knows the difference between good and evil.[249] Yet Paul urges his audiences to discern God's will in their lives.[250] Paul understands discernment of what is good and evil to take place in the context of community, because each believer in the community is a new creature in Christ, and each one's life is new life in the Spirit.[251] For Paul, "moral action is never a matter of an isolated actor choosing from among a variety of abstract ideals on the basis of how inherently 'good' or 'evil' each may be. Instead, it is always a matter

---

[243]Furnish, *Theology and Ethics in Paul*, 227.

[244]Furnish, *Theology and Ethics in Paul*, 227n47. For original citation in Tannehill, see Robert C. Tannehill, *Dying and Rising with Christ: A Study in Pauline Theology* (Berlin: A. Topelmann, 1967), 81.

[245]Furnish, *Theology and Ethics in Paul*, 232.

[246]Furnish, *Theology and Ethics in Paul*, 232.

[247]Furnish, *Theology and Ethics in Paul*, 233.

[248]Furnish, *Theology and Ethics in Paul*, 233.

[249]Furnish, *Theology and Ethics in Paul*, 233.

[250]Furnish, *Theology and Ethics in Paul*, 233.

[251]Furnish, *Theology and Ethics in Paul*, 233.

of choosing and doing what is good for the brother and what will upbuild the whole community of brethren."[252]

Believers, however, respond to God's "divine imperative" as "an expression of God's power to redeem and transform, not of man's power to comply and perform."[253] God gives the Christian new life in Christ, and the Spirit empowers the believer in this new life, which God displays in the believer as love (Rom 5:5) and liberates him to be a slave to God (Rom 7:6). The Christian's life is new because it is a redeemed life, not a reformed life. This redemption sets the believer free to obey, which is now realized because he has acknowledged both God's "call and claim."[254] God gives the believer the ability to do what he asks him to do. When believers hear the command, they receive the power to obey it (Phil 2:12-13; Gal 5:18-22; 6:8).[255] The fruit of the Spirit refer to the "modes of action" the believer does as "products of his life in the Spirit" (Gal 5:22).[256] The fruit are "expressions" of the power and grace of God by which believers live their lives in Christ, while they are never free from the forces of the present evil age and the flesh.[257] To the contrary, the believer's choice to obey God is at the same time a conscious decision to resist all things that stand in opposition to God's will.[258] Furnish says, "Insofar as one concretely acknowledges his dependence upon God's power, he is free to respond in obedience to God's claim; and insofar as one persists in relying on his own power to perform, he is bound in sin to the 'works of the flesh.'"[259]

THE SPIRIT AND THE CHARISMATIC EXPERIENCE OF THE FIRST CHRISTIANS: JAMES D. G. DUNN

In his classic monograph on the Holy Spirit, James D. G. Dunn focuses on baptism in the Spirit. His book exegetically argues against the

---

[252]Furnish, *Theology and Ethics in Paul*, esp. 233; cf. 234-41.

[253]Furnish, *Theology and Ethics in Paul*, 238.

[254]Furnish, *Theology and Ethics in Paul*, 238.

[255]Furnish, *Theology and Ethics in Paul*, 238-39.

[256]Furnish, *Theology and Ethics in Paul*, 239.

[257]Furnish, *Theology and Ethics in Paul*, 239.

[258]Furnish, *Theology and Ethics in Paul*, 239.

[259]Furnish, *Theology and Ethics in Paul*, 239.

Pentecostal movements of his day in the 1970s and earlier, when it was asserted that baptism in the Spirit was not an initiatory conversion experience but rather succeeded water-baptism and manifested itself in the speaking of tongues.[260] His thesis is the New Testament teaches "the baptism in or gift of the Spirit" is one of the steps in becoming a follower of Christ, including gospel-preaching, faith in Jesus of Nazareth as the Lord, and baptism in water in Jesus' name."[261] He calls this process "conversion-initiation." Baptism in the Spirit is "the chief element in conversion-initiation."[262] Only those baptized in the Spirit can be identified as Christians.[263] Dunn disagrees with Pentecostalism when Pentecostals separate baptism in the Spirit from "conversion-initiation."[264] According to Dunn, baptism in water must neither "be equated or confused with Spirit-baptism," nor should one make it the most important piece of conversion.[265] Rather "the high point in conversion-initiation is the gift of the Spirit, and the beginning of the Christian life is to be reckoned from the experience of Spirit-baptism."[266]

Dunn supports his thesis with an analysis of pertinent texts from the New Testament. When he briefly discusses Galatians, his aim is to show that the Spirit, even when baptism is not discussed, is either implied or explicitly appears in Paul's discussions about conversion-initiation.[267] For example, Dunn interprets Galatians 2:16-21 to refer to "spiritual transformation, which is conversion."[268] Dunn argues that as Paul reflects upon what conversion meant in his own experience, he articulates it as "an experience of spiritual death (to the law), resulting in new life (centered on and determined by the indwelling Christ)."[269] Dunn asserts this

---

[260]James D. G. Dunn, *Baptism in the Holy Spirit: A Re-examination of the New Testament Teaching on the Gift of the Spirit in Relation to Pentecostalism Today* (Philadelphia: Westminster, 1970), 1-7.
[261]Dunn, *Baptism in the Holy Spirit*, 4.
[262]Dunn, *Baptism in the Holy Spirit*, 4.
[263]Dunn, *Baptism in the Holy Spirit*, 4.
[264]Dunn, *Baptism in the Holy Spirit*, 4.
[265]Dunn, *Baptism in the Holy Spirit*, 4.
[266]Dunn, *Baptism in the Holy Spirit*, 4.
[267]Dunn, *Baptism in the Holy Spirit*, 106-7.
[268]Dunn, *Baptism in the Holy Spirit*, 106.
[269]Dunn, *Baptism in the Holy Spirit*, 107.

experience was not objective, "outside of Paul, operating externally on him."[270] Instead, Dunn says, Paul experienced this subjectively as "a spiritual transformation in the core of his personality."[271] Dunn admits neither baptism in the Spirit nor water-baptism occurs in this text.[272] Still, Dunn claims the Spirit's work in conversion is "implied more strongly than the rite of baptism."[273] He suggests Galatians 2:19 supports this assertion since it develops Paul's justification theology.[274] Paul, says Dunn, discusses justification later in chapter 3 "in terms of the Spirit" (Gal 3:2, 5).[275] And, Dunn says, Paul states that the life in him because of Christ "is the same thing as the life of the Spirit in me" (Gal 5:25), for Paul speaks of life as "the result of the Spirit's" work in him (Gal 3:11-14; 5:25; 6:8; cf. Rom 8:2, 10; 2 Cor 3:3, 6; 5:4).[276]

Dunn argues that Paul teaches believers receive the Spirit at the beginning of the Christian life (Gal 3:1-5, 14).[277] Justification by faith and the reception of the Spirit are different sides on the one coin of conversion.[278] Paul connects "the blessing of Abraham" with justification in 3:8 and with the Spirit in 3:14, and he states that both are experienced by faith.[279] The Spirit is the giver of life, not Torah.[280] God gives both "life and righteousness" by faith because he promised to do this.[281] The Spirit, Dunn says, according to Paul, is what God promised, and only those with faith in Christ experience this promise (3:14-22).[282] Therefore "it follows," says Dunn, that the Spirit creates those with faith into Abraham's sons, God's sons, and their faith places them "in Christ."[283] According to

---

[270]Dunn, *Baptism in the Holy Spirit*, 107.
[271]Dunn, *Baptism in the Holy Spirit*, 107.
[272]Dunn, *Baptism in the Holy Spirit*, 107.
[273]Dunn, *Baptism in the Holy Spirit*, 107.
[274]Dunn, *Baptism in the Holy Spirit*, 107.
[275]Dunn, *Baptism in the Holy Spirit*, 107.
[276]Dunn, *Baptism in the Holy Spirit*, 107.
[277]Dunn, *Baptism in the Holy Spirit*, 107-8.
[278]Dunn, *Baptism in the Holy Spirit*, 108.
[279]Dunn, *Baptism in the Holy Spirit*, 108.
[280]Dunn, *Baptism in the Holy Spirit*, 108.
[281]Dunn, *Baptism in the Holy Spirit*, 108.
[282]Dunn, *Baptism in the Holy Spirit*, 108.
[283]Dunn, *Baptism in the Holy Spirit*, 108.

Dunn, Paul thinks "becoming a Christian is therefore essentially a matter of receiving the Spirit."[284] "Faith alone," not water-baptism, in Galatians 3:2-5 is the sole reason from the perspective of humanity's experience of conversion, which Paul's remarks here suggest "revolves around preaching, faith and the Spirit."[285] Dunn argues that Galatians 3:27 (a text that interpreters often think refers to water-baptism) refers to the "conversion-initiation" of the Spirit and that Galatians 4:6 and Galatians 5:24 further support his thesis that the Spirit is received at the beginning of conversion, contrary to, as Dunn says, "Pentecostal theology."[286]

Dunn's most important work on the Spirit is his 1975 *Jesus and the Spirit*.[287] Here Dunn investigates the meaning of the "religious and Charismatic experience" of both Jesus and first-century Christians in the New Testament. Dunn's basic thesis is the New Testament reveals early Christianity's participation with God and the Spirit.

Regarding the Spirit and Paul's religious experience, Dunn argues Paul's experience of the Spirit should be understood together with his understanding of grace. He says the Spirit is "an experiential concept" to Paul.[288] That is, Paul understands the Spirit's content and importance the way he does in part because of his "experience" of the Spirit.[289]

Paul believes the Spirit works on believers' hearts, which is the center of their thoughts, feelings, and emotions, and the center of their consciousness.[290] Dunn calls this "experience I."[291] The Spirit is "the power of inner life."[292] This power helps believers turn away from all external rituals, and it makes faith in and worship of God "existentially real" (cf. Gal 4:6).[293] Dunn claims Paul presents the Spirit as a power that

---

[284]Dunn, *Baptism in the Holy Spirit*, 108.

[285]Dunn, *Baptism in the Holy Spirit*, 108-9.

[286]Dunn, *Baptism in the Holy Spirit*, 109-15.

[287]James D. G. Dunn, *Jesus and the Spirit: A Study of the Religious and Charismatic Experience of Jesus and the First Christians as Reflected in the New Testament* (Grand Rapids, MI: Eerdmans, 1997).

[288]Dunn, *Jesus and the Spirit*, 201.

[289]Dunn, *Jesus and the Spirit*, 201.

[290]Dunn, *Jesus and the Spirit*, 201.

[291]Dunn, *Jesus and the Spirit*, 201.

[292]Dunn, *Jesus and the Spirit*, 201.

[293]Dunn, *Jesus and the Spirit*, 201.

transforms humans both within and without to the point that Paul's references to "cleansing and consecration" refer to one's daily experience of walking in the Spirit (cf. 1 Cor 6:9-11).[294] The Spirit produces love and joy to overcome the evil forces of opposition that attack from outside (Rom 5:2).[295] The Spirit is the power that liberates from a rule-keeping mindset of specious reasoning and trepidation (Rom 8:2; 2 Cor 3:17) so that believers would make ethical decisions as "a matter of inward conviction and spontaneous love, of walking by the Spirit, rather than of unquestioning obedience to a law" (cf. Gal 5:25).[296]

The Spirit's work within and from humanity's heart is not "closet piety."[297] The Spirit verifies his works in the hearts of the people in whom he dwells by means of the marks of public baptism (1 Cor 12:13), by sealing believers as those who belong to Christ (2 Cor 1:22; Eph 1:13), and by believers' public obedience to the inward compulsions of the Spirit, who both "defines" and "determines" the believers' adoption in Christ.[298] In his discussion of the Spirit in Paul's letters, Dunn basically argues Paul suggests the Spirit's presence in believers is verified by clear manifestations of his presence in various experiences of gifts and ethical transformation.[299] Dunn says, the Spirit is an essential part of his theology.[300] Paul also connects the believer's experience of the Spirit to God's gracious power.[301] "Spirit" and "grace" occur in Paul's writings more than any two words to explain believers' experience of God.[302] In fact, Dunn says, "for Paul grace means *power*, an otherly power at work in and through the believer's life, the *experience* of God's Spirit."[303]

---

[294]Dunn, *Jesus and the Spirit*, 201.
[295]Dunn, *Jesus and the Spirit*, 201.
[296]Dunn, *Jesus and the Spirit*, 201.
[297]Dunn, *Jesus and the Spirit*, 202.
[298]Dunn, *Jesus and the Spirit*, 202.
[299]Dunn, *Jesus and the Spirit*, 202-361.
[300]Dunn, *Jesus and the Spirit*, 202-361.
[301]Dunn, *Jesus and the Spirit*, 202-5.
[302]Dunn, *Jesus and the Spirit*, 201-5.
[303]Dunn, *Jesus and the Spirit*, 202-3.

The Spirit and the Guarantee of Future Salvation: E. P. Sanders

Interpreters of Paul discussed matters related to the Spirit, obedience, and eternal life prior to modern scholarship.[304] Since E. P. Sanders' work on Paul changed the landscape of Pauline studies and forced a new conversation about the relationship between grace and obedience, my history of research views him as an important conversation partner in this chapter. Sanders' primary concern in *Paul and Palestinian Judaism* is to argue against the traditional view of the law and salvation in early Judaism and in Paul's soteriology. His basic thesis is Judaism was a religion of grace, not legalistic. God's election placed Jews into the covenant. Obedience enabled Jews to stay within the covenant. Paul's problem with the law was not legalism, but that Judaism was not Christianity. His reasoning worked backward from "solution to plight." Since Jesus is the Lord and Jewish Messiah, then the law must not be the pathway to covenant membership among the people of God. Since Christ is the solution, then there must be a problem. Since the solution is Christ, then the law must not be the solution.[305]

Sanders' work is relevant to my thesis on the Spirit in Galatians since he discusses the relationship between the Spirit, obedience, and life in the age to come. According to Sanders, there are two "most certain" aspects of Paul's soteriology that he "consistently" expresses: (1) God will save believers from his wrath and destroy all "unbelievers in the near future."[306] (2) All Christians possess the Spirit "as the present guarantee of future salvation."[307] Sanders says Paul states in texts like

---

[304]For additional work on the Spirit in Paul's theology that both predates Sanders and that is distinct from my argument here, see Davies, *Paul and Rabbinic Judaism*, 176-226. Davies's one chapter on the Spirit focuses on what he argues was, Paul's "Rabbinic" background. He argues Paul was a Pharisee that believed Jesus was the Jewish Messiah. He contends first-century Rabbinic Judaism provides the best background for understanding Paul. "The Pauline doctrine of the Spirit . . . is only fully comprehensible in the light of Rabbinic expectations of the Age to Come as an Age of the Spirit and community of the Spirit" (217).

[305]E. P. Sanders, *Paul and Palestinian Judaism* (Minneapolis: Fortress, 1977). See Frank Thielman's response in *From Plight to Solution* (Leiden: Brill, 1989).

[306]Sanders, *Paul and Palestinian Judaism*, 447.

[307]Sanders, *Paul and Palestinian Judaism*, 447.

1 Corinthians 15, Philippians 3:18-21, and 1 Thessalonians 4:15-17 a "generally coherent" point: "Christ will come, believers will be saved, unbelievers destroyed and all things put into subjection to God."[308] But, according to Sanders, Paul believed the Spirit's presence in believers guarantees their future salvation from his eschatological wrath in the age to come.[309] According to Sanders, participation is an integral part of Paul's soteriology.[310] Jesus' death washes/expiates previous sins.[311] His death is the means "by which one participated in Christ's death to the power of sin."[312] The Spirit guarantees that all who participate in Christ by means of his death do so in "one Spirit."[313] According to Sanders, "God has appointed Christ as Lord and savior of the world. All who believe in him have the Spirit as the guarantee of future full salvation and are at present considered to participate in Christ's body, to be one Spirit with him. As such, they are to act in accordance with the Spirit, which is also to serve Christ as the Lord to whom they belong."[314]

THE SPIRIT AND DIVINE POWER: DAVID JOHN LULL

In a monograph on the Spirit in Galatia, David John Lull argues Paul interprets the Spirit in Galatians as a "divine power."[315] Lull sets his thesis against the Gnostic myth view of Schmithals,[316] against Betz's view of "religious scrupulosity" to avoid slavery to the flesh,[317] and against Weber's theoretical view, which Lull claims suggests there was a "charismatic movement" with an "initial enthusiasm" that led to believers disregarding basic communal needs.[318] However, the believers

---

[308]Sanders, *Paul and Palestinian Judaism*, 448-52.
[309]Sanders, *Paul and Palestinian Judaism*, 450-52.
[310]Sanders, *Paul and Palestinian Judaism*, 453.
[311]Sanders, *Paul and Palestinian Judaism*, 453.
[312]Sanders, *Paul and Palestinian Judaism*, 453.
[313]Sanders, *Paul and Palestinian Judaism*, 453.
[314]Sanders, *Paul and Palestinian Judaism*, 463.
[315]David John Lull, *The Spirit in Galatia: Paul's Interpretation of Pneuma as Divine Power*, SBLDS 49 (Eugene, OR: Wipf & Stock, 1980).
[316]Lull, *Spirit in Galatia*, 3-7.
[317]Lull, *Spirit in Galatia*, 5-7.
[318]Lull, *Spirit in Galatia*, 7.

in Galatia eventually refocus their attention on the needs of the community.[319] Lull claims, however, this model does not make sense of the actual data in Galatians.[320] Instead, Lull argues the "Galatians took seriously problems with flesh" and that Paul's preaching attracted them "because it offered a solution" to the problems of the flesh.[321] Yet, the Galatians eventually thought they would not be "genuine Jews" unless they received the mark of circumcision, because they thought their conversion to Christ was actually a "conversion to Judaism."[322] The Galatians thought receiving circumcision finished the ministry that Paul began in their midst (Gal 3:3).[323]

According to Lull, Paul gave the Galatians specific instructions about ethics (Gal 5:13-6:10), but they preferred the law of Moses instead of the Spirit to help them live an ethical life.[324] Paul reminds them their course of action is "superstition," "religious scrupulosity" (Gal 4:8-10), and "apostasy" (Gal 1:6-7).[325] Lull suggests Paul informed the Galatians that because they have the Spirit, without the law of Moses, they were "genuine Jews" (i.e., members of Abraham's family) and that they were liberated from both the flesh and Torah.[326] Lull says Paul's preaching to them included instructions about ethics by their experience of the Spirit apart from obedience to the law.[327] Lull says,

> This study argues that while 6:1 is evidence that the Galatians were having "problems with the flesh," 5:13-6:10 does not provide evidence of "flagrant wrongdoing" in the Galatian churches. In these verses Paul confronts the Galatians' consideration of going the way of righteousness defined by the law of Moses, that is, of "religious scrupulosity," as the correct approach to ethics. Paul's argument is that the Galatians'

---

[319]Lull, *Spirit in Galatia*, 7.
[320]Lull, *Spirit in Galatia*, 7-8.
[321]Lull, *Spirit in Galatia*, 9.
[322]Lull, *Spirit in Galatia*, 9.
[323]Lull, *Spirit in Galatia*, 9.
[324]Lull, *Spirit in Galatia*, 9.
[325]Lull, *Spirit in Galatia*, 9.
[326]Lull, *Spirit in Galatia*, 9.
[327]Lull, *Spirit in Galatia*, 9.

experiences of the Spirit prove that without the intervention of the divine Spirit they were neither free nor able to live in accordance with the divine "will"; that the way of righteousness of obedience to the law of Moses is based on the contrary assumption; and that Scripture and tradition foretell the end of the law of Moses with the coming of Christ and of his Spirit received by faith.[328]

According to Lull, Paul wrote Galatians to inform them they did not need the law of Moses to perfect their ongoing experiences of the Spirit, for they had initially begun experiencing the Spirit by faith apart from the works of the law.[329] Paul refers to the Spirit in Galatians to remind them that the Spirit's work in their midst proves they had already received the Spirit through his preaching about the cross.[330] The Spirit's work in their midst demonstrates that Paul's gospel comes from God and that the Galatians did not need works of the law to experience the Spirit, for they received the Spirit by faith through Paul's preaching about the crucifixion of the Christ prior to their hearing about works of the Jewish law.[331]

THE SPIRIT AND ONGOING EXPERIENCES OF THE SPIRIT: CHARLES H. COSGROVE

In his book on Galatians, Charles H. Cosgrove argues the cross of Jesus is the ground for the Galatians' participation in the Spirit.[332] His thesis is, "Galatians is not about whether justification is by works or by faith, but about whether believers can promote their ongoing experience of the Sprit by doing the law."[333] By "ongoing experience of the Spirit," Cosgrove means supernatural experiences of the Spirit in the Galatian assemblies. The exegetical starting point for Cosgrove's analysis is

---

[328]Lull, *Spirit in Galatia*, 9-10.
[329]Lull, *Spirit in Galatia*, 38-39.
[330]Lull, *Spirit in Galatia*, 39.
[331]Lull, *Spirit in Galatia*, 39.
[332]Charles H. Cosgrove, *The Cross and the Spirit: A Study in the Argument and Theology of Galatians* (Macon, GA: Mercer University Press, 1988), viii.
[333]Cosgrove, *Cross and the Spirit*, 2.

Galatians 3:1-14.[334] Cosgrove claims in chapter three Paul addresses the central problem "head-on when he says 'I only want to know one thing.'"[335]

According to Cosgrove, Paul claims the Galatians experience and enjoy the Spirit because they participate in Christ. Jesus' cross is the Galatians' "sole condition for life in the Spirit."[336] The problem Paul fundamentally addresses in the letter pertains to how the Galatians received the Spirit: namely, by faith or by works of the law?[337] Paul wants the Galatians to know they received and experienced the Spirit by faith, and not by keeping Torah, before they began to contemplate life under the law.[338] According to Cosgrove, justification by faith is not the controversy in Galatia.[339] The issue is the opponents were challenging Paul's teaching that "ethical life in the Spirit forms the basis for future righteousness (justification); present righteousness (right living)—and certainly not the righteousness the Galatians think they have in the law—does not bring the Spirit."[340] However, Cosgrove argues the idea of walking in the Spirit or being led by the Spirit in Galatians does not refer to "ethical activity."[341] Instead, the question Paul answers is whether practicing Torah works, a kind of ethics, endorses "ongoing life in the Spirit, God's ongoing gift of the Spirit as sustaining presence and 'miracle.'"[342]

---

[334]Cosgrove, *Cross and the Spirit*, 2.

[335]Cosgrove, *Cross and the Spirit*, 38.

[336]Cosgrove, *Cross and the Spirit*, 38-86.

[337]When Cosgrove analyzes Gal 2:14-18, he argues Paul's point to Peter is that "he knows that the gospel does not require Jews to 'live as Jews.'" Furthermore, he argues that in a mixed Jewish and Gentile congregation, Jews were expected to surrender their allegiance to the law "insofar as it determines the scope of Judaizing, particularly the observance of dietary laws, which impedes fellowship between Jews and Gentiles" (Cosgrove, *Cross and the Spirit*, 133). He thinks verses 15-18 focus on the need for Jewish Christians to forfeit the law's boundaries for determining the scope of Judaizing. According to Cosgrove, "The concern dominating these verses is whether Jews who live in Christ 'as Gentiles' count as sinners before God." In other words, were Jewish Christians wrong to eat with uncircumcised Gentile Christians? Paul's answer, argues Cosgrove, is no.

[338]Cosgrove, *Cross and the Spirit*, 39-118.

[339]Cosgrove, *Cross and the Spirit*, 153.

[340]Cosgrove, *Cross and the Spirit*, 153.

[341]Cosgrove, *Cross and the Spirit*, 166.

[342]Cosgrove, *Cross and the Spirit*, 166.

THE SPIRIT, IDENTITY, AND BEHAVIOR: JOHN M. G. BARCLAY

In his published dissertation on Galatians, John M. G. Barclay discusses Paul's ethics.[343] Barclay's thesis is that Galatians 5:13–6:10 is an important part of Paul's argument and that his discussion in chapters 1–4 point to his ethical exhortations in Galatians 5:13–6:10.[344] Galatians is about "identity" and "behavior."[345] According to Barclay, Paul explains to the Galatians the Spirit, not the Torah, gives them everything they need to live an ethical life.[346] The Galatians' reception of the Spirit when they believed and their ongoing reliance upon the Spirit proves they need only the Spirit to live an ethical life.[347]

In a recent essay on grace in Galatians, Barclay focuses on Galatians 6:1-6, which he thinks is the "most neglected passage in the letter."[348] He argues Paul lists these specific sayings in these verses to safeguard the community from the deadly impact of "contest-culture."[349] Paul does this because "the flourishing of a community free from the usual competition for honor is integral to the meaning of the good news."[350] Barclay's argument claims "that social practice is, for Paul, the necessary expression of the Christ-gift, and that noncompetitive communities, ordered by a new calibration of worth, articulate and, in a certain sense, *define* the character of the Christ-event as an unconditioned gift."[351]

Barclay makes three precise arguments. First, Paul "re-calibrates" his understanding of the current institutions of value in the light of the "unconditioned Christ-gift."[352] By "unconditioned," Barclay means the

---

[343]John M. G. Barclay, *Obey the Truth: Paul's Ethics in Galatians* (Minneapolis: Fortress, 1988).

[344]Barclay, *Obey the Truth*, 36-251.

[345]Barclay, *Obey the Truth*, 36-251.

[346]Barclay, *Obey the Truth*, 114.

[347]Barclay, *Obey the Truth*, 85, 110-251.

[348]John M. G. Barclay, "Grace and the Countercultural Reckoning of Worth: Community Construction in Galatians 5-6," in *Galatians and Christian Theology: Justification, the Gospel, and Ethics in Paul's Letters*, ed. Mark W. Elliott et al. (Grand Rapids, MI: Baker, 2014), 306-17. For Barclay's recent monograph on grace in Romans and Galatians, see his *Paul and the Gift* (Grand Rapids, MI: Eerdmans, 2015).

[349]Barclay, "Grace and the Countercultural Reckoning of Worth," 307.

[350]Barclay, "Grace and the Countercultural Reckoning of Worth," 307.

[351]Barclay, "Grace and the Countercultural Reckoning of Worth," 307.

[352]Barclay, "Grace and the Countercultural Reckoning of Worth," 308-9.

expectation of an appropriate return of reciprocity to the gift-giver. Paul changed his view because he received "the gift of God" in the Son.[353] God's distribution of the "Christ-gift" came to Paul apart from his own value as a Torah-observant Jew and descendant of Abraham.[354] The "Christ-gift" was not given based on Paul's obedience to Torah.[355] Instead, he connects the "Christ-gift" back to the Abrahamic promises and bypasses an "incompetent Torah" with only an interim role as the pathway to the "Christ-gift."[356] According to Barclay, this is why in Christ neither Jewish nor Gentile identity matters: these real identities in Christ "cease to carry the symbolic value they enjoy outside Christ; they are relativized not by a doctrine of equality but because those baptized into Christ are reconstituted by a gift that disregards all traditional differentials in worth."[357] This explains Paul's new perception in Christ: he is "dead to the ultimate authority of the Torah."[358] This also explains why he ignores "ethnic boundaries and Torah restrictions" when he proclaims Christ to Gentiles.[359] It further explains the reason Paul says "only faith working through love," not circumcision or uncircumcision, has any worth.[360]

Because of his crucifixion to the world via his co-crucifixion with Christ, Paul now lives by a different rule.[361] This rule is "the allegiance to the Christ-event integral to the new creation (6:14-16)."[362] This new creation manifests itself in the creation of new communities with "cross-ethnic boundaries," while discounting dominant "criteria of worth."[363] This helps explain the reason Paul's first discussion of justification by faith in Galatians occurs in the context of "a cataclysmic failure" to put into practice

---

[353]Barclay, "Grace and the Countercultural Reckoning of Worth," 307.
[354]Barclay, "Grace and the Countercultural Reckoning of Worth," 307-8.
[355]Barclay, "Grace and the Countercultural Reckoning of Worth," 308.
[356]Barclay, "Grace and the Countercultural Reckoning of Worth," 308.
[357]Barclay, "Grace and the Countercultural Reckoning of Worth," 308.
[358]Barclay, "Grace and the Countercultural Reckoning of Worth," 308.
[359]Barclay, "Grace and the Countercultural Reckoning of Worth," 308.
[360]Barclay, "Grace and the Countercultural Reckoning of Worth," 308.
[361]Barclay, "Grace and the Countercultural Reckoning of Worth," 308-9.
[362]Barclay, "Grace and the Countercultural Reckoning of Worth," 309.
[363]Barclay, "Grace and the Countercultural Reckoning of Worth," 309.

the "Christ-gift" in social discourse (Gal 2:14),[364] when Peter withdrew from table fellowship with Gentile Christ followers.[365] Peter's actions suggest the "Christ-gift" is predicated upon the worth of the recipient.[366] As a result, he "betrays the gospel, which stands or falls with its revolutionary status as an unconditioned gift."[367] Communities on the receiving end of the "Christ-gift" must "recalibrate their systems of worth" or else they will "fail to enact the good news: a failure here would nullify the gift."[368]

Barclay's second argument relates to the Spirit in Galatians. It focuses on "constructing communities that reflect the gift."[369] He argues Galatians 5:13–6:10 describes and exhorts "the social expression of the good news."[370] The Galatians are free in Christ from the conventions of societal value, and they must submit to the Spirit.[371] The Spirit's authority is "the presence of the Christ-gift in their hearts and in their midst."[372] The best example of the life that comes from the Spirit is love (Gal 5:6, 13-14, 22).[373] This love is "life derived from the Spirit."[374] In Galatians, "love is the social commitment to others that forms the foundation of the community."[375] The chief manifestation of "existence in Christ" is not knowledge of the self or one's individual mastery of self for his "individual perfection,"[376] but "a pattern of prosocial behavior represented by the fruit of the Spirit (5:22-23)."[377] The Galatians' entire social discourse and social privileges must be reoriented around and by the "Christ-event."[378] The crucifixion of Jesus Christ destroyed "previous structures of allegiance."[379] Love, not law, is now "the

---

[364]Barclay, "Grace and the Countercultural Reckoning of Worth," 309.
[365]Barclay, "Grace and the Countercultural Reckoning of Worth," 309.
[366]Barclay, "Grace and the Countercultural Reckoning of Worth," 309.
[367]Barclay, "Grace and the Countercultural Reckoning of Worth," 309.
[368]Barclay, "Grace and the Countercultural Reckoning of Worth," 309.
[369]Barclay, "Grace and the Countercultural Reckoning of Worth," 309-16.
[370]Barclay, "Grace and the Countercultural Reckoning of Worth," 309-16.
[371]Barclay, "Grace and the Countercultural Reckoning of Worth," 309.
[372]Barclay, "Grace and the Countercultural Reckoning of Worth," 309.
[373]Barclay, "Grace and the Countercultural Reckoning of Worth," 309.
[374]Barclay, "Grace and the Countercultural Reckoning of Worth," 309.
[375]Barclay, "Grace and the Countercultural Reckoning of Worth," 309.
[376]Barclay, "Grace and the Countercultural Reckoning of Worth," 309.
[377]Barclay, "Grace and the Countercultural Reckoning of Worth," 309.
[378]Barclay, "Grace and the Countercultural Reckoning of Worth," 309.
[379]Barclay, "Grace and the Countercultural Reckoning of Worth," 309-10.

essence" of the new community.[380] Paul's discourse on love is neither random nor general, but it speaks to the core of "intra-communal rivalry" that was pervasive in the ancient Mediterranean world.[381] This would also challenge the culture's impulse toward demeaning someone to attain honor or the impulse toward seeing one's worth in his or her self-worth.[382]

Barclay's third argument focuses on "social practice as the definition and realization of the gift."[383] God's gift in Christ is an "unconditioned gift" in the construction of the community.[384] The "Christ-gift" neither "mirrors nor endorses" the dominant value systems.[385] The "incongruous gift" in a transformed community complies with a different set of values.[386] The obedient walk of this newly constructed community is "recognized" and "achieved" by practicing the new values of the community in Christ.[387] Because the community has crucified the flesh (Gal 5:24) when it became crucified with Christ (Gal 2:20), it shatters its former posture toward the values that are antithetical to the Spirit.[388] The community's new loyalty flows from its "alternative source of life."[389] This "alternative source of life" makes the new life in Christ recognizable when and only when the community's members resist normal procliv-ities for social honor by focusing on mutual love for one another in Christ.[390] "Social practice is not, for Paul, an addition to belief, a sequel to a status realizable in other terms: it is the expression of belief in Christ, the enactment of a life that otherwise can make no claim to be alive."[391]

---

[380]Barclay, "Grace and the Countercultural Reckoning of Worth," 310.
[381]Barclay, "Grace and the Countercultural Reckoning of Worth," 310.
[382]Barclay, "Grace and the Countercultural Reckoning of Worth," 311.
[383]Barclay, "Grace and the Countercultural Reckoning of Worth," 316.
[384]Barclay, "Grace and the Countercultural Reckoning of Worth," 316.
[385]Barclay, "Grace and the Countercultural Reckoning of Worth," 316.
[386]Barclay, "Grace and the Countercultural Reckoning of Worth," 316.
[387]Barclay, "Grace and the Countercultural Reckoning of Worth," 316.
[388]Barclay, "Grace and the Countercultural Reckoning of Worth," 316.
[389]Barclay, "Grace and the Countercultural Reckoning of Worth," 316.
[390]Barclay, "Grace and the Countercultural Reckoning of Worth," 316-17.
[391]Barclay, "Grace and the Countercultural Reckoning of Worth," 317. F. W. Horn argues the Spirit's ethical relevance in Paul's pneumatology only pertains to brotherly love. *Das Angeld des Geistes: Studien zur paulinischen Pneumatologie*, FRLANT 154 (Göttingen: Vandenhoeck & Ruprecht, 1992).

THE SPIRIT AND THE COMPLETION OF LIFE FOR GENTILE BELIEVERS: GORDON FEE

Gordon Fee produced the most comprehensive publication on the Spirit in Paul's letters and theology.[392] Fee's thesis is that the Spirit is the center of Paul's theology. His discussion of the Spirit in Galatians argues the Spirit is more significant to Paul's theology in Galatians than traditionally argued.[393] Fee thinks the Spirit "plays a leading role" in Paul's argument from Galatians 3:2 to Galatians 6:10.[394] According to Fee, Paul's argument focuses on the Galatians' experience of the Spirit instead of on their justified position before God.[395] Paul's opponents in Galatia preach a message that focuses on how "life is brought to completion (Gal 3:3)—especially for Gentile believers."[396]

Fee declares that the opponents agreed with Paul that one enters into the believing community through Jesus' death and resurrection.[397] Contrary to Paul, the opponents preached Torah observance (especially circumcision) was the means by which the Galatians' faith would come to completion.[398] They may have believed that the prophets foresaw the day when God's Spirit would help the people of God obey Torah (Jer 31:31-34; Ezek 11:19-20; 36:26-27).[399] However, Paul suggests "the gift of the Spirit, along with the death and resurrection of Christ, meant the *end* of the time of Torah."[400] The Mosaic "covenant failed precisely because it was not accompanied by the Spirit."[401] The coming of the "Christ and the Spirit" brought a new covenant, which God "ratified through the death of Christ."[402] God instituted this new covenant "through the gift of the Spirit."[403] Jesus' coming also "replaced Torah."[404]

---

[392]Gordon Fee, *God's Empowering Presence: The Holy Spirit in the Letters of Paul*, 2nd ed. (Grand Rapids: Baker, 2011).

[393]Fee, *God's Empowering Presence*, 368-69.

[394]Fee, *God's Empowering Presence*, 368-69.

[395]Fee, *God's Empowering Presence*, 368-69.

[396]Fee, *God's Empowering Presence*, 369.

[397]Fee, *God's Empowering Presence*, 369.

[398]Fee, *God's Empowering Presence*, 369.

[399]Fee, *God's Empowering Presence*, 369.

[400]Fee, *God's Empowering Presence*, 369.

[401]Fee, *God's Empowering Presence*, 369.

[402]Fee, *God's Empowering Presence*, 369.

[403]Fee, *God's Empowering Presence*, 369.

[404]Fee, *God's Empowering Presence*, 369.

Fee argues the importance of the Spirit is implicit and explicit from chapters two through six. In Galatians 2:2, Fee says the "revelation," which led Paul and Barnabas up to Jerusalem to present his gospel to the pillars, relates to the Spirit.[405] This revelation was a Spirit-guided and community-tested revelation.[406] Paul's remarks about co-crucifixion and Christ living in him attest to the Spirit living in Paul.[407] Paul, Fee observes, does not explicitly mention the Spirit.[408] Yet, if Christ dwells in believers, then the Spirit dwells in believers since Paul identifies the Spirit as the Spirit of God's Son who dwells in the hearts of Christ followers.[409]

Galatians 3:1–4:11 spells out how the believer's experiential righteousness is "predicated on Christ by his Spirit living out God's own life in us."[410] Paul's argument in chapter three is not primarily that justification by faith is the blessing of Abraham, but justification by faith "points toward the eschatological life now available to Jews and Gentiles alike."[411] This life is accomplished by Jesus' death and "realized through the dynamic ministry of the Spirit—and all of this by faith."[412]

THE SPIRIT AND AN ESCHATOLOGICAL ETHICAL CRISIS: YON-GYONG KWON

In a 2002 monograph on eschatology in Galatians,[413] Yon-Gyong Kwon's comments on the Spirit in Galatians are in the context of his discussion of the letter's eschatology. Kwon claims Paul's argument in Galatians is against the Galatians, not against his so-called opponents. Paul emphasizes their deviation from his gospel threatens the "not-yet" aspects of

---

[405]Fee, God's Empowering Presence, 369.
[406]Fee, God's Empowering Presence, 372-73.
[407]Fee, God's Empowering Presence, 374.
[408]Fee, God's Empowering Presence, 374.
[409]Fee, God's Empowering Presence, 374.
[410]Fee, God's Empowering Presence, 377-416.
[411]Fee, God's Empowering Presence, 395.
[412]Fee, God's Empowering Presence, 395.
[413]Yon-Gyong Kwon, Eschatology in Galatians: Rethinking Paul's Response in Galatia, WUNT 183 (Tübingen: Mohr Siebeck, 2002).

the blessing of Abraham. It does not focus on the "already" experiences of the Spirit. Accordingly, Paul's argument to dissuade the Galatians from turning away from his gospel is eschatological. However, his argument focuses on the not yet without ignoring or denying the already aspects of his eschatology.[414]

Kwon divides his analysis in three sections: (1) "fully realized eschatology," (2) "the eschatological tension between the 'already and not yet,'" and (3) "future eschatology."[415] Kwon also discusses Betz's view of "future eschatological justification."[416] Kwon's analysis focuses primarily on eschatology in Galatians, not on what scholars have said about eschatology in Galatians.[417]

Kwon discusses Burton under the *fully realized* eschatological view.[418] He states that Burton's traditional view of justification, which focuses on the Galatians' present justification by faith as the reason for their standing in the family of Abraham, does not deny the not-yet elements of Paul's eschatology. Instead, Kwon claims that Burton asserts Paul doesn't emphasize the not yet as an important part of his argument as to why the Galatians should not turn away from his gospel.

Kwon next discusses the "realized eschatological convictions of Paul."[419] According to Kwon, this view says that Paul's argument against Torah combats the Galatians' "realized eschatological convictions of Paul."[420] He says, "the coming of Christ has established a new era and thereby rendered the law obsolete."[421] This view is, Kwon says, "often combined with a strong Christological or theocentric orientation."[422] Kwon claims this approach is attractive because it avoids having to explain Paul's critiques of the law.[423]

---

[414]Kwon, *Eschatology in Galatians*, 18-19.
[415]Kwon, *Eschatology in Galatians*, 2.
[416]Kwon, *Eschatology in Galatians*, 2-3.
[417]Kwon, *Eschatology in Galatians*, 3.
[418]Kwon, *Eschatology in Galatians*, 3-4.
[419]Kwon, *Eschatology in Galatians*, 7.
[420]Kwon, *Eschatology in Galatians*, 7.
[421]Kwon, *Eschatology in Galatians*, 7.
[422]Kwon, *Eschatology in Galatians*, 7-8.
[423]Kwon, *Eschatology in Galatians*, 8.

Kwon next discusses the "eschatological already and not yet" view.[424] Yet, he suggests the "future eschatological" force of Paul's argument is maintained within the "already and not yet" scheme.[425] Kwon discusses "libertinism and Paul's future eschatology view."[426] This view basically argues that Paul warns that libertinism will cause the Galatians to miss out on future eschatology,[427] and that justification always points to the future. This is Kwon's view.[428]

Kwon argues Paul's remarks in Galatians 1:6, 8-9, 3:1-5, and 4:18-20 support the premise that his polemic is against the Galatians who are turning away from the gospel instead of against those who entered the churches of Galatia preaching another gospel contrary to Paul's.[429] Kwon argues Paul understands the Galatian problem from a "future-oriented perspective."[430] According to Kwon, Paul thinks the Galatians' "deviation" is dangerous because it both threatens their future and Paul's.[431] This is why Paul fears perhaps his ministry among them was in vain; he speaks of the Galatians as beginning in the Spirit but trying to finish by the flesh, of Christ not benefiting them in the future, and of quitting the race.[432] Kwon argues justification is central and awaits the Galatians in the future.[433] According to Kwon, Paul says nothing about a present justification in Galatians, unlike in Romans.[434]

Kwon claims the promise and inheritance are distinct in Paul's argument in Galatians.[435] He argues the promise and Spirit are different.[436] Paul's remarks about the Spirit as a fulfillment of the promise refer to the

---

[424]Kwon, *Eschatology in Galatians*, 13-16.

[425]Kwon, *Eschatology in Galatians*, 13-16.

[426]Kwon, *Eschatology in Galatians*, 16-17.

[427]Kwon, *Eschatology in Galatians*, 16-18.

[428]Kwon thinks Betz's view of justification in Galatians contradicts his exposition of Paul's argument in the letter because Betz identifies the blessing with justification (18).

[429]Kwon, *Eschatology in Galatians*, 26-50, esp. 31-50.

[430]Kwon, *Eschatology in Galatians*, 42.

[431]Kwon, *Eschatology in Galatians*, 42.

[432]Kwon, *Eschatology in Galatians*, 42-49.

[433]Kwon, *Eschatology in Galatians*, 51-77.

[434]Kwon, *Eschatology in Galatians*, 51-77.

[435]Kwon, *Eschatology in Galatians*, 101-29.

[436]Kwon, *Eschatology in Galatians*, 107-17.

fulfillment of the "prophetic promise."[437] He argues against the idea that the Spirit "signifies the time of fulfillment."[438] The Spirit identifies those who are sons, but Paul nowhere says the Spirit is the inheritance.[439] Thus, Paul's christological argument in Galatians to discourage them from apostasy is not an argument based on "realized eschatology."[440] In Galatians, when Paul says "by faith" or "in Christ," he means "through the Spirit."[441]

Kwon concludes the crisis in Galatia is mainly ethical.[442] He supports this premise by arguing that circumcision and the law are moral issues.[443] He further argues Paul makes a moral argument in Galatians.[444] Kwon argues Paul's problem with circumcision is that the Galatians neglect faith working through love because they embrace circumcision. That is, circumcision causes them to deviate from the ethics of love.[445]

ESCHATOLOGICAL OUTPOURING OF THE SPIRIT: FINNY PHILIP

In a 2005 monograph, Finny Philip investigates the origins of pneumatology in Paul's theology.[446] His thesis is Paul's view of the Holy Spirit derives from his belief that God poured out his Spirit on Gentiles without requiring them to observe Torah.[447] His personal experience on the Damascus Road and his personal work as a missionary among the Gentiles in Antioch are foundational to Paul's thinking about the Spirit's presence among the Gentiles.[448] Philip's work is primarily seeking to answer questions of origins, not to discuss the relationship between the Spirit, agency, ethical transformation, and eternal life.

---

[437]Kwon, *Eschatology in Galatians*, 117-27.
[438]Kwon, *Eschatology in Galatians*, 138-41.
[439]Kwon, *Eschatology in Galatians*, 141-43.
[440]Kwon, *Eschatology in Galatians*, 155-82.
[441]Kwon, *Eschatology in Galatians*, 181-82.
[442]Kwon, *Eschatology in Galatians*, 184-212, esp. 191.
[443]Kwon, *Eschatology in Galatians*, 192-98.
[444]Kwon, *Eschatology in Galatians*, 198-212.
[445]Kwon, *Eschatology in Galatians*, 192-95.
[446]Finny Philip, *The Origins of Pauline Pneumatology: The Eschatological Bestowal of the Spirit Upon Gentiles in Judaism and in the Early Development of Paul's Theology*, WUNT 194 (Tübingen: Mohr Siebeck, 2005).
[447]Philip, *Origins of Pauline Pneumatology*, 27.
[448]Philip, *Origins of Pauline Pneumatology*, 27.

His monograph has one primary aim: to investigate Paul's belief of the outpouring of the Spirit on Gentile Christians apart from works of the law.[449] This aim has two objectives. First, Philip seeks to identify both the essence and the size of Paul's belief of Gentile reception of the Spirit by answering whether Paul foresaw a bestowal of the Spirit upon the Gentiles apart from Torah observance, whether he expected the Spirit would come upon the Gentiles during his missionary work in their midst, and whether he was baffled when the Gentiles received the Spirit without their becoming proselytes to Judaism.[450] Second, Philip seeks to offer a compelling explanation as to why Paul thought the way he did about the outpouring of the Spirit among the Gentiles. Philip endeavors to offer his explanation by answering how one can make sense of Paul's belief that God bestowed the Spirit upon Gentile Christians, and to what degree Paul's personal experience of the Spirit's work in his own life and interaction with and work among the earliest Christ-following communities informed his understanding of the Spirit.[451] Philip argues Paul's understanding of the Spirit must be understood against the background of Jewish anticipation of an eschatological outpouring of the Spirit on all flesh as a sign of the coming age.[452]

LIVING IN THE REALM OF THE SPIRIT VERSUS ETERNAL LIFE BY THE SPIRIT: ANDREW H. WAKEFIELD

In his 2003 monograph on Galatians 3:1-14, Andrew H. Wakefield offers a detailed analysis of what he calls Paul's "intertextual" citations of Scripture. He contends that focusing on the "ungrammaticalities" and the "presuppositions" of Paul's "intertextual" citations of Old Testament texts gives insight into Paul's use of Old Testament texts in Galatians 3:1-14 and on the meaning of the text. He thinks scholars have wrongly focused on soteriological issues in the text and, as a result, have offered no solutions to the apparent problems of Paul's scriptural citations in 3:1-14. Wakefield

---

[449]Philip, *Origins of Pauline Pneumatology*, 28.
[450]Philip, *Origins of Pauline Pneumatology*, 28.
[451]Philip, *Origins of Pauline Pneumatology*, 28.
[452]Philip, *Origins of Pauline Pneumatology*, 32.

contends that an "intertextual approach," which he thinks includes both Paul's use of texts and places where Paul imparts meaning into the text from certain cultural signals from his cultural context, offers insight into why Paul cites the Old Testament texts to prove a point in his argument that seems to make the opposing point in the original contexts of these Old Testament texts. Wakefield argues that Paul's concern is on "where to live" in Galatians 3:1-14. That is, Paul's emphasis is the Galatians live in the realm of the Spirit in the new age in the realm of Christ. His focus is not on how one personally gains eternal life.[453]

Wakefield argues for an "eschatological matrix" instead of a soteriological one, while he acknowledges that "soteriology is an eschatological issue (or at least has eschatological implications)."[454] He declares many interpreters of the letter have a misplaced focus on the concept of personal salvation, and this misplaced focus has contributed to some of the hermeneutical challenges of this text in the history of interpretation.[455] Paul's focus on where to live in Galatians 3–4 ties together his ethical exhortations in Galatians 5–6.[456] His emphasis in Galatians 5–6 is how to live in the present evil age while keeping in step with the Spirit on a path of righteousness toward the new age in which the Spirit frees one from the lusts of the flesh of the old age.[457] One walks both "by the Spirit" and in the realm of the Spirit.[458] As a result, Wakefield says this reading has important implications for Paul's criticism of the law.[459] He criticizes the law because it is part of the old age, not because it is defective.[460] To turn away from Christ to the law is to "return to the old age" prior to Christ.[461] The law neither leads one to life nor is the path toward living righteously because it is part of the old age.[462]

---

[453] Andrew H. Wakefield, *Where to Live: The Hermeneutical Significance of Paul's Citations from Scripture in Galatians 3:1-14* (Atlanta: SBL, 2003).
[454] Wakefield, *Where to Live*, 9n32.
[455] Wakefield, *Where to Live*, 9n32.
[456] Wakefield, *Where to Live*, 9n32.
[457] Wakefield, *Where to Live*, 9n32.
[458] Wakefield, *Where to Live*, 9n32.
[459] Wakefield, *Where to Live*, 9n32.
[460] Wakefield, *Where to Live*, 9n32.
[461] Wakefield, *Where to Live*, 9n32.
[462] Wakefield, *Where to Live*, 187.

THE SPIRIT, NEW EXODUS, NEW CREATION, AND
THE RESTORATION OF ISRAEL: RODRIGO J. MORALES

In a 2010 monograph, Rodrigo J. Morales focuses on the Spirit and multiple prophetic eschatological restoration themes in Galatians.[463] He argues the authors' use Old Testament restoration themes in the Prophets and in Second Temple Judaism to connect the pouring out of the Spirit and Israel's restoration. These texts with these themes give insight into (and is "key" to) Paul's understanding of the reception of the Spirit in Galatians 3–6.[464] The Spirit's manifestation proves the redemption of Israel from the Torah's curse pronouncement upon the nation for failing to obey the Torah covenant, and the Spirit's manifestation further envisages Paul's remarks about the "kingdom of God" in Galatians 5:21 and his reference to Christians as the "Israel of God" in Galatians 6:16.[465] Paul's remarks about the eschatological anticipation of the Spirit sustain his paranetic sections in Galatians 5–6, but they do so in a way contrary to many of his Jewish contemporaries' understanding of Torah.[466]

Morales claims the significance of his study is threefold: First, it offers a "fuller picture" of ways Second Temple Judaism understood the Spirit in relation to various eschatological expectations.[467] One way, claims Morales, Paul demonstrates this connection is the relationship between his comments about the Spirit's outpouring and Israel's redemption from the law's curse.[468] Second, the relationship between the outpouring of the Spirit and Israel's redemption in the Old Testament prophets and in Second Temple Jewish texts illuminates Paul's phrase "curse of the law" in Galatians 3:13.[469] Paul's discussion of the Spirit and restoration is analogous to the way certain Jewish texts (e.g., Words of the Luminaries and the Testament of Judah) present the solution to Israel's plight under the Torah's curse.[470]

---

[463]Rodrigo J. Morales, *The Spirit and the Restoration of Israel: New Exodus and New Creation Motifs in Galatians*, WUNT 282 (Tübingen: Mohr Siebeck, 2010).

[464]Morales, *Spirit and the Restoration of Israel*, 1, 4-5. For the texts he discusses, see 43-69.

[465]Morales, *Spirit and the Restoration of Israel*, 4.

[466]Morales, *Spirit and the Restoration of Israel*, 4-5.

[467]Morales, *Spirit and the Restoration of Israel*, 5.

[468]Morales, *Spirit and the Restoration of Israel*, 5.

[469]Morales, *Spirit and the Restoration of Israel*, 5.

[470]Morales, *Spirit and the Restoration of Israel*, 5.

In Galatians, the Spirit's presence in believers signals the realization of Israel's redemption from the law's curse and the nation's "empowerment of believers to order their lives rightly before God."[471] Third, Morales highlights the importance of the relationship between the Spirit and life in the letter. He argues the concepts of life and death are themes that can be seen from Galatians 2:15-21, in 3:21, and in 6:8. Paul is justified by faith (Gal 2:16), crucified with Christ, dead to the law so that he lives to God, and lives his new life in Christ by faith (Gal 2:19-20),[472] and the Spirit gives life instead of the law (cf. Gal 3:21 with 6:8).[473] Paul's eschatological pouring out of the Spirit supports his paranetic sections in Galatians 5–6. The flesh-versus-Spirit antithesis in Galatians 5 is not a warfare between two powers (the flesh and the Spirit), but Paul's point is the flesh (represented by circumcision) and the law together belong to the old age (cf. Gal 3:23-25; 4:5-6). In this age, "frail humanity" (flesh) experiences all sorts of temptations to give into the desires of the flesh, but flesh, according to Morales, is not a personified power.[474] Those in Christ fulfill the law by loving their neighbors as themselves since the whole law is fulfilled by Christ's sacrificial love for those in Christ (cf. Gal 2:20; 5:14).[475] These chapters assume the inauguration of the eschatological new age discussed by the Prophets and in Second Temple Jewish texts.[476]

THE SPIRIT, ETHICAL TRANSFORMATION, AND PAUL'S PASTORAL CONCERN: JAMES W. THOMPSON

In a 2011 book on moral formation in Paul's letters,[477] James W. Thompson argues Paul's ethical instructions are the result of his pastoral concern for the communities he helped establish with other

---

[471]Morales, *Spirit and the Restoration of Israel*, 5.

[472]Morales, *Spirit and the Restoration of Israel*, 6.

[473]Morales, *Spirit and the Restoration of Israel*, 6.

[474]Morales, *Spirit and the Restoration of Israel*, 143.

[475]Morales, *Spirit and the Restoration of Israel*, 143-45.

[476]Morales, *Spirit and the Restoration of Israel*, 7, 78-163.

[477]James W. Thompson, *Moral Formation According to Paul: The Context and Coherence of Pauline Ethics* (Grand Rapids, MI: Baker, 2011).

missionaries.[478] He claims Paul's ethical instruction directly addresses the moral transformation in those communities.[479] He suggests both Paul's Hellenistic and Jewish contexts influence his understanding of ethical formation, and he used the moral teachings in the relevant Hellensitic and Jewish texts to address specific ethical concerns in the Christian communities he helped establish.[480]

Thompson argues the vice lists in Hellenistic Jewish texts show the importance of Wisdom literature "for the paranesis within Hellenistic Judaism."[481] Hellenistic Jewish writers do not always quote the Jewish law when they offer ethical exhortations, but they suppose their instructions for a Jewish way of life comes from the Jewish law.[482] According to Thompson, Paul's moral instruction shapes his communities' identity as the people of God,[483] the foundation of which is God's saving action in Christ via Jesus' life, death, and resurrection.[484] The Christ-event is likewise the "turning point" for story of Israel.[485]

Thompson argues "faith, hope, and love" in 1 Thessalonians are important for Paul's ethical instructions.[486] Paul, for example, specifically places Gentile Christians in Thessalonica within "Israel's narrative world" with his commands about sexual morality.[487] Thompson contends that Torah shapes Paul's ethical discourse with Gentile communities. Paul does not expect Gentile Christians to obey the so-called boundary markers of the law (Sabbath-keeping, circumcision, and food laws). However, Paul expects the Gentiles to follow the moral aspects of the law as interpreted by Christ (e.g., abstaining from sexual immorality, idolatry, etc.).[488] Paul's discussion of overcoming the passions have

---

[478]Thompson, *Moral Formation According to Paul*, 7.
[479]Thompson, *Moral Formation According to Paul*, 7.
[480]Thompson, *Moral Formation According to Paul*, 18.
[481]Thompson, *Moral Formation According to Paul*, 19-41, esp. 26.
[482]Thompson, *Moral Formation According to Paul*, 41.
[483]Thompson, *Moral Formation According to Paul*, 43-62.
[484]Thompson, *Moral Formation According to Paul*, 44.
[485]Thompson, *Moral Formation According to Paul*, 44-45.
[486]Thompson, *Moral Formation According to Paul*, 63-86.
[487]Thompson, *Moral Formation According to Paul*, 63-86.
[488]Thompson, *Moral Formation According to Paul*, 111-34.

both Greek philosophical and Jewish antecedents, both of which are informative for him. Both emphasize that humans can do good.[489] For Paul, this good is possible because of God's work in the people of God through Christ.[490]

THE SPIRIT, DIVINE ENABLEMENT, AND DIVINE EMPOWERMENT: PRESTON M. SPRINKLE

In a recent monograph on divine and human agency in early Judaism and Paul, Preston M. Sprinkle discusses the relationship between the Spirit, obedience, and eternal life.[491] According to Sprinkle, Qumran and Paul discuss the same five theological motifs: (1) God's deliverance of the covenant people from the curse of the law, (2) the essence of the "eschatological spirit's work" in the midst of the covenant, (3) the human plight of "anthropological pessimism," (4) "justification," and (5) the relationship between judgment and works for the covenant community.[492]

This thesis contributes to a discussion of soteriology in Qumran and in Paul. Sprinkle cautiously defines soteriology as "the restoration God brings to those who belong to his covenant community." He recognizes the difficulty of talking about a soteriology of any ancient sect since the term has unshakable Christian ideas.[493] The point of Sprinkle's comparison is "to compare soteriological motifs in Paul and Qumran in order to better understand how these two Second Temple Jewish communities understood divine and human agency in salvation."[494]

According to Sprinkle, there is continuity and discontinuity between the scrolls and Paul in their understanding of the eschatological Spirit in Ezekiel 36–37.[495] There is an "even spread" of continuity and discontinuity among the scrolls surveyed of their use of Ezekiel 36–37's

[489]Thompson, *Moral Formation According to Paul*, 135-56.
[490]Thompson, *Moral Formation According to Paul*, 141-56.
[491]Preston M. Sprinkle, *Paul and Judaism Revisited: A Study of Divine and Human Agency in Salvation* (Downers Grove, IL: InterVarsity Press, 2013).
[492]Sprinkle, *Paul and Judaism Revisited*, 34.
[493]Sprinkle, *Paul and Judaism Revisited*, 33.
[494]Sprinkle, *Paul and Judaism Revisited*, 36.
[495]Sprinkle, *Paul and Judaism Revisited*, 115.

eschatological invasion of the Spirit and Paul. However, according to Sprinkle, at times the scrolls express a Deuteronomic understanding of cognitive restoration (1QH 5.24-25; 10.11-12; 21.14). They express complete human transformation found in Ezekiel in both the present (1QH 8.19-20) and in the future (1QS 4.10-22).[496] 4QPseudo-Ezekiel, on the other hand, contrasts with God's unilateral work of the Spirit to effect this transformation.[497]

Sprinkle claims Paul and Qumran believe works are necessary for the final judgment, but they disagree as to origins of those works. Paul believes the works that will vindicate one in the judgment are "divinely empowered" works.[498] However, Sprinkle claims several Qumran scrolls parallel Paul on this point (1QH, 1QS 10, 11, 4Q434, 4Q504).[499] Sprinkle says Paul, however, states Christ and the Spirit both "enable" and "empower" obedience.[500]

THE SPIRIT AND RELATIONAL TRANSFORMATION: VOLKER RABENS

Volker Rabens has contributed much to the discussion of the Spirit in Paul's theology. In a recent essay, he argues the old imperative and indicative ways of discussing Paul's ethics in Galatians are not helpful.[501] He posits instead an "implicit" indicative and an "implicit" imperative approach.[502] Indicatives and imperatives are in Galatians even without imperative forms, but Paul uses implicit imperatives where he explains what one "ought" to do in contrast with what one "is" doing.[503] Hence, Rabens uses the phrase "implicit imperative."[504]

---

[496]Sprinkle, *Paul and Judaism Revisited*, 115.
[497]Sprinkle, *Paul and Judaism Revisited*, 115.
[498]Sprinkle, *Paul and Judaism Revisited*, 201.
[499]Sprinkle, *Paul and Judaism Revisited*, 201.
[500]Sprinkle, *Paul and Judaism Revisited*, 203.
[501]Volker Rabens, "Indicative and Imperative as the Substructure of Paul's Theology and Ethics in Galatians?" in *Galatians and Christian Theology: Justification, the Gospel, and Ethics in Paul's Letters*, ed. Mark W. Elliott et al. (Grand Rapids, MI: Baker, 2014), 285-305.
[502]Rabens, "Indicative and Imperative," 289.
[503]Rabens, "Indicative and Imperative," 289.
[504]Rabens, "Indicative and Imperative," 289.

Rabens critically interacts with Zimmerman's article in which he challenges the "indicative-imperative schema" and argues for an "implicit ethics" template. Barring his criticisms of Zimmerman, Rabens accepts his model and modifies it with a discussion of divine agency and with the labels of "implicit indicatives" and "implicit imperatives."[505] Rabens argues for a "relational model of divine and human agency in Galatians."[506] He suggests the Spirit transforms and empowers believers by drawing them to God through the body of Christ, a transformation that believers forfeit if they remove themselves from the body of Christ.[507]

Rabens' most extensive work on the Spirit and ethics in Paul discusses numerous Pauline texts.[508] He, however, spends most of his time discussing texts outside of Galatians. Rabens argues the Holy Spirit is the reason for Paul's ethical reasoning.[509] He claims the ethical work of the Spirit in Paul is "relational."[510] That is, "it is primarily through deeper knowledge of, and an intimate relationship with, God, Jesus Christ and with the community of faith that people are transformed and empowered by the Spirit for religious-ethical life."[511] Rabens argues against what he calls "an infusion-transformation approach."[512] He asserts that this model of transformation states Paul teaches that one experiences the "ethical life" by means of "the transformation of the inner nature of a person by the infusion with a material" spirit.[513] Rabens also calls this view the "substance-ontological" approach.[514] This approach emphasizes, according Rabens, the "interior" or "substance" of a person, and "to the depreciation of the person's relationships."[515]

---

[505]Rabens, "Indicative and Imperative," 287-99, esp. 288-99.
[506]Rabens, "Indicative and Imperative," 299-302.
[507]Rabens, "Indicative and Imperative," 304.
[508]Volker Rabens, *The Holy Spirit and Ethics in Paul: Transformation and Empowering for Religious-Ethical Life*, 2nd ed. (Minneapolis: Fortress, 2014).
[509]Rabens, *Holy Spirit and Ethics in Paul*, 1.
[510]Rabens, *Holy Spirit and Ethics in Paul*, 21.
[511]Rabens, *Holy Spirit and Ethics in Paul*, 21.
[512]Rabens, *Holy Spirit and Ethics in Paul*, 21.
[513]Rabens, *Holy Spirit and Ethics in Paul*, 18-19.
[514]Rabens, *Holy Spirit and Ethics in Paul*, 18-19.
[515]Rabens, *Holy Spirit and Ethics in Paul*, 2-13.

Rabens sets Paul's view of the Spirit and ethics in conversation with the Stoics on the material spirit.[516] Rabens explains Stoics had a material view of the Spirit, but their view was not built upon the Spirit transforming humans.[517] He continues to note that Stoics had similarities with and dissimilarities from infusion-transformation approaches of the Spirit.[518] Rabens says Stoics affirmed "cognitive transformation through philosophy and active reasoning."[519] Making an observation about the Dead Sea Scrolls, Rabens suggests interpreters of Paul's metaphorical language about the Spirit should be careful not to make the incorrect assumption that Paul's letters speak of the "materiality/immateriality of the Spirit"[520] for, Rabens claims, neither canonical nor extra-canonical Jewish texts state the Spirit is a material substance infused into the people of God.[521]

Rabens argues the "infusion transformation" view of the Spirit is wrong,[522] and he claims Paul nowhere in his letters describes the Spirit as a substance.[523] Rather, "the ethical work of the Spirit . . . is primarily through deeper knowledge of, and an intimate relationship with, God, Jesus Christ and with the community of faith that people are transformed and empowered by the Spirit for religious-ethical life."[524] Rabens argues for a "relational-transformational view of the Spirit." Transformation, according to Rabens, has an enduring impact, but the empowerment of the Spirit ebbs and flows.[525] Rabens' understanding of transformation is different from the "infusion-transformation" approach, for he does not think the Spirit transforms the believer by becoming a material Spirit.[526] Rabens, however, affirms the Spirit empowers the believer in the Pauline sense, but Paul refers to the transformation of the Spirit instead of the

---

[516]Rabens, *Holy Spirit and Ethics in Paul*, 25-35.
[517]Rabens, *Holy Spirit and Ethics in Paul*, 25-35.
[518]Rabens, *Holy Spirit and Ethics in Paul*, 31-32.
[519]Rabens, *Holy Spirit and Ethics in Paul*, 31-32.
[520]Rabens, *Holy Spirit and Ethics in Paul*, 54.
[521]Rabens, *Holy Spirit and Ethics in Paul*, 40-78.
[522]Rabens, *Holy Spirit and Ethics in Paul*, 80-120.
[523]Rabens, *Holy Spirit and Ethics in Paul*, 80-120.
[524]Rabens, *Holy Spirit and Ethics in Paul*, 123.
[525]Rabens, *Holy Spirit and Ethics in Paul*, 123-25.
[526]Rabens, *Holy Spirit and Ethics in Paul*, 123-25.

empowerment of the Spirit when Paul speaks of the "lasting change of character" in the life of the believer.[527]

Rabens agrees the Spirit divinely enables believers to live a transformed ethical life.[528] But, unlike what he calls the "infusion-transformation model," he does not think the Spirit infuses and transforms the believer by "ontologically transforming" the believer by means of the "ontologically transforming effect" of the Spirit's "physical nature."[529] Rabens' "relational approach" suggests "that the Spirit effects ethical life predominately by means of intimate relationships created by the Spirit with God (Abba), Jesus and fellow believers."[530] Rabens emphasizes that "it is not the relationships themselves that are the enabling factor as if they could be separated from those to whom the believers are related."[531] Instead, God the Father, Christ, and believers "give shape to these Spirit-created relationships."[532]

Rabens illustrates the differences between the two models with two diagrams. In the "infusion-transformation model," the Spirit breaks into the fleshly existence of the believer through a sacramental transfer of the "Spirit-substance," at which point the Spirit transforms the believer to live the ethical life.[533] The "ethical life" is the result of transformation.[534] Rabens calls this model "static."[535]

According to Rabens, the "relational" model is "dynamic."[536] The starting point for this model is God the Father, Christ, and the community of fellow believers.[537] The Spirit breaks into the believer's fleshly existence with "dynamic Spirit-designed relationships between God the Father, Christ, and fellow believers." The Spirit creates these relationships

---

[527]Rabens, *Holy Spirit and Ethics in Paul*, 125-26.
[528]Rabens, *Holy Spirit and Ethics in Paul*, 126.
[529]Rabens, *Holy Spirit and Ethics in Paul*, 126.
[530]Rabens, *Holy Spirit and Ethics in Paul*, 126.
[531]Rabens, *Holy Spirit and Ethics in Paul*, 126.
[532]Rabens, *Holy Spirit and Ethics in Paul*, 126.
[533]Rabens, *Holy Spirit and Ethics in Paul*, 127.
[534]Rabens, *Holy Spirit and Ethics in Paul*, 127.
[535]Rabens, *Holy Spirit and Ethics in Paul*, 127-28.
[536]Rabens, *Holy Spirit and Ethics in Paul*, 127-28.
[537]Rabens, *Holy Spirit and Ethics in Paul*, 126-28.

and uses them to enable believers to walk in a pattern of ethical living by means of them.[538] In this model, the transformation is "gradual" or "dynamic" instead of "static" or "instant."[539] Rabens cites a litany of biblical texts to support that humans are created to be in relationship with God through Christ and with others.[540] Many of these texts are from Paul's writings. Rabens argues Paul believed personal relationships with God, Christ, and believers are how the Spirit empowers believers.[541] However, Rabens admits Paul's view of the Spirit and ethics is both ontological and transformational.[542]

Rabens suggests "there is adequate material in Paul's religious and philosophical context against which our relational model of the ethically empowering work of the Spirit can be read."[543] Rabens discusses evidence from both Jewish and Greek sources.[544] He argues "the Spirit enables ethical life" through a "conversion-initiation" process whereby humans "are transferred from the existence in the flesh to being in the Spirit."[545] The result of this transference is "freedom from sin, the flesh, the law, the enslaving powers, etc., and a new, intimate relationship with God, Christ, the Spirit and the Christian community."[546] The believer changes his allegiance "with the consequence of a new belonging." Believers "are now united with Christ by the Spirit—they are in Christ . . . in the Spirit . . . , and Christ by his Spirit indwells them."[547]

This transference does not result in an automatic and sudden comprehensive change.[548] Rather, walking in the flesh is still a real possibility for the believer. The believer must choose to walk in the Spirit to experience enablement for ethical transformation, that is, so that they

---

[538]Rabens, *Holy Spirit and Ethics in Paul*, 127-29.
[539]Rabens, *Holy Spirit and Ethics in Paul*, 129.
[540]Rabens, *Holy Spirit and Ethics in Paul*, 133-38.
[541]Rabens, *Holy Spirit and Ethics in Paul*, 135-38.
[542]Rabens, *Holy Spirit and Ethics in Paul*, 141.
[543]Rabens, *Holy Spirit and Ethics in Paul*, 146.
[544]Rabens, *Holy Spirit and Ethics in Paul*, 147-69.
[545]Rabens, *Holy Spirit and Ethics in Paul*, 171-242, esp. 171.
[546]Rabens, *Holy Spirit and Ethics in Paul*, 172.
[547]Rabens, *Holy Spirit and Ethics in Paul*, 172.
[548]Rabens, *Holy Spirit and Ethics in Paul*, 172-73.

will grow in living "christomorphic" lives.[549] This growth happens, Rabens says, in Paul's view because the Spirit is lively in the believer by enabling an ongoing ethical transformation.[550] The Spirit enables God's people to live an ethical life apart from the law because of their "Christ-created and Spirit-sustained filial relationship with God."[551] This relationship is "the reason" they do not need Torah to live an ethical life pleasing to God.[552] The believer experiences a transfer from the realm of the flesh to the realm of the Spirit by the Spirit "into a new relationship with God, Christ and the Christian community."[553] However, this transferal from one realm to another "is not merely a transforming event in the converts' lives" at the moment of their conversion.[554] Instead, Rabens argues, the Spirit transforms and empowers Christ followers to obey God by energizing and escalating these relationships between God, Jesus, and the church.[555]

THE SPIRIT AND FUTURE JUSTIFICATION: CHEE-CHIEW LEE

In a 2013 monograph, Chee-Chiew Lee investigates the Abrahamic blessing, the Spirit, and justification by faith in Galatians.[556] Her thesis is twofold. First, she argues that Paul does not state the Abrahamic blessing is the Spirit in Galatians 3:14. Second, she argues Paul's discussion of the Abrahamic blessing and the Spirit in Galatians gives insight into his argument in the letter and his theology of justification.[557] Lee admits some readers of Galatians in the history of interpretation have focused too much on the importance of justification in

---

[549]Rabens, *Holy Spirit and Ethics in Paul*, 172-73.
[550]Rabens, *Holy Spirit and Ethics in Paul*, 173.
[551]Rabens, *Holy Spirit and Ethics in Paul*, 233.
[552]Rabens, *Holy Spirit and Ethics in Paul*, 233-34.
[553]Rabens, *Holy Spirit and Ethics in Paul*, 233-34.
[554]Rabens, *Holy Spirit and Ethics in Paul*, 233-34.
[555]Rabens, *Holy Spirit and Ethics in Paul*, 233-34.
[556]Chee-Chiew Lee, *The Blessing of Abraham, the Spirit, and Justification in Galatians* (Eugene, OR: Pickwick, 2013).
[557]Rodrigo Jose Morales, however, argues the blessing of Abraham is the Spirit (e.g., "The Words of the Luminaries, the Curse of the Law, and the Outpouring of the Spirit in Gal 3:10, 14," *Zeitschrift für die neutestamentliche Wissenschaft und die Kunde der älteren Kirche* 100, no. 2 [2009]: 269-77).

Galatians, but she states minimizing justification in Paul's argument in the letter "does not do justice to the letter."[558] She cites numerous examples where Paul mentions justification just as much as he comments on the Spirit.[559] According to Lee, "both justification by faith and life in the Spirit are Paul's answer to the controversy at Galatia."[560] Paul argues, says Lee, Gentiles are free from obeying the law since God justifies Jews and Gentiles by faith in Christ apart from works of the law (Gal 2:15–3:25) and since the Gentiles prove their status of justification when they received the Spirit by faith (Gal 3:2-5).[561] She agrees with previous commentators that "justification cannot be understood and experienced apart from the Spirit."[562]

Lee claims Paul borrows from the "divine empowerment" tradition in Ezekiel.[563] The Galatians obey God "through the Spirit" because the Spirit empowers them to do so.[564] According to Paul, since humans are enslaved to sin's power,[565] neither Jews nor Gentiles can perfectly obey the law.[566] The Galatians need the Spirit to work in them to enable them to resist sin and righteously obey in accordance with the law.[567] "It is the Spirit who ensures believers of the hope of righteousness and eternal life" (Gal 5:5-6; 6:8; cf. Ezek 36:26-27; 37:14).[568] In agreement with the prophet, Paul suggests, says Lee, those who receive the Spirit by faith in Christ and who are justified by faith in Christ obey Torah because of the Spirit's work of obedience in the believer.[569] Obedience is not the "prerequisite" to justification by faith and the reception of the Spirit by faith.[570]

---

[558]Lee, *Blessing of Abraham*, 23.
[559]Lee, *Blessing of Abraham*, 23.
[560]Lee, *Blessing of Abraham*, 23.
[561]Lee, *Blessing of Abraham*, 23.
[562]Lee, *Blessing of Abraham*, 23.
[563]Lee, *Blessing of Abraham*, 191.
[564]Lee, *Blessing of Abraham*, 191.
[565]Lee, *Blessing of Abraham*, 191.
[566]Lee, *Blessing of Abraham*, 191.
[567]Lee, *Blessing of Abraham*, 194-98.
[568]Lee, *Blessing of Abraham*, 194-98.
[569]Lee, *Blessing of Abraham*, 192.
[570]Lee, *Blessing of Abraham*, 192.

THE SPIRIT, PERSONAL AGENCY, AND DIVINE ACTIVITY:
OLIVER O'DONOVAN AND JEAN-NOEL ALETTI

In a 2014 collection of essays on Galatians and Christian theology, the authors address the topics of justification, the gospel, and ethics.[571] I have already discussed the essays of Barclay and Rabens above. Two additional essays on the Spirit and ethics in Galatians are pertinent.

O'Donovan emphasizes personal agency because of the work of the Spirit. He argues Paul's flesh-versus-Spirit antithesis represents "a pneu-matological conception of the moral life."[572] Those who walk in the flesh live in a disconnected way from God's commands and are "restricted to the disconnected building blocks of moral learning."[573] The Spirit adds to these fragmented elements "the missing meaning and coherence in the command of love, and there with the authority to interpret and direct our lives accordingly."[574] To walk in the Spirit and contrary to the flesh takes up "life as a moral privilege and task instead of merely reacting."[575] Walking in the Spirit leads believers to order their lives in consistent rhythms of faith and liberation that manifest their presence in love as those with the Spirit live by the Spirit because of God's promise.[576]

Aletti's essay focuses on "divine activity" and "personal agency." He discusses Galatians 5:17 and the way this verse relates to the flesh-versus-Spirit antithesis. This essay argues Paul's remarks in Galatians 5:17 refer to the active role of the flesh in its fight against the Spirit to stop those who have the Spirit from doing the good things they desire to do, while "the Spirit's role is precisely to thwart the designs of the flesh."[577] The flesh "directly" works against the Spirit, but Christ followers are not under any

---

[571]Mark W. Elliott, Scott J. Hafemann, and N. T. Wright, eds., *Galatians and Christian Theology: Justification, the Gospel, and Ethics in Paul's Letter* (Grand Rapids, MI: Baker, 2014).

[572]Oliver O'Donovan, "Flesh and Spirit," in *Galatians and Christian Theology: Justification, the Gospel, and Ethics in Paul's Letter*, ed. Mark W. Elliott et al. (Grand Rapids, MI: Baker, 2014), 271-84, esp. 273.

[573]O'Donovan, "Flesh and Spirit," 281.

[574]O'Donovan, "Flesh and Spirit," 281.

[575]O'Donovan, "Flesh and Spirit," 281.

[576]O'Donovan, "Flesh and Spirit," 282, 284.

[577]Jean-Noel Aletti, "Paul's Exhortations in Galatians 5:16-25: From the Apostle's Techniques to His Strategies," in *Galatians and Christian Theology: Justification, the Gospel, and Ethics in Paul's Letter*, eds. Mark W. Elliott, et al. (Grand Rapids, MI: Baker, 2014), 318-34, esp. 324-25.

real threat because of the flesh's opposition.[578] The flesh opposes the Spirit to keep those who have the Spirit from pursuing the good behavior patterns that Christ followers desire to pursue.[579] As an active agent, the Spirit helps those who have the Spirit to act in accordance with the good and contrary to the flesh.[580] The Spirit's agency is much more powerful than the agency of the flesh, and the Spirit is able to defend believers against the flesh.[581] Aletti infers from this that Galatians 5:17 "does not reflect a negative soteriology according to which believers cannot be freed from the mastery of the flesh."[582] The Galatians must not become the law's subjects because this results in slavery to the law and subjugation to the flesh (Gal 5:13).[583] There are both soteriological and ethical interests on the line if the Galatians turn to the law (Gal 1–6) since the Galatians would be returning to bondage to the power of the flesh.[584] The active verbs with the Galatians as their subjects reveal that "ethical behavior is conditioned by one's salvific status: a doing by being."[585]

THE SPIRIT AND APOCALYPTIC CRUCIFORMITY: MICHAEL J. GORMAN

In a 2019 book on participation and spirituality in Paul's theology, Michael J. Gorman argues, "Participation is not merely one aspect of Pauline theology and spirituality, or a supplement to something more fundamental; rather it is at the very heart of Paul's thinking and living. Pauline soteriology (theology of salvation) is inherently participatory and transformative."[586] By participation, Gorman means "cruciformity," "theosis," or "participating in the life of God."[587]

---

[578] Aletti, "Paul's Exhortations," 331.
[579] Aletti, "Paul's Exhortations," 331.
[580] Aletti, "Paul's Exhortations," 331.
[581] Aletti, "Paul's Exhortations," 331.
[582] Aletti, "Paul's Exhortations," 331.
[583] Aletti, "Paul's Exhortations," 332.
[584] Aletti, "Paul's Exhortations," 332.
[585] Aletti, "Paul's Exhortations," 332.
[586] Michael J. Gorman, *Participating in Christ: Explorations in Paul's Theology and Spirituality* (Grand Rapids, MI: Baker, 2019), xviii.
[587] Gorman, *Participating in Christ*, xviii.

Regarding the Spirit's role in participation, Gorman argues that life in Christ is life in the Spirit by discussing the intersection between covenant theology and apocalyptic theology in Paul's thought.[588] Gorman agrees with Rowland's thesis that Paul's soteriology is apocalyptic because God revealed Jesus to him and not because of "a particular theological perspective or agenda that could be called 'apocalyptic.'"[589] However, Gorman modulates Rowland's remarks.[590] His nuances relate to "the rejection of the possible implications" of Rowland's assertion. Those implications could be "(1) experience and theology should be pitted against each other and (2) Paul is only, or at least primarily, apocalyptic experientially."[591] Gorman argues readers of Paul should "resist" this false distinction.[592] According to Gorman, "Paul's apocalyptic experience shaped his apocalyptic theology (including his 'politics')."[593] Furthermore, Paul's "apocalyptic theology" both "helped him interpret" and "shaped his apocalyptic experience."[594]

With a discussion of Galatians 1, Gorman offers four points about Paul as an "apocalyptic figure."[595] Gorman discusses these four points under the "rubric of the apocalyptic new covenant and the shape of life in the Spirit."[596] This is Gorman's effort to hold in tension "Paul's apocalyptic experience and his apocalyptic theology."[597] Gorman also attempts to hold together both Paul's "apocalyptic" thinking and his "new-covenant" mindset.[598]

Gorman's arguments take the following shape in this chapter. First, he argues, with Wright, Paul is "both an apocalyptic and a *new*-covenant theologian."[599] God reveals to Paul "the radically unexpected and new

---

[588]Gorman, *Participating in Christ*, 96-114.
[589]Gorman, *Participating in Christ*, 97.
[590]Gorman, *Participating in Christ*, 97.
[591]Gorman, *Participating in Christ*, 97.
[592]Gorman, *Participating in Christ*, 97.
[593]Gorman, *Participating in Christ*, 97.
[594]Gorman, *Participating in Christ*, 97.
[595]Gorman, *Participating in Christ*, 97.
[596]Gorman, *Participating in Christ*, 97.
[597]Gorman, *Participating in Christ*, 97.
[598]Gorman, *Participating in Christ*, 97.
[599]Gorman, *Participating in Christ*, 97.

way in which the new covenant has come to fruition."[600] Second, Gorman claims Paul "reworked" new covenant theology "in light of God's apocalyptic" invasion within history in Jesus and in the Spirit.[601] Gorman argues Paul especially reworks his theology of the new covenant because of his "experience of the Messiah and the Spirit."[602] Third, a crucial element in the "content" of God's revelation to Paul is "the gracious invasion of God's Spirit (Ezekiel) and the Law (Jeremiah) into the hearts of God's people" has been realized in a "shocking, cruciform mode."[603] Paul articulates the fulfillment of this new covenant theology by discussing the faithfulness and love of the Messiah, who lived in Paul and all believers by the Spirit (Gal 2:19-20; 4:6), and when he says those in Christ fulfill the law of Christ (Gal 6:2).[604]

Fourth, the revelation God gave "to" Paul in Galatians 1:12 and the revelation God gave "in" Paul in Galatians 1:16 are interconnected.[605] The interconnectedness of the two becomes most apparent in 2 Corinthians.[606] Gorman says, "By means of the invading and indwelling Messiah/Spirit/Law of the Messiah, Paul becomes his gospel (i.e., embodies his gospel), and he expects others do so similarly—to live out the new covenant of faithfulness and love, the beginning of the new creation."[607] In other words, "the in-breaking of God into human history in Jesus' new-covenant-inaugurating death and in the gift of the Spirit necessarily includes a divine inbreaking into the lives of individual human beings to create a new community of the new covenant community that embodies the character of that divine invasion."[608] Gorman infers, "The result is both shockingly new and surprisingly continuous with the prophetic promises in Scripture."[609]

---

[600]Gorman, *Participating in Christ*, 97.
[601]Gorman, *Participating in Christ*, 98.
[602]Gorman, *Participating in Christ*, 98.
[603]Gorman, *Participating in Christ*, 98.
[604]Gorman, *Participating in Christ*, 96, 98.
[605]Gorman, *Participating in Christ*, 98.
[606]Gorman, *Participating in Christ*, 98.
[607]Gorman, *Participating in Christ*, 98.
[608]Gorman, *Participating in Christ*, 98.
[609]Gorman, *Participating in Christ*, 98.

Gorman continues that the Old Testament promises of a "renewed" or "new covenant" appear in Deuteronomy, Jeremiah, and Ezekiel.[610] Both of the two latter major prophets in the preceding sentence use the term covenant in similar contexts.[611] Jeremiah mentions "new covenant."[612] He further states God places his law inside of his people.[613] Ezekiel refers to the indwelling presence of the Spirit without mentioning the term "covenant."[614]

Gorman notes the prophets' remarks use the "language of divine-human interaction."[615] He further asserts this is language of "presence and participation, and implicitly of transformation."[616] Gorman states both prophets speak of God doing something to the hearts of his people (Jer 31:33; Ezek 11:19; 36:26).[617] God performs a circumcision of their heart (Jer 4:4; cf. Ezek 44:7, 9),[618] gives them one heart (Jer 32:39; Ezek 11:19),[619] gives his people a heart of flesh in the place of a heart of stone (Jer 32:39; Ezek 18:31; 36:26),[620] gives them a new heart (Ezek 11:19; 36:26),[621] and puts the law on the hearts of his people (Jer 31:33).[622] Gorman says the prophets think "the heart is the heart of the problem."[623] Ezekiel clearly states God works in the hearts of his people so that they would obey his law (Ezek 11:20; cf. 36:27).[624] Gorman calls this language "covenant fulfillment," "covenant formula," and "transformation."[625] Deuteronomy 30:6-10 pledges a renewal of the covenant.[626] These prophets affirm both an apocalyptic moment

---

[610]Gorman, *Participating in Christ*, 98-99.
[611]Gorman, *Participating in Christ*, 98-99.
[612]Gorman, *Participating in Christ*, 98-99.
[613]Gorman, *Participating in Christ*, 98-99.
[614]Gorman, *Participating in Christ*, 99.
[615]Gorman, *Participating in Christ*, 99.
[616]Gorman, *Participating in Christ*, 99.
[617]Gorman, *Participating in Christ*, 99.
[618]Gorman, *Participating in Christ*, 99.
[619]Gorman, *Participating in Christ*, 99.
[620]Gorman, *Participating in Christ*, 99.
[621]Gorman, *Participating in Christ*, 99.
[622]Gorman, *Participating in Christ*, 99.
[623]Gorman, *Participating in Christ*, 99.
[624]Gorman, *Participating in Christ*, 99.
[625]Gorman, *Participating in Christ*, 99.
[626]Gorman, *Participating in Christ*, 99-100.

whereby God writes his law/places his Spirit within them, transforms them, and God's people faithfully respond in obedience to the covenant.[627] Gorman says Paul likewise merges this new covenant and renewed creation language to speak about life in Christ as life in the Spirit.[628]

Gorman describes the apocalypse "in" Paul in the following way: the moment when God broke into Paul's life to reveal Jesus "in" him so that he irrevocably and completely changed from a violent opponent of the church to preacher of Christ.[629] Paul exemplifies God's "radical" discontinuous and invasive division between the old age and the new age.[630] God did in Paul what he's done for the cosmos.[631] Gorman argues, "Paul's self-portrayal as the apocalyptically 'invaded' persecutor, who has been crucified (and raised) with the Messiah, is simultaneously a self-portrayal as the recipient of the surprising Spirit of the new covenant that enables him, and all believers to embody the cruciform pattern of the Messiah's self-giving love: the 'Law of the Messiah.'"[632] Gorman claims Galatians 4:4-6 has three apocalyptic movements. First, Paul refers to the sending of God's Son as the "fullness of time." However, this divine invasion occurs in two parts: (1) God sends his Son, and (2) God sends his Spirit within us.[633] Second, Paul describes God's action as his sending his Son's Spirit into our hearts.[634] Third, the "apocalyptic Spirit" is the Spirit of the Messiah.[635]

Gorman claims Paul links the Spirit and the Messiah as he did in Galatians 3:1-5.[636] "The Spirit of the Jesus who has been apocalypsed, and the Spirit who participates in the divine apocalyptic activity of liberating people from this age and giving them a share in the life of the

---

[627]Gorman, *Participating in Christ*, 100-101.
[628]Gorman, *Participating in Christ*, 101.
[629]Gorman, *Participating in Christ*, 101-3.
[630]Gorman, *Participating in Christ*, 102.
[631]Gorman, *Participating in Christ*, 102.
[632]Gorman, *Participating in Christ*, 103.
[633]Gorman, *Participating in Christ*, 103.
[634]Gorman, *Participating in Christ*, 103.
[635]Gorman, *Participating in Christ*, 104.
[636]Gorman, *Participating in Christ*, 103-4.

age to come that was inaugurated by God's action in Christ."[637] Gorman
continues Paul's remarks about the Spirit in us crying out "Abba,
Father" restates the new covenant formula, expressing that the Spirit is
the one who "relates" people with God in this renewed covenant relationship.[638] Shockingly, says Gorman, this association includes both
Jews and Gentiles.[639] "In the giving of the Messiah and the Spirit of the
Messiah, God is speaking the language of (new) covenant, saying 'I am
your Father, and you are my children (cf. Rev 21:7).'"[640] Both Jews and
Gentiles are the people of God and cry out to God together with the
words, "Abba, Father."[641]

Gorman argues justification is "transformation into justice/right-
eousness (faithfulness and Love)."[642] Gorman claims Paul's remarks in
Galatians 3:8 about Abraham's righteousness should be understood in connection with his statement about life in Galatians 3:11 and the Spirit in
Galatians 3:14.[643] This connection entails that righteousness or life is the
result of faith,[644] or that faith "takes on the quality of righteousness" in a
transformative sense.[645] This righteousness, says Gorman, is the transformed life in the Spirit.[646] He supports this reading by citing Paul's remarks
in Galatians 3:21.[647] There, Paul links "righteousness" and "life" again.[648]
Thus, Gorman thinks the life to which Paul refers is the transformative life
in the Spirit, a transformation that Gorman identifies as "righteousness."[649]
According to Gorman, to be justified or to receive righteousness as a gift
from God is to receive transformational life in the Spirit.[650] Gorman uses

---

[637]Gorman, *Participating in Christ*, 104.
[638]Gorman, *Participating in Christ*, 104-5.
[639]Gorman, *Participating in Christ*, 105.
[640]Gorman, *Participating in Christ*, 105.
[641]Gorman, *Participating in Christ*, 105.
[642]Gorman, *Participating in Christ*, 138-42.
[643]Gorman, *Participating in Christ*, 138-42.
[644]Gorman, *Participating in Christ*, 138-42.
[645]Gorman, *Participating in Christ*, 138-42.
[646]Gorman, *Participating in Christ*, 138-42.
[647]Gorman, *Participating in Christ*, 138-42.
[648]Gorman, *Participating in Christ*, 138-42.
[649]Gorman, *Participating in Christ*, 138-42.
[650]Gorman, *Participating in Christ*, 139-40.

the terms "theosis" and "deification" to express justification as transformational life in the Spirit and to assert that "transformation into Godlikeness is constitutive of justification itself."[651]

THE SPIRIT AS AN AGENT OF TRANSFORMATION: DAVID A. DESILVA

In 2020, Nijay K. Gupta and John K. Goodrich edited a collection of essays titled *Sin and Its Remedy in Paul*.[652] David A. deSilva's essay, "Sin, Slavery, Sacrifice, and the Spirit," is the only one devoted to Galatians.[653] He argues sin is both an act of transgression and a structural power in Galatians.[654] He admits that Paul does not speak of sin as a power in Galatians with the language and force as he does in Romans, but this concept is still present in the letter.[655] For Paul, the Spirit is the agent God uses to transform those enslaved to sin from its structural power and transgressions.[656] DeSilva argues that "righteousness" in Galatians refers to an "ethical quality," not to "acquittal."[657] Ethical behavior (i.e., righteousness) comes by means of Christ by the Spirit.[658] "Christ," says deSilva, "died in order to make possible what the law had not made possible, namely for human beings to live righteously and, thus, to become righteous in God's sight rather than remain sinners."[659]

---

[651]Gorman, *Participating in Christ*, 142.

[652]Nijay K. Gupta and John K. Goodrich, eds., *Sin and Its Remedy in Paul* (Eugene, OR: Cascade, 2020).

[653]DeSilva, "Sin, Slavery, Sacrifice, and Redemption," in Gupta and Goodrich, eds., *Sin and Its Remedy in Paul*, 99-113.

[654]DeSilva, "Sin, Slavery, Sacrifice, and Redemption," in Gupta and Goodrich, eds., *Sin and Its Remedy in Paul*, 100-102.

[655]DeSilva, "Sin, Slavery, Sacrifice, and Redemption," in Gupta and Goodrich, eds., *Sin and Its Remedy in Paul*, 99-106.

[656]DeSilva, "Sin, Slavery, Sacrifice, and Redemption," in Gupta and Goodrich, eds., *Sin and Its Remedy in Paul*, 106, 111.

[657]DeSilva, "Sin, Slavery, Sacrifice, and Redemption," in Gupta and Goodrich, eds., *Sin and Its Remedy in Paul*, 107.

[658]DeSilva, "Sin, Slavery, Sacrifice, and Redemption," in Gupta and Goodrich, eds., *Sin and Its Remedy in Paul*, 108.

[659]DeSilva, "Sin, Slavery, Sacrifice, and Redemption," in Gupta and Goodrich, eds., *Sin and Its Remedy in Paul*, 108.

DeSilva agrees Christ's death "for our sins" (Gal 1:4) brought "acquittal for past transgressions."[660] Yet, he asserts, his death also "secured" for believers the necessary provisions to live a righteous life— "a life that would be acquitted as righteous indeed by the just and impartial Judge of all."[661] Sinful acts preclude those who commit them from inheriting the kingdom of God (Gal 5:19-21). But God "intervened" in the lives of believers by the Spirit "to effect radical change in orientation and practice."[662] Consequently, "the sins—the self-serving actions that reflected non-alignment with God's good desires for human life and human community—that formerly characterized his or her life, necessitating the self-giving death of Jesus, no longer have any place in the believer's life, which is instead to be characterized by the virtues identified as the Spirit's 'fruit' (Gal 5:22-23) or, in a word, 'righteousness.'"[663] God "empowers and directs" believers to live righteously in Christ by the Spirit,[664] but believers must walk in the Spirit as they live out the reality of their being crucified with Christ to the powers "of ungodliness and his or her coming alive with Christ to the new life, the Spirit-led life."[665]

In his 2018 Galatians commentary, deSilva discusses in further detail his understanding of righteousness and walking in the Spirit. He claims, "In Galatians . . . Paul *anticipates* justification—being acquitted before God at the judgment—as a result of trusting in Jesus and walking in the new life and the new power of the Spirit that Jesus's death made available to human beings."[666] According to deSilva, Paul nowhere in

---

[660]DeSilva, "Sin, Slavery, Sacrifice, and Redemption," in Gupta and Goodrich, eds., *Sin and Its Remedy in Paul*, 108.

[661]DeSilva, "Sin, Slavery, Sacrifice, and Redemption," in Gupta and Goodrich, eds., *Sin and Its Remedy in Paul*, 108.

[662]DeSilva, "Sin, Slavery, Sacrifice, and Redemption," in Gupta and Goodrich, eds., *Sin and Its Remedy in Paul*, 109.

[663]DeSilva, "Sin, Slavery, Sacrifice, and Redemption," in Gupta and Goodrich, eds., *Sin and Its Remedy in Paul*, 109.

[664]DeSilva, "Sin, Slavery, Sacrifice, and Redemption," in Gupta and Goodrich, eds., *Sin and Its Remedy in Paul*, 111.

[665]DeSilva, "Sin, Slavery, Sacrifice, and Redemption," in Gupta and Goodrich, eds., *Sin and Its Remedy in Paul*, 111-12.

[666]David A. deSilva, *The Letter to the Galatians*, NICNT (Grand Rapids, MI: Eerdmans, 2018), 218.

Galatians speaks of "justification" or "acquittal" in terms of "an already-accomplished fact."[667] Even in Galatians 2:16, says deSilva, when Paul discusses justification by faith, he uses a purpose clause instead of a result clause. The purpose clause is not "determinative," says deSilva, but a result clause would have clearly asserted justification is an already-accomplished fact in this present evil age.[668] Yet, he continues, Paul clearly speaks of future justification in Galatians 2:16 with a future-tense verb and with his echo of LXX Psalm 143:2. Paul asserts with clarity no one will be justified by works of law.[669] This future reference to justification supports Paul and others hoped to be justified/acquitted in the future, a hope of which those seeking to be justified by works of law would fall short.[670]

DeSilva claims "seeking to be justified in Christ" is an ongoing pursuit even "after" the initial act of one placing faith in Christ.[671] In deSilva's view, Paul describes justification as "the still-future goal driving an entire lifestyle shift."[672] Paul supports this reading, says deSilva, in Galatians 3:3 when he discusses the Galatians began this process of justification when they placed faith in Christ.[673] Paul exhorts the Galatians to continue walking in step with the Spirit on the path that God opened for them the moment they placed faith in Jesus "so that they arrive at the desired goal."[674] DeSilva defines "seeking to be justified" to mean "investing oneself in that path that would lead to being acquitted before God's judgment seat by virtue of having fallen in line with God's righteous standards."[675]

DeSilva argues those who trust in Christ and consequently walk in step with the Spirit have begun the journey that is "the basis" upon

---

[667]DeSilva, *Letter to the Galatians*, 218.
[668]DeSilva, *Letter to the Galatians*, 218.
[669]DeSilva, *Letter to the Galatians*, 218.
[670]DeSilva, *Letter to the Galatians*, 218.
[671]DeSilva, *Letter to the Galatians*, 218-19.
[672]DeSilva, *Letter to the Galatians*, 219.
[673]DeSilva, *Letter to the Galatians*, 219.
[674]DeSilva, *Letter to the Galatians*, 219.
[675]DeSilva, *Letter to the Galatians*, 219.

which they attain and "the means to attain righteousness (alignment with God's standards)."[676] DeSilva is clear the relationship between justification and the Spirit is a transformative one rather than forensic.[677] According to deSilva, "Paul is not talking about the goal as merely being declared righteous while not actually being righteous in God's sight."[678] Instead, he says, Paul presents the hope of the Christian as "transformation into Spirit-led and Spirit-empowered people who do and are what pleases God" (cf. Gal 5:13–6:10).[679] In this sense, δικαιοσύνη is "an ethical quality" in Galatians, and the Spirit nurtures this quality "within the believer," and righteousness is the believer's goal.[680] Torah does not make people righteous because God has eradicated the boundary markers of Torah for the people of God in Christ.[681] Rather, God "justifies," that is, "God makes people righteous, bringing them in line with God's standards, through the Spirit."[682]

THE SPIRIT, IDENTITY, AND AGENCY: GRANT BUCHANAN

In a short article in 2020, Grant Buchanan discusses "identity and human agency in Galatians 5–6." Buchanan argues that Galatians 5:13–6:10 explains the Galatians should obey the gospel because of their identity in Christ. That is, the imperatives and hortatory subjunctives in this section emphasize the Galatians should walk in step with the Spirit and choose to be influenced and directed by the Spirit in their pursuit of virtue because of God's saving action in Christ. Their identity as sons of God liberates them from the bondage under Torah so that they can now walk in obedience in the path of the Spirit, and they should resist the opposing power of the flesh as those who are now free in Christ to walk in the path of the Spirit that leads to life.[683] According to Buchanan,

---

[676]DeSilva, *Letter to the Galatians*, 219.
[677]DeSilva, *Letter to the Galatians*, 422.
[678]DeSilva, *Letter to the Galatians*, 422.
[679]DeSilva, *Letter to the Galatians*, 422.
[680]DeSilva, *Letter to the Galatians*, 422.
[681]DeSilva, *Letter to the Galatians*, 422.
[682]DeSilva, *Letter to the Galatians*, 422.
[683]Grant Buchanan, "Identity and Agency in Galatians 5-6," *ABR* 68 (2020): 54-66.

"When believers are walking with the Spirit, being attentive to their life and the context they are in, then it will be the character and desire of the Spirit that will be the guiding framework out of which choice and action will be made—including ethical responses. In other words, they will know what to *do* because they will know *who they are*—that is, children (υἱοί)—in light of *who they are of*—that is, God (θεοῦ)."[684]

CONCLUSION

In chapters three to five, I turn my attention to an exegesis of specific texts to support my thesis. My thesis is Paul describes God's saving action in Christ in Galatians as vertical, horizontal, and cosmic for Jews and Gentiles and for the cosmos, and his vertical, horizontal, and cosmic saving action in Christ is *the* reason Paul *commands* the Galatians to walk in the Spirit, *the* reason they *can* walk in the Spirit, *the* reason they have life by the Spirit, and *the* reason they *must* walk in the Spirit in order to participate in eternal life now in the present evil age and inherit it in the age to come. My thesis emphasizes five primary points about the Spirit, moral agency, ethical transformation, and eternal life in Galatians. First, God's vertical, horizontal, and cosmic saving action in Christ for Jews and Gentiles and for the cosmos is the foundational reason the Galatians received the Spirit by faith (cf. Gal 3:1-14; 4:5-6). Second, because of God's saving action in Christ, the Galatians have the capacity to act as free moral agents so that they can and will choose to walk in the Spirit and not gratify the lust of the flesh (Gal 5:1; 5:13–6:10). Third, only those Galatian Christ followers who walk in the Spirit in obedience to the gospel in the present evil age would participate in eternal life in the present evil age and inherit eternal life in the age to come. Fourth, the Spirit's presence in and among the Galatian Christ followers was both the result and proof of God's saving action *for* and *in* them in Christ. Fifth, the Spirit indwells (cf. Gal 3:2, 3, 5, 14; 4:6), transforms (Gal 3:3), enlivens (Gal 3:21; 5:25;

---

[684]Buchanan, "Identity and Agency," 61.

6:8; cf. 6:15), and empowers (Gal 5:5, 18, 22, 25; 6:1) Christ-following Jews and Gentiles in the assemblies of Galatia to walk in the Spirit and to walk contrary to the flesh and the present evil age—even as they continue to live in the present evil age, and the present evil age continues to triumph.

3

THE SPIRIT AND GOD'S REVELATION
OF THE RESURRECTED AND CRUCIFIED
CHRIST IN PAUL

IN THIS CHAPTER, I argue the foundational reason the Galatians received the Spirit, experienced free moral agency and ethical transformation, and participated in eternal life by faith in this age and in the age to come is because of God's vertical, horizontal, and cosmic saving action in Christ for Jews, Gentiles, and for the cosmos via Jesus' cross and resurrection (Gal 1:1, 4; 3:1-14). Paul articulates God's saving action with apocalyptic language (e.g., Gal 1:4, 15-16; 5:16-26; 6:15), with forensic language (Gal 2:16; 3:6-8; 5:5), and with salvation-historical language (Gal 4:5-6).[1]

APOCALYPTIC IN GALATIANS

The epistolary context of God's revelation of Christ. A brief word about the epistolary context of God's revelation of the resurrected and crucified Christ in Paul is necessary to remind readers of the polemical context in Galatians in which he discusses God's revelation of Christ, God's vertical, horizontal, and cosmic saving action in Christ, and Paul's transformational experience of the Spirit. Paul first mentions the resurrection in Galatians 1:1 and the crucifixion in Galatians 1:4. These two verses are part

---

[1]For a recent argument for an apocalyptic, forensic, and salvation-historical reading of Paul, see Michael F. Bird, *An Anomalous Jew: Paul among Jews, Greeks, and Romans* (Grand Rapids, MI: Eerdmans, 2016).

of Paul's appeal to the Galatians not to turn away from his gospel to the distorted message preached by the teachers in the churches of Galatia, whom Paul identifies as troublemakers ("those who trouble you") and as those "who desire to distort the gospel about/from Christ" (Gal 1:7).[2] Paul wrote Galatians to persuade Gentile Christians in the churches of Galatia not to turn away from his gospel (Gal 1:6–2:10). His gospel in Galatians focuses on the announcement of the good news about Jesus: that God has fulfilled all of his redemptive promises for Jews, Gentiles, and for the cosmos through Jesus' death for sins and through his victorious resurrection from the dead (Gal 1:1, 4; 3:13-14; esp. 3:1–5:1).[3]

Based on Paul's remarks in Galatians, the teachers in Galatia were preaching a distorted message to these Galatian (Gentile) Christians (Gal 1:7). Their message focused on circumcision (Gal 2:3; 5:3; 6:12-13) and other "works of the law" (Gal 2:16; 3:10; 4:10) as prerequisites for these Gentiles to perform before they could inherit the blessing of Abraham and become part of the people of God (cf. Gal 3:2–4:31). Evidently, the teachers were gaining some converts in Galatia since Paul begins the letter expressing shock that the Galatians "were turning so quickly from the one who called them by the grace of Christ to another gospel" (Gal 1:6). Paul clarifies the teachers' gospel is actually "not another gospel," since there's only one gospel. Rather, their message is a distortion of the true gospel of Christ (Gal 1:7). Paul later attacks the teachers and their distorted gospel by asserting they have zeal for the Galatians' circumcised flesh because they want to save face in the Jewish community (Gal 4:17). He criticizes them for their boasting in the Jewish community because of a performance of cultic circumcision on these Gentile Christians' uncircumcised flesh (Gal 6:12-13).

---

[2] Unless otherwise indicated, all translations of New Testament texts are mine.

[3] Both the Greek nouns and verbs Paul uses to refer to the gospel mean an announcement. The terms are used in multiple texts in the Old Testament (Nouns: LXX 2 Sam 4:10; 2 Sam 18:22, 25, 27; 2 Kings 7:9; verbal forms: LXX 1 Sam 31:9; 2 Sam 1:20; 4:10; 18:19-20, 26, 31; 1 Kings 1:42; 1 Chron 10:9; Ps 39:10; 67:12; 95:2; Sol. 11:1; Joel 3:5; Nah 2:1; Is 40:9; 52:7; 60:6; 61:1; Jer 20:15) and Jewish literature to refer to an announcement (Verbal forms: Asen. 19:2; 4 Bar. 3:15; 5:19; 9:20; Pss. Sol. 11:1). This announcement also pertained to good news regarding his churches' progress in the gospel (1 Thess 3:6).

Paul consequently wrote this letter with urgency to inform the Galatians that when they received his gospel by faith through his apostolic gospel ministry, they had already begun to participate in and experience every one of God's redemptive promises in Christ for Jews and Gentiles and for the cosmos because of their faith (Gal 3:1–4:31). One of those redemptive promises is the realization of the blessing of Abraham in their midst, which is the Spirit (Gal 3:14), because Jesus is the seed of Abraham (Gal 3:16). And in Christ Jesus, by faith, they too are sons of God (Gal 3:26), heirs of the promises to Abraham, and members of the seed of Abraham (Gal 3:29). By believing in Paul's gospel, which focuses on Jesus' death and resurrection (Gal 1:1, 4; 3:13), they received the Spirit because they became children of God and heirs of the promises to Abraham (Gal 3:1–4:31). Paul warns the Galatians if they give in to the teachers' distorted message, they forfeit the grace of God in Christ and will not inherit eternal life (Gal 1:8-9; 5:16–6:9). Paul's remarks about God's apocalypse of the resurrected and crucified Christ in him are rooted in a real historical threat of apostasy in Galatia, the apostolic urgency to defend his apostolic gospel authority, and the superiority of his gospel over the troublemakers' distorted gospel. He needed to win the Galatians back to his gospel so that they would as a result inherit eternal life and escape the curse of the present evil age, a curse he argues would only lead to eschatological destruction (cf. Gal 1:4; 1:8-9; 3:1–4:31; 5:2-6; 6:11-16).

The resurrected and crucified Christ. By Paul's own admission, God's vertical, horizontal, and cosmic saving action in Christ for Jews and Gentiles and for the world transforms Paul in Galatians because of his personal encounter and experience of God's apocalypse of the resurrected and crucified Christ. He began to understand God's saving action in Christ when he revealed his Son in him and transformed him so that he might "announce him as the good news among the Gentiles" (cf. Gal 1:15-16; 2:19-21; 3:1-14; 4:5-6). However, the first place in Galatians to begin discussing the transformational nature of God's apocalypse of the resurrected and crucified Christ in Paul is not his reference to his vision on the Damascus Road in Galatians 1:15-16, as important as this event and text are for my thesis, but with his remarks about Jesus' victorious resurrection in Galatians 1:1 and his death "for our sins" in Galatians 1:4.

The good news of the fulfillment of God's redemptive promises for Jews and Gentiles and for the cosmos in the risen and crucified Christ is the content of what God revealed in Paul on the Damascus Road (cf. Gal 3:1–5:1). Without Jesus' resurrection and crucifixion, Paul would have never received a vision from God of the resurrected and crucified Christ. The risen and crucified Christ is foundational to God's apocalypse of his Son in Paul. Paul explicitly references Jesus' resurrection three times in the letter (Gal 1:1, 16; 2:20). A case can be made, however, that each time he refers to the crucifixion, he assumes or implies the resurrection, for Paul mentions the death of Jesus or the crucifixion of Jesus in Galatians when articulating the saving benefits that Jews and Gentiles have already received by faith in Christ because of God's saving action through Jesus' death for Jews, Gentiles, and the cosmos.[4]

Andrew K. Boakye argues Galatians has a "Spirit-life soteriology" throughout the letter.[5] According to Boakye, "Jesus was crucified and God raised him; God's people are those who have shared in the crucifixion, and, through the Spirit, shared in the risen life of Jesus; God's new world has itself suffered crucifixion and been newly created."[6] Boakye claims this language in Galatians is similar to the narrative of Ezekiel 36–37 and the new covenant story in Jeremiah 31.[7] These texts emphasize the Spirit enlivens the spiritually "dead people of God."[8] As a result, the Spirit secures Israel's liberation and resurrects them to accept his commands.[9] God never gave the law with the intent of resurrecting the spiritually dead people of God.[10] Boakye claims "the

---

[4]For a work on the importance of the resurrection in Galatians, see Andrew K. Boakye, *Death and Life: Resurrection, Restoration, and Rectification in Paul's Letter to the Galatians* (Eugene, OR: Pickwick, 2017).

[5]Boakye, *Death and Life*, 4.

[6]Boakye, *Death and Life*, 4.

[7]Boakye, *Death and Life*, 4.

[8]Boakye, *Death and Life*, 4.

[9]Boakye, *Death and Life*, 4.

[10]Boakye, *Death and Life*, 4.

mediation of Jesus' risen life by the Spirit, a life Paul saw enshrined in Israel's scripture, as the soteriological centre of Galatians," distinguishes his reading of Galatians from other readings of the letter.[11] Boayke's thesis argues the entire letter should be read with an eye on God's act of raising Jesus from the dead (Gal 1:1-5) and the "rectification of humanity in terms of life-coming-from-death," which is seen in Galatians 2:19-20; 3:21; 5:24-25; 6:8, 14-15.[12] The source of this life-from-death theme comes from God's revelation of the crucified and resurrected Christ in Paul.[13]

Readers of Boayke's monograph must determine for themselves whether his reading strategy of Galatians is better than other approaches. As can be seen in my exegesis throughout this monograph, I disagree with him on some specific exegetical and theological matters in Galatians. However, when one considers the entire letter, his observations about the importance of life flowing from the resurrection seem right.

For example, after Paul explicitly states his apostolic ministry of the gospel comes from Jesus Christ and God the Father, "who raised him from the dead" (Gal 1:1), he immediately states in Galatians 1:4 Jesus died "for our sins to deliver us from the present evil age." Jesus' incarnation, ministry, death, and resurrection signal the arrival of the new age (cf. Gal 1:4; 3:13-14; 4:6). But his resurrection especially accentuates this, proving the new age of God's vertical, horizontal, and cosmic saving action in Christ has begun.[14] Paul's reference to Jesus' resurrection in Galatians 1:1 and to his death in Galatians 1:4 should inform readers to see an implicit reference to the resurrection going forward when he refers only to Jesus' death in the letter and when he refers to life in the Spirit. Without the resurrection (Gal 1:1), the cross has no redemptive power in Paul's soteriology in Galatians (cf. Gal 1:1, 4; 3:13-14 with 1 Cor 15:1-58), and those in Christ have no life in the Spirit without the resurrection (Gal 1:1; 3:14; 4:6; 5:25).

---

[11]Boakye, *Death and Life*, 4.
[12]Boakye, *Death and Life*, 16.
[13]Boakye, *Death and Life*, 16.
[14]For a similar point, see Robert A. Bryant, *The Risen Crucified Christ in Galatians*, SBL 185 (Atlanta: SBL, 2001), 147.

Because of Jesus' resurrection (Gal 1:1), his death for Jews and Gentiles delivers from the present evil age those for whom he died (Gal 1:4). In Galatians 2:16-17, Paul refers to justification by faith. In Galatians 2:19-21, he asserts he has been crucified with Christ because he died to the law so that he would live to God; he no longer lives, but Christ lives in him, and he claims the life he lives, he lives it by faith in God's Son who both loved him and who gave himself for him. Consequently, Paul refuses to nullify God's gift of grace to him in the gift of Christ, because he knows that if Torah brings righteousness (= justification), then Christ's death would have been in vain (Gal 2:21).[15]

In Galatians 3:13 and Galatians 4:5-6, Paul states those whom Christ redeems receive the blessing of the Spirit. In Galatians 3:1, Paul calls the Galatians "foolish" because he preached the good news of Jesus' crucifixion to them as the pathway to their personal experience of the Spirit by faith (Gal 3:2-14) while they were contemplating a turn away from his gospel that leads to life in the Spirit to the curse of the law that leads to slavery (Gal 4:8-11). Instead of preaching circumcision, Paul preached Jesus (cf. Gal 1:15-16 with 5:11). In Christ Jesus, the Galatians crucified the flesh when they participated in co-crucifixion with Jesus by dying to the law by faith (cf. Gal 2:19-20 with 5:24). By faith in Christ, God gives life by the Spirit apart from works of the law (Gal 3:10-14, 21; 5:25) because Jesus died (Gal 1:4; 3:13) and because God resurrected him from the dead (Gal 1:1). This crucifixion of the flesh with its passions and lusts was their reality because they had life in the Spirit through the cross by participating in Jesus' death by faith, and this life gave them the ability to conduct their daily pattern of life in obedience by the Spirit because they crucified the flesh with its passions and desires (cf. Gal 3:1–4:9 with 5:24-25).

Those who preached circumcision did so to avoid persecution for the cross of Jesus, but Paul boasted in the cross because he was crucified to the world through the cross and the world to him because of his co-crucifixion with Christ (Gal 6:13-14). Because of the cross (and resurrection),

---

[15]For recent work arguing the concept of grace should be understood as a gift in Paul's theology, see John M. G. Barclay, *Paul and the Gift* (Grand Rapids, MI: Eerdmans, 2015).

Paul no longer lived to promote either circumcision or to shame the uncircumcision, but he lived as one who participates in new creation; he experienced the blessing of God with all the other followers of Christ who lived in accordance with the standard of new creation (Gal 6:15-16). Based on his efforts throughout the letter to persuade the Galatians not to turn away from his gospel about Jesus Christ, the standard of new creation is the gospel of Jesus Christ (cf. Gal 1:1–2:21). This gospel focuses on the announcement that God has fulfilled all of his vertical, horizontal, and cosmic saving promises for Jews and Gentiles and for the cosmos in Christ because of Jesus' death for our sins to deliver us from the present evil age (Gal 1:4) and because of his resurrection from the dead (Gal 1:1).

Elsewhere in Paul's letters, he states Jesus died for our sins to deliver us from God's wrath, to justify us by faith, and to reconcile us to God (Rom 5:6-10; 2 Cor 5:21). In Galatians 1:4, he asserts Jesus' death "for our sins" results in deliverance from the "present evil age," to which Jews, Gentiles, and the cosmos are enslaved, as the present evil age continues to triumph until the full realization of new creation (cf. Gal 5:16-26; 6:15). The phrase "present evil age" (τοῦ αἰῶνος τοῦ ἐνεστῶτος πονηροῦ) refers to the old age (cf. Gal 3:15–4:7). It is a realm of bondage, enslaved to and ruled by sin (Gal 3:22), subjected to the curse and slavery of the law (Gal 3:10; 3:15–4:7), and in bondage under the τὰ στοιχεῖα τοῦ κόσμου ("the elementary principalities and powers of the world" or the "evil anti-God powers") (Gal 4:3, 9).[16]

The present evil age refers to the cursed universe because of sin's cosmic power (Gen 3:1-19; Rom 6). The cosmic power of sin is one reason Paul speaks of the need for a "new creation" (Gal 6:15; 2 Cor 5:18-21; cf. Is 65:17-25; Rev 21–22).[17] The present evil age includes false ideas

---

[16]For the apocalyptic phrase "evil anti-God powers," see J. Louis Martyn, *Galatians,* AB 33A (New York: Doubleday, 1997), 97n51.

[17]My above discussion of the present evil age was originally published in Jarvis J. Williams and Curtis A. Woods, "Jesus, Deliver Us from This Present Racist Age," *Christianity Today,* August 6, 2019, www.christianitytoday.com/ct/2019/august-web-only/deliver-us-from-this-racist -evil-age.html. Material published here with permission. Same material also used with permission in Jarvis J. Williams, *Redemptive Kingdom Diversity: A Biblical Theology of the People of God* (Grand Rapids, MI: Baker, 2021), 115-16.

(cf. Gal 1:8-9; 4:8-11; Col 1:21; 2:8), wicked behavior (cf. Gal 5:19-21; Col 1:21), and spiritually dead and morally ruined human beings walking in a pattern of life in their trespasses and sins contrary to the Spirit (Eph 2:1-10), and the present evil age refers to corrupt institutions, systems, authorities, and rulers (earthly and demonic) (cf. Eph 1:20-21; 2:1-3; Col 2:14-15; Rev 17:1–18:24). The present evil age enslaves people under sin's power (cf. Gal 4:3), is enslaved to sin's power (Rom 6:6, 20) and the demonic forces of evil (Gal 4:9-11; Eph 4:17-19; Col 2:20), and enslaves everything within the present evil age (cf. Gal 1:4; 4:3). The present evil age also includes the enemy of physical death (1 Cor 15:26). However, Jesus brings good news (Mk 1:14-15), and Jesus *is* the good news (Gal 1:15-16). The good news of the gospel of Jesus Christ is he delivers Jews and Gentiles from everything within the present evil age, including the last enemy of death (1 Cor 15), by his death for our sins (Gal 1:4; 3:13; 4:6) because he physically resurrected from the dead (Gal 1:1, 15-16; 1 Cor 15). Jesus' death delivers the entire creation from its bondage to the present evil age because of his resurrection (Gal 1:1, 4; 3:13-14; 4:5-6; 6:15-16; cf. 1 Cor 15).

Paul's remarks about the present evil age in Galatians 1:4 anticipate his comments about Jewish and Gentile slavery to the στοιχεῖα (Gal 4:3, 9).[18] Prior to their faith in Christ, the Galatians, as Gentiles, showed their enslavement to the present evil age by their idolatry because they did not know God (Gal 4:8). Paul warns them that a turn to Torah is analogous to their return to idolatry and to slavery to "weak and poor elements" (Gal 4:9). In Galatians 4:3, Paul said Jews, prior to their faith in Christ, were likewise enslaved under the τὰ στοιχεῖα τοῦ κόσμου.

Interpreters have suggested στοιχεῖα refers to the "fundamental principles of learning," the "elements of nature," "heavenly bodies," or to "spirits worshiped as deities."[19] The term Paul uses for "elements"

---

[18]For a recent monograph on the concept of evil in Galatians, see Tyler A. Stewart, *The Origin and Persistence of Evil in Galatians*, WUNT (Tübingen: Mohr Siebeck, 2021).

[19]For a discussion of the different views, see Craig S. Keener, *Galatians* (Grand Rapids, MI: Eerdmans, 2019), 326-33.

(στοιχεῖα) occurs in Jewish texts to refer to the elements of which humans are made (4 Macc 12:13), the elements of which the world was made (Wis 7:17), the elements of creation (Wis 19:18), and the demons/ rulers of darkness (T. Sol 8.2, 4; 18.1-2). Absent the term στοιχεῖα, the elements of the world are present in another Jewish text in reference to Gentile worship of the elements of creation (e.g., fire, wind, air, stars, water, and other non-angelic heavenly luminaries) (Wis 12:2-3). These "weak and poor elements" (τὰ ἀσθενῆ καὶ πτωχὰ στοιχεῖα) to which the Galatians are wishing to enslave themselves all over again[20] are the same elements in the present evil age under which Paul and other Jews apart from faith in Christ were enslaved (ὑπὸ τὰ στοιχεῖα τοῦ κόσμου ἤμεθα δεδουλωμένοι) (Gal 4:3; cf. Wis 13:1-19).

In Galatians, I am not convinced, however, Paul refers only to one specific thing with his reference to the στοιχεῖα.[21] Because of the phrase τὰ στοιχεῖα τοῦ κόσμου in the context of Galatians 4:3-11 and the context of the letter, στοιχεῖα in Galatians 4:3 and Galatians 4:9 does not simply refer to the law or to life under the law.[22] Rather, τὰ στοιχεῖα τοῦ κόσμου at least refers to everything contrary to the Spirit and enslaved within and by the present evil age (cf. Gal 1:4 with 3:1–5:26). The occurrence of a form of τὰ στοιχεῖα τοῦ κόσμου in Colossians 2:8 and 2:20, in an epistolary context that emphasizes the supremacy of Jesus Christ over all things (Col 1:15-20) and that critiques a pattern of life and worship contrary to exclusive devotion to Jesus Christ (Col 1:21–3:17), supports Clinton Arnold's claim that "the κόσμος is not solely the sphere of human activity, but is simultaneously the sphere of demonic activity which wields a powerful and compelling influence on human behavior."[23] Indeed, the Galatians are in danger of becoming enslaved all over again to their former deities.[24] But more than that,

---

[20]ὡς ἐπιστρέφετε πάλιν ἐπὶ τὰ ἀσθενῆ καὶ πτωχὰ στοιχεῖα οἷς πάλιν ἄνωθεν δουλεύειν θέλετε.
[21]Keener takes a similar position in *Galatians*, 333.
[22]Clinton Arnold clearly argues this point, although his thesis is that the στοιχεῖα refers to demonic powers. For example, see his "Returning to the Domain of the Powers: Stoicheia as Evil Spirits in Galatians 4:3, 9," *Novum Testamentum* 38, no. 1 (1996): 55-76.
[23]Arnold, "Returning to the Domain of the Powers," 65.
[24]For a similar point, see Arnold, "Returning to the Domain of the Powers," 61.

they are in danger of becoming enslaved again to every single aspect of the present evil age and to everything opposed to the Spirit and new creation that falls short of the hope of righteousness in Christ. The latter point appears correct because if the Galatians embrace the law, Paul claims they renounce God's saving action for them in Christ, an action that includes their reception and experience of the Spirit by faith (Gal 1:6; cf. 3:1–6:15). Their rejection of Christ would result in an eschatological anathema (Gal 1:8-9).

In Galatians 4:3 and in Galatians 4:8-9, Paul attaches στοιχεῖα to slavery, prior to faith in Christ, to those who do not know God, and to idolatry. He also attaches στοιχεῖα to special days, months, seasons, and years (Gal 4:10). The slavery of the present evil age contrasts with the liberation of "new creation" (cf. Gal 1:4; 3:1–6:10 with 6:15) and with the new age, both of which are inaugurated by Christ and have the Spirit as its emblem and signpost (cf. Gal 1:4 with 3:1–6:10).

The στοιχεῖα includes the political and social regimes that are enslaved to the "anti-God powers" that both enslave and press against the entire creation, and from which Jews, Gentiles, and the entire creation need to be rescued, resurrected, and transferred into a new creation in the realm of the Spirit (Gal 1:4; 6:15).[25] The στοιχεῖα age also includes Jews living in accordance with the law apart from faith in Jesus and Gentiles enslaved to a life of idolatry apart from faith in Christ because they do not know God (cf. Gal 2:15-21 with 4:3-11). The στοιχεῖα are part of this present evil age. Paul sharply criticizes the Gentiles as returning to lives of pagan idolatry if they walk away from his gospel toward the στοιχεῖα and embrace the Jewish law as a way of life (Gal 4:8-11), for God's new creation has dawned in Christ for Jews and Gentiles by the indwelling presence of the Spirit and the entire creation. Jews and Gentiles in Christ have both received the Spirit by faith and conduct their daily lives by walking in step with the Spirit as an emblem and a signpost of new creation's reality since they have life by the Spirit (Gal 3:1–6:10).

---

[25]A similar thought in H. D. Betz, *Galatians* (Minneapolis: Fortress, 1979), 190.

This new creation language in Galatians 6:15 draws on language from Isaiah 65:17-25 (cf. Jer 31:31-33 and Ezek 36–37). In its Old Testament context, Isaiah 65 is a promise of both national and cosmic hope in the context of God's judgment of his people during a time of exile because of their sin. The Lord declares he revealed himself to a people who did not seek him, to a nation that did not call upon his name, and he daily stretched out his hands to a disobedient people who refused to walk in accordance with his precepts (Is 65:1-7). The Lord, then, promises that he will be merciful to the people who repent and follow him (Is 65:8-10). He likewise promises to bring the sword of judgment against those who refuse to repent but instead who would disobey his statutes (Is 65:11-16). In Isaiah 65:17-25, the Lord promises to bring cosmic renewal to both the earthly Jerusalem by means of deliverance from exile and future restoration, but most strikingly the restored Jerusalem (that is, the city of God) actually functions as a metaphor for the cosmic regeneration and resurrection of the entire world (see also Tobit 13 and Rev 21–22).

The Lord says through the prophet Isaiah that he would "create new heavens and a new earth" and that "the former things shall not be remembered or come into mind" (Is 65:17). He will create Jerusalem to be a joy to her inhabitants as he brings his people out of exile and restores the fortunes of the earthly Jerusalem (Is 65:18-25). But when Isaiah says the Lord will "create new heavens and a new earth," he points beyond deliverance from exile to a comprehensive cosmic new creation of the entire universe (Is 65:17). The latter reading is supported in Isaiah's second line when he states, "The former things shall not be remembered or come to mind" (Is 65:17). Isaiah, then, moves from this promise of cosmic redemption to the local redemption of the earthly Jerusalem in Isaiah 65:18-25.

Paul picks up on this language of new creation from Isaiah, focuses on the cosmic aspect of new creation, and understands God to bring this promise of cosmic redemption to full realization via his saving action in Christ for Jews and Gentiles and for the cosmos as he justifies Jews and Gentiles by faith and renews the entire creation (Gal 2:16; 3:6-9; 5:5; 6:15;

cf. 2 Cor 5:17-19; Rev 21–22). The emblem of God's new, universal, and cosmic creative act of resurrection is the indwelling presence and power of the Spirit within Jews and Gentiles justified by faith, and only these justified ones have the Spirit and receive by faith their portion in the Abrahamic blessing in Christ because of God's saving action for them in Christ, who is the seed of Abraham (Gal 1:4; 3:1-14; 4:6, 21-31; 5:5).

Paul later refers to the revelation of God's Son in him so that he would announce Jesus as the good news among the Gentiles (Gal 1:15-16). This announcement of good news to the Gentiles was the message, if believed by faith, that granted Jews and Gentiles membership in and made them participants of the full blessing of Abraham (Gal 2:16; 3:2–4:31). The reference in Galatians 1:1 unquestionably highlights the Father's raising of Jesus from the dead (τοῦ ἐγείραντος αὐτὸν ἐκ νεκρῶν). His comments in Galatians 1:16, however, do not mention God's resurrection of Jesus. Instead, Paul refers to God's act of revealing his Son in him so that he would announce Jesus as the good news among the Gentiles (Gal 1:16). In Galatians 2:19-20, he says he died to the law so that he would "live" to God; he was crucified with Christ, and Christ lives in him. This life perhaps includes more than eternal life in Galatians 2:19-20, but it is not less than eternal life since Paul associates this life with death to the law (which promised life but did not give it) and with co-crucifixion with Christ. Furthermore, Paul later declares that life comes by faith in Christ, not by works of the law (Gal 3:12, 21), and that since "we live by the Spirit," we must also conduct our daily lives by the Spirit (Gal 5:25; cf. 5:16).

Paul describes God's revelation of Jesus in him as both good news to be announced among the Gentiles and as a revelation about his Son (Gal 1:16). The sonship language connects with Paul's earlier remarks in Galatians 1:1 that God the Father (Jesus' Father and our Father) raised Jesus from the dead. Paul's description of Jesus as God's Son is in the context of Paul calling him the Christ (Gal 1:1, 3, 7, 12) and the Lord (Gal 1:3).[26] Labeling

---

[26]For other references to Jesus as the Christ in Galatians, see Gal 1:1, 3, 6-7, 10, 12, 22; 2:4, 16-17, 19-3:1; 3:13-14, 16, 22, 24, 26-29; 4:14, 19; 5:1-2, 4, 6, 24; 6:2, 12, 14. For references to Jesus as Lord, see Gal 1:3, 19; 4:1; 5:10; 6:14, 18.

his vision of Jesus as a revelation of/about God's Son in Galatians 1:16 is the language of exaltation/resurrection since the revelation God gave Paul of his Son was a vision of the resurrected and exalted Christ (Acts 9:1-22; 22:6-21). God's revelation of his exalted Son in Paul caused him to participate in Jesus' death and resurrection by the Spirit by becoming crucified with Christ and living his life by faith in the Son of God who loved him, gave himself for him, and lives in him (Gal 2:19-20; 5:25; 6:14).

As more than one scholar has observed, the term *Son* in Galatians communicates a filial relationship between God and Jesus (Gal 1:15-16; 4:5-6) and between God and the people of God (Gal 3:7, 26; 4:7, 22, 30).[27] Yet, here in Galatians 1:16, the term is connected to the filial relationship between God the Father and his *resurrected* crucified Son, Jesus Christ (cf. Gal 1:1, 15-16). Paul assumes the resurrection of Jesus when he refers to the death of Jesus; when he talks about Jesus' death in Galatians, he does so in the context of discussing the efficacy of Jesus' death for Jews and Gentiles to extend to them the blessing of Abraham and to deliver them from the present evil age and from the curse of the law (e.g., Gal 1:4; 3:10-14; etc.). In Romans 1:4, written several years after Galatians, Paul states Jesus was "appointed to be God's Son with power in accordance with the Spirit of holiness at the resurrection from the dead."[28] Because Jesus is the Father's eternal, resurrected, exalted, and Spirit-anointed, crucified Son, Jews and Gentiles by faith in Christ become children of God and fulfill the righteous requirements of the law as they walk in step with the Spirit in obedience to the gospel and as the Spirit dwells in them (Rom 8:14, 19; 9:26; cf. 8:1-11).

As I have argued elsewhere, Paul mentions Jesus' death numerous times in Galatians.[29] When Paul identifies Jesus as the resurrected Son, he does so in the context of framing the letter with an explicit reference

---

[27]Paul also uses τέκνα ("children") in Galatians to express a filial relationship between God and the people of God because of his saving action for them in Christ (Gal 4:19, 25, 27-28, 31).

[28]τοῦ ὁρισθέντος υἱοῦ θεοῦ ἐν δυνάμει κατὰ πνεῦμα ἁγιωσύνης ἐξ ἀναστάσεως νεκρῶν.

[29]Jarvis J. Williams, *Christ Redeemed "Us" from the Curse of the Law: A Jewish Martyrological Reading of Galatians 3.13*, LNTS 524 (New York: T&T Clark, 2019), 2-3; *A Commentary on Galatians*, NCC (Eugene, OR: Cascade, 2020), 4-5.

to Jesus' resurrection ("who raised him from the dead"; Gal 1:1), to his cross ("who gave himself for our sins"; Gal 1:4) at the beginning of the letter, and to an explicit reference to Jesus' cross (Gal 6:14) and new creation at the end of the letter (Gal 6:15). The latter reference to new creation is another way of talking about cosmic resurrection (cf. Gal 6:15 with Is 65:17-25; Jer 31:31-34; Ezek 36–37).[30] Commenting on Jesus' crucifixion, Paul identifies Jesus as the "Son of God, who loved me and gave himself for me" (Gal 2:20), so that righteousness would come by faith because of Christ's death (and resurrection) instead of by law (Gal 2:21). He refers to Jesus as God's Son, whom he sent to "redeem us from the curse of the law" (Gal 3:13; 4:4-6).

Elsewhere in the letter, when Paul mentions the cross/crucifixion of Christ, he assumes his resurrection. He says he died with respect to the law (Gal 2:19), and he was crucified with Christ (Gal 2:20). Christ "died in vain" if righteousness comes to Jews and Gentiles by Torah observance (Gal 2:21). The Galatians, before whom Christ was publicly proclaimed as having been crucified, were foolish for being duped to think they had supernatural experiences of the Spirit by works of the law instead of by faith (Gal 3:1-5).

Finny Philip points out that in selected Old Testament texts, the Prophets anticipate a future outpouring of the Spirit upon all Jews (cf. Is 44:1-5; Ezek 36:25-29; 37:1-14; 39:29) and possibly Gentiles who join themselves to the covenant community of the Jewish people (MT Joel 3:1-5).[31] He further argues that in numerous Second Temple Jewish texts, God pours out his Spirit only upon the covenant community of Jews (Jub. 1:22-23; 1QH 6.11-13; 7.6-7; 12.11-13; 13.18-14.13; 16.11b-129),[32] and that Qumran texts offer no explanation of the process by which Gentiles could proselytize and become part of the covenant community.[33] He says there are texts that list requirements for the "various stages" by which

---

[30]See also the vertical, horizontal, and cosmic redemptive promises in Isaiah 40-66.

[31]Finny Philip, *The Origins of Pauline Pneumatology*, WUNT 194 (Tubingen: Mohr Siebeck, 2005), 34-76.

[32]Philip, *Origins of Pauline Pneumatology*, 81, 85-86.

[33]Philip, *Origins of Pauline Pneumatology*, 86.

Gentiles are admitted into the covenant community (1QS 5.8-9; 6.20-21).[34] Philip infers that this evidence only suggests that if Gentiles proselytized and participated in the Spirit, they would only do so when they purified themselves from every transgression of Torah (1QS 5.14) and became members within the Jewish covenantal community.[35]

Psalms of Solomon 17–18 state that the Davidic Messiah will rule his people and conquer the Gentiles by the Spirit (17:37; 18:6). Yet, these Psalms say nothing about the outpouring of the Spirit upon the Gentiles. Wisdom of Solomon, says Philip, associates Spirit with wisdom.[36] There wisdom, and by association the Spirit, is available to anyone (Jew or Gentile) who seeks it (e.g., Wis 1:1-2; 6:12, 21-24; 7:7, 27; 8:1).[37] Likewise, says Philip, Philo suggests the Spirit is "probably" available to Gentiles (cf. *Her.* 56; *Leg.* 1.31-38; cf. *Det.* 80; *Her.* 259; *Virt.* 212-19).[38]

To the contrary, Paul states Christ (the Jewish Messiah) redeemed Jews and Gentiles from Torah's curse by becoming an accursed victim of the law on behalf of them via his crucifixion so that both groups would receive the Abrahamic blessing of the Spirit (Gal 3:13-14; 4:5-6) and become equal members of the new covenant community in Christ by faith apart from the works of the law as Jews and Gentiles in Christ (Gal 3:1–4:31). God's Son redeemed those under the law as one who also lived under the law so that they would become heirs and no longer slaves (Gal 3:13-14; 4:4-7).

The stumbling block of the cross would be no more if Paul still preached circumcision as the mark of the people of God (Gal 5:11). Those in Christ crucified the flesh with its lustful passions (Gal 5:24). Those who preached circumcision did so simply to avoid persecution for the cross of Christ (Gal 6:12). Paul boasts only in Jesus' cross because the cross is the agent through which he was crucified to the world and the world to him (Gal 6:14).

---

[34]Philip, *Origins of Pauline Pneumatology*, 86.

[35]Philip, *Origins of Pauline Pneumatology*, 86.

[36]Philip, *Origins of Pauline Pneumatology*, 97-100.

[37]Philip, *Origins of Pauline Pneumatology*, 100.

[38]Philip, *Origins of Pauline Pneumatology*, 103; esp. 103-8. For a monograph discussing the Spirit in Pseudo-Philo, and Josephus, see John Levison, *The Spirit in First-Century Judaism* (Leiden: Brill, 1999).

In the same letter where Paul proclaims Christ lives in him and the life he lives in this world he lives (in resurrection life) by faith in God's Son, who died for him (Gal 2:19-20), he also appeals to the marks of Jesus in his body (likely a reference to his sufferings for the cross [cf. Gal 4:12-20]) as the reason the troublemaking teachers in Galatia should stop troubling his apostolic gospel labors in Galatia (Gal 6:17). Thus, the resurrection and the death of Jesus together in Galatians are foundational elements to everything Paul says in the letter about God's vertical, horizontal, and cosmic saving action in Christ and about personal agency, ethical transformation, and Jewish and Gentile participation in eternal life by the Spirit.[39]

God's revelation of the resurrected and crucified Christ in Paul. Paul would have likely never been convinced of the good news about Jesus for Jews, Gentiles, and the cosmos unless God himself revealed his Son in Paul and caused an epistemological shift in his thinking. This epistemological shift was in fact "retrospective" in Galatians,[40] and the revelation Paul received about Christ from God was apocalyptic.

An apocalyptic reading of Paul is complex,[41] but it is an important soteriological piece to understand in Paul's theology in order to better discern the connection between the Spirit, personal agency, ethical transformation, and eternal life in Galatians.[42] There are disagreements

---

[39]Bryant, *Risen and Crucified Christ in Galatians*, 150-94, also argues the resurrection plays a prominent role in Paul's argument in Galatians. His project is very different from Boayke's and mine. Bryant frames the importance of the resurrection in Galatians within the context of Greco-Roman rhetoric and epistolary writing in antiquity. Boayke's thesis focuses on the life-from-death motif in Galatians. My primary concern in this section is the relationship between the resurrection and life in the Spirit, ethical transformation, and eternal life in Galatians.

[40]For perhaps the most comprehensive retrospective apocalyptic reading of Paul's soteriology, see Douglas A. Campbell, *The Deliverance of God: An Apocalyptic Rereading of Justification in Paul* (Grand Rapids, MI: Eerdmans, 2009). Campbell devotes a few pages to an apocalyptic reading in Galatians. My reading and Campbell's reading differ at many points. Still, he is correct to point out Paul's apocalyptic understanding is "retrospective." He looks back on God's saving action in Christ in the light of God's revelation of Christ in him.

[41]For a recent discussion of apocalyptic, see Brendan Byrne, *Paul and the Economy of Salvation: Reading from the Perspective of the Last Judgment* (Grand Rapids, MI: Eerdmans, 2021), 9-34. For essays on the application of apocalyptic soteriology to political resistance and the liberation of the oppressed, see Ernst Käsemann, *Church Conflicts: The Cross, Apocalyptic, and Political Resistance*, ed. Ry O. Siggelkow, trans. Roy A. Harrisville (Grand Rapids, MI: Baker, 2021).

[42]Richard B. Hays goes a step further and asserts, "Paul's moral vision is intelligible only when his apocalyptic perspective is kept clearly in mind: the church is to find its identity and vocation

and various nuances among the numerous scholars who primarily read Paul through an apocalyptic lens.[43] However, according to J. P. Davies, those scholars tend to affirm rightly an "epistemology of revealed knowledge, the eschatological doctrine of the two ages, a cosmology characterized by two realms, and a soteriology which emphasizes divine victory."[44] Yet, Davies points out, they also wrongly downplay, or out-right deny, the presence of human agency, salvation history, the reve-lation of God's continued presence, and justification by faith.[45] To save space, I simply define how I understand apocalyptic in this monograph and then interact with Martinus C. de Boer,[46] an important conversation partner when discussing an apocalyptic reading of Paul's soteriology in Galatians.[47] The concept of apocalyptic in Galatians occurs first in Galatians 1:4 and again in Galatians 1:15-16. Before I engage with de Boer, I must interact with a recent article that questions identifying Paul's soteriology in Galatians as apocalyptic since I argue his soteriology is apocalyptic. However, I do not argue it is only apocalyptic.

Logan Williams compares the *Apocalypse of Weeks* in 1 Enoch (Apocalypse) with Galatians in order to answer whether Paul's "dis-junctive" soteriology in Galatians can properly be called "apocalyptic."[48] Williams makes a compelling argument that Paul's "disjunctive" sote-riology neither derives from nor is similar to the soteriology in the

---

by recognizing its role within the cosmic drama of God's reconciliation of the world to himself." See Richard B. Hays, *The Moral Vision of the New Testament: A Contemporary Introduction to New Testament Ethics* (New York: HarperCollins, 1996), 19. He quotes 2 Cor 5:14-18 to support this statement.

[43]For a few representatives of and a critique of the so-called apocalyptic school, see discussion in N. T. Wright, *Paul and His Recent Interpreters* (Minneapolis: Fortress, 2015), 135-218.

[44]For recent discussion, see J. P. Davies, *Paul Among the Apocalypses? An Evaluation of the "Apoca-lyptic Paul" in the Context of Jewish and Christian Apocalyptic Literature*, LNTS 562 (New York: T&T Clark, 2016), 1-2.

[45]For this critique, see Davies, *Paul Among the Apocalypses?*, 1-2.

[46]Although I interact with de Boer's discussion of apocalyptic in his Galatians commentary, his most important work on Paul's apocalyptic soteriology is his *The Defeat of Death: Apocalyptic Eschatology in 1 Corinthians 15 and Romans 5*, JSNTSup 22 (Sheffield: JSOT Press, 1988).

[47]The most important voice in English-speaking scholarship in the apocalyptic reading of Paul is J. Louis Martyn. His Galatians commentary was the first commentary that set forth a compre-hensive apocalyptic reading of Galatians.

[48]Logan Williams, "Disjunction in Paul: Apocalyptic or Christomorphic? Comparing the Apoca-lypse of Weeks with Galatians," *NTS* 64 (2018): 64-80.

Apocalypse of Weeks since God's revelation of Christ comes, to use John M. G. Barclay's language, to undeserving recipients in Galatians, while the *Apocalypse of Weeks* states God's revelation comes to those who are progressing in righteousness.[49] The revelation to Enoch is "apocalyptic," but it does not contain a "disruptive," "irruptive," or "invasive" inbreaking into the present evil age to create a new age out of something old.[50] Rather, Williams argues Paul's "disjunctive" soteriology is "christomorphic, not apocalyptic," because it is retrospectively grounded in and shaped by Jesus' death and resurrection. According to Williams, a comparison with the *Apocalypse of Weeks* shows at the very least readers should not call Paul's soteriology in Galatians a quality of apocalyptic, when in fact the *Apocalypse of Weeks* is a clear example of apocalyptic soteriology but does not have in it this so-called apocalyptic "invasive" and "irruptive" ingredient.[51]

Williams's article is a helpful corrective to scholars who generally assert "disruption" is a key piece to "apocalyptic" when in fact he has shown with his comparison at least one Jewish apocalypse does not parallel what scholars have identified as Paul's apocalyptic language. Williams is also correct to point out Paul's understanding of God's saving action in Christ is reconsidered in the light of Jesus' death and resurrection and Paul's association with Jesus' death and resurrection by faith.

When I identify Paul's soteriology in Galatians as apocalyptic in this monograph, I do not mean every feature of Paul's apocalyptic soteriology is likewise present in every Jewish text that scholars identify as apocalyptic. I assume there are both similarities and discontinuities between Paul's apocalyptic soteriology and Jewish apocalyptic texts because of Jesus' death and resurrection and because of Paul's participation in God's saving action in Christ by faith. By apocalyptic soteriology in Galatians, I mean both individuals and the entire cosmos are

---

[49]Williams, "Disjunction in Paul," 64-80.
[50]Williams, "Disjunction in Paul," 64-80.
[51]Williams, "Disjunction in Paul," 64-80.

enslaved to sin's power and to the present evil age. As a result, every-thing and everyone in the cosmos needs to be delivered from the present evil age and transferred into a new age because the entire creation (Jews, Gentiles, and everything else) is imprisoned under the power of sin and the demonic forces of evil (Gal 3:22; 4:3, 9-11).

Jews and Gentiles need to be forensically justified by faith in Christ before God (Gal 2:16-21), redeemed and liberated from the curse of the law and from slavery to the present evil age (Gal 3:13–5:26), and become part of Abraham's universal reconciled family through Christ so that they can freely choose to walk in step with the Spirit in love for one another in obedience to the gospel (Gal 3:1–6:10). The entire creation is enslaved within and to the present evil age and needs to be liberated from its oppressive bondage (Gal 6:15) apart from works of the law (Gal 5:3). The law itself is both part of and enslaves those under it to the present evil age (cf. Gal 2:11-16; 3:15-5:1). God in Christ invaded the present evil age (Gal 1:1, 4; 3:13-14; 4:5-6) to provide the vertical (Gal 2:16), horizontal (Gal 2:11-14; 5:16–6:2), and cosmic redemption from sin's enslavement (Gal 6:15).

De Boer discusses the concepts of "forensic apocalyptic eschatology" and "cosmological apocalyptic eschatology" as they occur in the primary Jewish texts.[52] He explains the "two-age scheme" (the old age and the new age) is foundational to both Jewish and Christian "apocalyptic eschatology."[53] God reveals the truth about both ages.[54] The new age reveals and "unmasks" the present age "as the old age that is doomed to pass away."[55] The two ages reveal two different paths in the relevant Second Temple Jewish texts: a "cosmological" track and a "forensic" track.[56] The "cosmological" track suggests the current world that God created became a slave to the power of wicked, demonic powers and forces of evil because of the rebellion of angels at some point in an

---

[52]For this summary and citations of primary texts, see Martinus C. de Boer, *Galatians*, TNTL (Louisville: Westminster John Knox, 2011), 31-36.

[53]De Boer, *Galatians*, 31.

[54]De Boer, *Galatians*, 31.

[55]De Boer, *Galatians*, 31.

[56]De Boer, *Galatians*, 31.

antediluvian history of the world; this fall likely occurred at some point in the days of Noah.[57]

The demonic forces of evil have seized God's supreme rule.[58] The demonic powers and forces of evil also took control over and dominance of everyone and everything in the entire cosmos, and they led the entire creation into many patterns of idolatry.[59] However, "a righteous remnant" of God's elect people testify, by their obedience to Israel's one and true living and sovereign God over the entire creation, that the wicked, cosmic angelic and demonic powers are destined to be destroyed.[60] God's elect remnant patiently anticipates his liberation when he will "invade the world, now under the dominion of the evil powers, and defeats them in a cosmic war."[61] Only God himself has the ability "to defeat and to overthrow the demonic and diabolical powers" that have dominion over and have seduced the entire creation by evil.[62] In the immediate future, God will exercise his sovereign power over the entire creation by "delivering the righteous and bringing about a new age in which he will reign unopposed."[63] In this moment, God will make right all things that have gone terribly wrong both in his creation and with his creation.[64] De Boer cites 1 Enoch 1-36 as "perhaps its purest form" of "cosmological apocalyptic eschatology."[65] He suggests that a passage from Assumption of Moses 10 elucidates this kind of eschatology:

> Then his [God's] kingdom (rule) will appear throughout his
>   whole creation,
> Then the devil will have an end,
> Yes, sorrow will be led away with him.

---

[57]De Boer, *Galatians*, 31. De Boer cites the following primary texts to support his point: Gen 6:1-6; 1 En. 6-19; 64.1-2; 69.4-5; 86.1-6; 106.13-17; Jub. 4:15, 22; 5:1-8; 10:4-5; T. Reub. 5:6-7; T. Naph 3.5; CD 2.17-3.1; 2 Bar 56.12-15; L.A.B. 34.1-5; Wis 2:23-24; Jude 6; 2 Pet 2:4.

[58]De Boer, *Galatians*, 31.

[59]De Boer, *Galatians*, 31.

[60]De Boer, *Galatians*, 31.

[61]De Boer, *Galatians*, 31.

[62]De Boer, *Galatians*, 31.

[63]De Boer, *Galatians*, 31.

[64]De Boer, *Galatians*, 31.

[65]De Boer, *Galatians*, 32.

> For the Heavenly One will arise from his royal throne,
>
> Yes, he will go forth from his holy habitation
>
> With indignation and wrath on behalf of his sons.
>
> And the earth will tremble . . .[66]

De Boer further suggests "cosmological apocalyptic eschatology" contains a "cosmic drama."[67] This drama consists of both "divine" and "cosmic" powers simultaneously working against one another.[68] This act playing out within the creation reveals the two ages are both temporary periods of time in the current "cosmic drama" and "two spheres or zones in which certain powers hold sway or in which certain kinds of activity take place."[69]

The second type of apocalyptic eschatology is "forensic apocalyptic eschatology."[70] De Boer describes this pattern as excluding, minimizing, or overtly rejecting the cosmological demonic forces of evil (cf. 1 En. 98.4-5; Pss. Sol. 9:4-5).[71] In the Jewish texts where this scheme occurs, both "free will and individual human decision" coexist.[72] Sin is a free choice to reject God, the sovereign Creator of the universe.[73] By willfully rejecting God, sinners freely violate the foundational commandment in the Hebrew Scriptures: only worship God, and do not commit idolatry.[74] God punishes this "fundamental sin" with the judgment of death.[75] God gave the law to provide the solution to this plight.[76] One's relationship to the law sets in motion one's eschatological fate.[77] The day of judgment is conceived of as a courtroom where all people will stand in the presence of God, the righteous Judge, instead of the

---

[66]De Boer, *Galatians*, 32.
[67]De Boer, *Galatians*, 32.
[68]De Boer, *Galatians*, 32.
[69]De Boer, *Galatians*, 32.
[70]De Boer, *Galatians*, 32.
[71]De Boer, *Galatians*, 32.
[72]De Boer, *Galatians*, 32.
[73]De Boer, *Galatians*, 32.
[74]De Boer, *Galatains*, 32.
[75]De Boer, *Galatians*, 32.
[76]De Boer, *Galatians*, 32.
[77]De Boer, *Galatians*, 32.

judgment being presented as a cosmic war between good and evil.[78] On that day of judgment, God will give eternal life to those who honored him and who obeyed the law.[79] These are the righteous.[80] But he will pay eternal destruction to the wicked who disobeyed his law.[81] God will condemn the wicked, but he will justify, that is declare the righteous to be in the right and vindicate them in his law court, by virtue of their allegiance to his law.[82]

De Boer finds examples of "forensic (legal, judicial) apocalyptic eschatology" in 4 Ezra and 2 Baruch.[83] In both traditions, the authors accentuate Adam's fall into disobedience and his personal responsibility as "the first and paradigmatic transgressor (4 Ezra 3:5-7, 20-21; 4:30-31; 7:118-19; 2 Bar. 17:2-3; 23:4; 48:42-43; 54:14, 19; 56:6; cf. 1 En. 69:6; Jub. 3:17-25; 4:29-30; L.A.B. 13:8-9; Sir 25:24; Wis 10:1)."[84] The current age of evil and wickedness is the moment when the righteous must make the decision to obey the law to participate in life in the age to come (2 Bar. 17:4; 38:1-2; 48:22; 54:5).[85] De Boer claims the Dead Sea Scrolls contain patterns of personal responsibility, predestination, cosmic warfare against wicked forces of evil and their agents in the eschatological age, and judgment according to works (1 QS 1-4; 1 QM; CD).[86] When one chooses the law, one chooses to live under God's realm of protection from the cosmological forces of evil that are constantly threatening both the entire community and its members.[87] God uses the protection of his law to help the righteous resist the supernatural cosmic forces of evil (CD 16.1-3).[88] The individual's experience in the present time is a constant difficulty between two diametrically opposed "groups

---

[78]De Boer, *Galatians*, 32.
[79]De Boer, *Galatians*, 32.
[80]De Boer, *Galatians*, 32.
[81]De Boer, *Galatians*, 32.
[82]De Boer, *Galatians*, 32.
[83]De Boer, *Galatians*, 32.
[84]De Boer, *Galatians*, 32.
[85]De Boer, *Galatians*, 32.
[86]De Boer, *Galatians*, 33.
[87]De Boer, *Galatians*, 33.
[88]De Boer, *Galatians*, 33.

of cosmological powers or spirits that seek to lay their claim on human beings."[89] This cosmic struggle is present both in the severing of the righteous within the community from the wicked outside of the community and personal decisions that all individuals must daily make to live in obedience to God and his law.[90] This choice is particularly pertinent for those who want to remain within the community.[91]

De Boer thinks Paul's letters make use of both "cosmological apocalyptic eschatology" and "forensic apocalyptic eschatology" (cf. Rom 5:12-21; 1 Cor 15:21-22 with 4 Ezra and 2 Baruch),[92] but he argues Paul's references to Satan's hostility toward God and the gospel support that he was more indebted to a "cosmological apocalyptic eschatology."[93] In certain places in Second Temple Jewish literature, "cosmological apocalyptic eschatology" has a strong presence, and there the present evil age and the new age are "spatial" and temporal categories or realms of power vying for comprehensive dominance over the entire creation, in addition to being temporal and discontinuing specific periods of history.[94] In the present evil age, demonic powers have sovereignty over everything in the entire cosmos, and they have also "perverted" the cosmos with wicked behavior.[95] The present age is "the realm of sin, death, and evil," which is why Paul calls it the present evil age in Galatians 1:4.[96] All humans are enslaved to wickedness and to violent powerful forces of evil that have taken over God's sovereignty over the world.[97] In the coming age, which is already but not yet, "God will (once more) reign unopposed over the whole creation."[98] Thus, the coming age is the sphere "of righteousness, life, and peace."[99] The

---

[89]De Boer, *Galatians*, 33.
[90]De Boer, *Galatians*, 33.
[91]De Boer, *Galatians*, 33.
[92]De Boer, *Galatians*, 33.
[93]De Boer, *Galatians*, 33. He cites the following verses as support for his premise: Rom 8:38; 16:20; 1 Cor 2:6-8; 5:5; 7:5; 15:24, 26, 56; 2 Cor 2:11; 6:4, 15; 11:14; 12:7; 1 Thess 2:18.
[94]De Boer, *Galatians*, 33.
[95]De Boer, *Galatians*, 33.
[96]De Boer, *Galatians*, 32-33.
[97]De Boer, *Galatians*, 33.
[98]De Boer, *Galatians*, 33.
[99]De Boer, *Galatians*, 34.

opposing powers of the already-but-not-yet age are God, the Messiah, and others whom God appoints, and they will give a revelation of themselves from heaven as "they will invade the orb of the powers on earth below (the orb of Satan and his minions) and aggressively defeat them, thereby removing them from the creation and liberating human beings from their malevolent, destructive control."[100]

This end time judgment will develop in four stages. (1) It will be "cosmic."[101] It will include the entire creation.[102] (2) This judgment will be God's act of liberation of the entire creation.[103] (3) It will be God's act of *rectification*, or justification, whereby "God puts right what has gone wrong in and with the world."[104] (4) It will be "eschatological."[105] That is, God's judgment will be "final, definitive, and irrevocable."[106] When the ages definitively turn, that turn will signal "God's eschatological act of cosmic rectification."[107] According to de Boer, Paul believes God has accomplished this "cosmic rectification" in Jesus Christ.[108] God sent Jesus into the cosmos to liberate humans from malevolent oppressive powers (Gal 4:3-4).[109] God's act to send Jesus "began a unified apocalyptic drama of cosmic rectification" that will be consummated when he returns (cf. 1 Thess 4:13-18; 1 Cor 15:20-28).[110] Christians live at the intersection of both ages where both the kingdom of God (the new age) and the present evil age are in a constant battle with the powers of the old age, such as sin, Torah, and death.[111]

De Boer argues that similar to Jewish apocalyptic, Paul's eschatology is already and not yet.[112] But, says de Boer, Paul emphasizes God's act

---

[100]De Boer, *Galatians*, 34.
[101]De Boer, *Galatians*, 34.
[102]De Boer, *Galatians*, 34.
[103]De Boer, *Galatians*, 34.
[104]De Boer, *Galatians*, 34.
[105]De Boer, *Galatians*, 34.
[106]De Boer, *Galatians*, 34.
[107]De Boer, *Galatians*, 34.
[108]De Boer, *Galatians*, 34.
[109]De Boer, *Galatians*, 34.
[110]De Boer, *Galatians*, 34.
[111]De Boer, *Galatians*, 34.
[112]De Boer, *Galatians*, 34.

of already sending Jesus to liberate humans from demonic enslaving powers in Galatians (cf. Gal 3:13; 4:1-6).[113] In Galatians, this liberation, according to de Boer, is what Paul means by justification: namely, "God's justifying act is interpreted by Paul as God's act of cosmic rectification involving a 'rescue from the present evil age' (1:4), liberation from the malevolent cosmic powers that hold sway there (3:13, 22-23; 4:3-5; 5:1, 16-24)."[114] The preachers in Galatia preached a message about "forensic-eschatological justification." That is, God declares to be in the right, vindicates, or approves.[115] They preached justification is "God's declaration of vindication or approval and/or the resulting status of having been vindicated."[116] However, Paul also understands the verb "to justify" and the noun "justification" in "a cosmological-eschatological" sense.[117] He interprets "God's justifying act as God's act of cosmic rectification involving a "rescue from the present evil age (1:4), liberation from the malevolent cosmic powers that hold sway there (3:13, 22-23; 4:3-5; 5:1, 16-24)."[118]

Because of the present evil age, everyone is enslaved to the violent and oppressive powers within the present evil age apart from God's apocalyptic action in Christ.[119] According to de Boer, in Galatians, Paul needs to address the slavery to the malevolent and oppressive powers under which the entire creation finds itself, not "sins" as a violation of God's commands.[120] Paul addresses "Sin" as an enslaving power instead of sin as the free acts of the disobedience of humans against God's law.[121] Agreeing with J. Louis Martyn,[122] de Boer says Torah is "an oppressive, enslaving power from which those under its power need redemption

---

[113]De Boer, *Galatians*, 34.
[114]De Boer, *Galatians*, 34-35.
[115]De Boer, *Galatians*, 34.
[116]De Boer, *Galatians*, 34.
[117]De Boer, *Galatians*, 34.
[118]De Boer, *Galatians*, 34.
[119]De Boer, *Galatians*, 35-36.
[120]De Boer, *Galatians*, 35-36.
[121]De Boer, *Galatians*, 35-36.
[122]J. Louis Martyn, *Galatians*, AB 33A (New York: Doubleday, 1997), 370-73.

and deliverance."[123] Paul's primary issue in the letter is the law, not sin(s).[124] De Boer points out Paul only mentions sin twice in the letter (Gal 2:17; 3:22) after his reference to "sins" in Galatians 1:4.[125] Christ's death "for our sins" delivers/rescues us "from the present evil age," where sin's power currently rules and reigns in oppressive dominance over the entire creation.[126] Until Jesus returns, this deliverance in Christ is always in danger and depends upon God's constant "rescuing activity as and through the Spirit (4:1-6)."[127]

De Boer has made a compelling case that Paul's soteriology is apocalyptic. However, I argue in this chapter that it is *not only* apocalyptic. As I argue elsewhere in the book, justification in Galatians is God's forensic declaration of making the wrongs right. However, contrary to de Boer, justification in Galatians is a Pauline way of referring to God's forensic declaration of "not guilty" upon individual Jewish and Gentile sinners (not the liberation of the cosmos) who place faith in Jesus Christ (Gal 2:16). The wrongs that God will put in the right in the moment of justification relate only to the statuses of Jews and Gentiles before God in the judgment, whom God will declare in the right by faith in Christ in this present evil age and exonerate them from their sins because of Jesus' death for their sins and because of his resurrection (Gal 1:1, 4; 2:16; 3:13-14; 5:2-5; cf. Rom 4:25).[128]

The "by faith" in "justification by faith" refers to the individual faith of Jewish and Gentile sinners who place faith in Christ (Gal 2:16-17). Even if one argues for the faithfulness of Christ as the proper way to read the phrase διὰ πίστεως Ἰησοῦ Χριστοῦ in Galatians 2:16, Paul still says "we

---

[123]De Boer, *Galatians*, 36. For another example of an apocalyptic reading of Galatians, see Campbell, *Deliverance of God*, 839-95.

[124]De Boer, *Galatians*, 36.

[125]De Boer, *Galatians*, 36.

[126]De Boer, *Galatians*, 36.

[127]De Boer, *Galatians*, 36.

[128]Peter Oakes and Andrew K. Boakye make a similar point in response to Martyn's cosmological apocalyptic reading of soteriology in Galatians: "Christ is not presented in Galatians as one who acts primarily in relation to the Cosmos. The Christ of Galatians acts primarily in relation to his people." See *Rethinking Galatians: Paul's Vision of Oneness in the Living Christ* (New York: T&T Clark, 2021), 36. Oakes wrote the chapter where this quote occurs.

believed in Christ Jesus"[129] (εἰς Χριστὸν Ἰησοῦν ἐπιστεύσαμεν) in Galatians 2:16, with the result that "we are justified by faith." God counts the
personal faith of Jews and Gentiles in Christ as a righteous status before
him now and in the day of judgment because he reckons to their account
Christ's righteousness and reckons to his account the sins of Jews and
Gentiles for whom Christ died (cf. Rom 3:21–4:25 with Gal 2:16-21; 3:12-13;
5:5). Paul's soteriology is vertical, horizontal, and cosmic in Galatians.
However, justification by faith is only vertical in Galatians (Gal 2:16), not
cosmic, for Paul applies justification by faith only to individual sinners
in Galatians who place personal faith in Christ (Gal 2:16-17, 21; 3:6, 8, 11,
21, 24; 5:4-5). Justification by faith is a specific (and narrow!)[130] piece of
Paul's soteriology in Galatians that refers only to God's forensic declaration of "not guilty" upon Jews and Gentiles by faith in this present evil
age. This is because of their union with Christ by faith and because God
reckoned righteousness to their accounts by faith (Gal 2:16; 3:6, 8) so that
they can participate in his vertical, horizontal, and cosmic salvation in
Christ in this present evil age and in the age to come (Gal 5:2-5).

While both individuals and the entire cosmos are liberated from the
slavery of the present evil age because of the death and resurrection of
Jesus (Gal 1:1, 4; 3:13–6:15), only individual Jews and Gentiles who place
faith in Jesus Christ are justified (Gal 2:16-17, 21; 3:6, 8, 11, 21, 24; 5:4-5).
Deliverance from the present evil age and the concept of cosmic liberation
are both present in Galatians, and both are important soteriological pieces
in Paul's theology in Galatians. Paul says Christ "gave himself for our sins
to deliver us from the present evil age" (Gal 1:4). He also says he would
only boast in the cross of Jesus Christ because he was crucified to the

---

[129]Contra Campbell, *Deliverance*, 840. Campbell takes the clause to mean "we believed concern-
ing [or *about* or *with respect to*] Christ Jesus that we are delivered through the faithfulness
of Christ."

[130]The above parenthetical statement does not intend to minimize the importance of justification
by faith for Paul's soteriology, but to emphasize that justification by faith is a very specific piece
of his soteriology that only refers to the justification of individual sinners who place personal
faith in Christ. In my view, Paul never calls cosmic liberation (another important part of his
soteriology) justification in Galatians. Rather, he calls it new creation (Gal 6:15). Jews and
Gentiles are justified by faith in Christ, and they are liberated from slavery to sin's power. But
the material universe is liberated from sin's power.

world, and the world was crucified to him (Gal 6:14). Therefore, what matters to him is neither circumcision nor uncircumcision but "new creation" (Gal 6:15). However, neither deliverance from the present evil age nor cosmic liberation is called justification in Galatians. In Galatians, justification is only experienced by faith in Christ (Gal 2:16). Only those who have faith are justified (Gal 2:16). But both individuals and the entire creation are liberated from slavery (Gal 6:15). Only individual Jews and Gentiles who are justified by faith in Christ are delivered from the curse of the law (Gal 3:10-14) because only they are under the curse of the law (Gal 3:10; 4:5-6). The entire creation is under the power and curse of sin (Gal 3:22), and creation will experience "new creation" and cosmic liberation (Gal 6:15) with Jews and Gentiles who are justified by faith in Christ and who have received the Spirit by faith (Gal 2:16; 3:13-14; 4:5-6).

I reframe de Boer's description of Paul's so-called forensic apocalyptic eschatology and his so-called cosmic apocalyptic eschatology as *forensic apocalyptic soteriology* and *cosmic apocalyptic soteriology*. His soteriology is vertical, horizontal, and cosmic. It involves God making right individual Jewish and Gentile relationships with himself through Christ (Gal 2:16-21; 3:2–4:31); it involves God restoring Jewish and Gentile relationships with one another through Christ (Gal 2:11-14; 5:1; 5:13–6:10); and it involves God completely restoring the entire creation through Christ (Gal 6:15). But justification only refers to the vertical relationship between God and Jews and Gentiles who are declared righteous (i.e., not guilty) in God's presence by faith in Christ (Gal 2:16-17).

One part of God's saving action in Christ is that creation receives liberation, resurrection, and new creation because of Jesus' death and resurrection (cosmic apocalyptic soteriology) (Gal 1:1, 4; 6:15). A foretaste of this cosmic resurrection is Jesus' physical resurrection from the dead (Gal 1:1), Paul's own resurrection to life in the present evil age (Gal 2:20), and the life that all in Christ have by the Spirit by faith in Christ (Gal 3:12, 14; 4:6; 5:25). Christ lives because God the Father resurrected him from the dead (Gal 1:1); Christ lives in Paul because of the indwelling presence of the Spirit by faith in Christ (Gal 2:20; 3:14; 4:6).

All who are justified by faith receive the Spirit and live by the Spirit (Gal 2:16; 3:6-14; 4:6; 5:25) because of God's vertical and horizontal saving action in Christ (Gal 1:4; 2:11-14; 3:1-14; 5:16–6:10), and all therefore participate in God's cosmic saving action in Christ by faith in Christ (cf. Gal 6:15). However, Paul does not call this justification.

Jews and Gentiles participate in liberation, resurrection, and new creation by individually being justified by faith in Christ. He died for their sins to deliver them from the present evil age and was resurrected from the dead (forensic apocalyptic soteriology) (Gal 1:1, 4; 3:13; 6:15). Evidence that Jews and Gentiles have participated in present liberation and new creation and that they will participate in future liberation and new creation is their current experience of the Spirit who lives in them and works in them to create life and to help them freely choose to live in step with that life they have received by the Spirit by faith (Gal 3:2-14; 4:6; 5:16–6:10). God accomplishes both forensic apocalyptic soteriology and cosmic apocalyptic soteriology because of his vertical, horizontal, and cosmic saving action in Christ. God invasively disrupted the present evil age via the incarnation, death, and resurrection of Jesus to accomplish his vertical, horizontal, and cosmic saving action in Christ for Jews and Gentiles and for the world (Gal 1:1, 4; 3:13-14; 4:5-6).[131]

Prior to this invasion, both individuals and the entire creation were enslaved to the present evil age and to all the spiritual powers opposing God within it (Gal 1:4; 3:10–5:26). God's invasive disruption of the present evil age via his saving action through Jesus' death and resurrection has begun the process of both individual (forensic) and cosmic renewal. Individuals participate in God's saving action in Christ and this cosmic renewal by justification by faith in Jesus Christ (2:16; 3:6-8; 5:5). As justified sons and daughters of God by faith in Christ, God gives them his Spirit to walk in, to live by, and as the proof that cosmic renewal has begun because of God's disruptive and invasive saving action in Christ (3:2-5, 13-14; 4:5-7; 5:16, 18, 21-22, 25). As Paul was viciously seeking to

---

[131]For an example of Second Temple Jewish apocalyptic texts, see 1 Enoch, 4 Ezra, and 2 Baruch. For a canonical example, see Daniel.

destroy the church (Gal 1:13-14), in one life-altering moment God apocalyptically revealed his Son in him so that he would announce Jesus as the good news among the Gentiles (Gal 1:15-16). The result of this revelation in Paul was the belief that God through Christ's death and his resurrection would render both Jews and Gentiles not guilty in the judgment by faith (Gal 1:15-16; 2:16-17) and would liberate the cosmos from its enslavement to the present evil age (Gal 6:14-15).

As I discuss below, God revealed his Son as good news to and in Paul. This revelation dramatically worked in him to change his perspective and his entire mindset toward the church, toward the Gentiles, and toward his previous actions under the law (Gal 1:15-23) so that he retrospectively looked back on his previous manner of life in Judaism apart from Christ and realized that it did not lead to life (cf. Gal 3:21). The revelation from God about Jesus in Paul caused an epistemological shift in his thinking about God (Gal 1:11–2:21; 4:4-7); about the identity of Jesus (Gal 1:1, 4; 3:13-14); about his relationship to the righteousness of God; about Gentile participation in salvation in his age and in the age to come; about the irrelevance of the role of the law in the personal agency and ethical transformation of Jews and Gentiles (Gal 3:2–6:10); about their participation with Jews in eternal life now and in the age to come by faith in Christ for Jews and Gentiles (Gal 3:2–6:10); and about the renewal of the entire creation (Gal 6:15). This epistemological shift is evident in his "transformed thinking" about life in Christ apart from the works of the law (cf. Gal 2:16; 3:10-14; 5:16, 18, 25; 6:8; see also Rom 12:1-2).[132]

Paul does not state in Galatians exactly when or where this revelation of Christ in him took place. However, based on Luke's narrative in Acts, Paul's remarks in Galatians 1:13-16 likely refer to his Damascus Road experience. Luke states Paul's encounter with Jesus on the

---

[132]For a book on transformed thinking in Paul, see Craig S. Keener, *The Mind of the Spirit: Paul's Approach to Transformed Thinking* (Grand Rapids, MI: Baker, 2016). Keener, however, does not engage Galatians. But he does discuss the relationship between the mind and the Spirit in 1 Corinthians 2.

Damascus Road was both a visual and audible revelation (cf. Acts 9:1-22; 22:6-21). As he journeyed to Damascus in his efforts to incarcerate followers of the Way (Acts 9:1-2), a light shined around him (Acts 9:3), and "he heard a voice saying: 'Saul, Saul, why do you persecute me?'" (Acts 9:4). In Acts 22:6-21, Paul recounts this story while speaking to a crowd about Jesus of Nazareth. There, he says that both he and his companions saw a light (Acts 22:7, 9), but that only he heard the voice (Acts 22:9).

In both accounts, the Lord convinces a man named Ananias to go to Paul and explain to him next steps once he arrived in Damascus (Acts 9:10-19; 22:12-16). A key piece to Luke's discussion of Ananias's visit in Acts 9 is he specifically mentions that Ananias tells Paul that the Lord, who appeared to him, sent him so that Paul would see and so that "he would be filled with the Holy Spirit" (Acts 9:17). Once Ananias uttered these words, things analogous to scales fell from Paul's eyes (Acts 9:18). Immediately thereafter, Paul was baptized and began to preach Christ in the synagogues (Acts 9:20-22).

Luke does not mention the Spirit in Paul's encounter on the Damascus Road, but, as I have already argued above, the Spirit was present at Jesus' resurrection (Rom 1:4), and he died to give believing Jews and Gentiles the Spirit by faith (Gal 3:13-14; 4:5-6). Of course, neither Luke nor Paul says anything about the role of the Spirit in persuading Paul that Jesus was the risen and exalted Lord and Messiah. However, both Luke and Paul set Paul's experience on the Damascus Road in contexts where the Spirit is important to the messages each author presents (cf. Acts 2–9 with Gal 1:15–6:10). The Spirit appears the first time in Galatians in 3:2, not in 1:15-16. However, Paul's description of his Damascus Road experience speaks directly to the impact of God's revelation of his Son in Paul, a revelation of which the Spirit was part. Paul elucidates this latter point in 1 Corinthians 2 with his comments about the Spirit, God's revelation about the deep things of God, and the Spirit's work to help him understand the deep things of God.

Paul tells the Corinthians, "God revealed to us by means of the Spirit" the deep things of God related to Jesus Christ (1 Cor 2:10; cf. esp. 2:1-16).[133] In the context of communal conflict due to division in the Corinthian assembly, Paul reminds the Corinthians the message he received and preached to them came from God by his Spirit (1 Cor 2:11-12). Paul insists he and his fellow missionaries speak by the Spirit, not with words taught by human wisdom, as he explains spiritual things to them with words taught to him by the Spirit (1 Cor 2:13). Because he received the Spirit of God instead of the spirit of this world (1 Cor 2:12), he has the mind of Christ (1 Cor 2:16). The Spirit of God in him gives him and everyone who receives the Spirit the ability to understand the spiritual things given to them as a gift by God (1 Cor 2:12). They can discern spiritual things (1 Cor 2:13). But the "fleshly man," that is, the one without the Spirit, does not receive the spiritual things given by the Spirit of God because they are "foolish to him" and because he is not able "to understand them," since they must be spiritually assessed (1 Cor 2:14-15).

Paul's discussion of the Spirit and the enlightenment of the mind in 2 Corinthians 3:12-18 does not use the exact same language as in 1 Corinthians 2:10-16. Still, the former text provides a conceptual parallel with his remarks in 1 Corinthians 2:10-16. He connects life by the Spirit (2 Cor 3:3, 6, 8; cf. 1 Cor 2:10-13); the new covenant in Christ (2 Cor 3:6; cf. 1 Cor 2:14-16); the unveiling of God's glory through the new covenant ministry of the Spirit (2 Cor 3:6-14; cf. 1 Cor 2:10-16), which removes the veil put up by the old covenant ministry of Moses (2 Cor 3:7-14; cf. 1 Cor 2:10-16); the hardening of the mind because of the absence of the Spirit in the old covenant ministry until those hardened turn to the Lord Jesus and the veil is removed (2 Cor 3:16; cf. 1 Cor 2:10-16); and the freedom given by the Spirit to those who turn to the Lord (2 Cor 3:17; cf. 1 Cor 2:10-16) so that they all know and see his glory with an unveiled face as they are being transformed from one stage of glory to another by the power of the Spirit (2 Cor 3:18; cf. 1 Cor 2:10-16).

---

[133]ἡμῖν δὲ ἀπεκάλυψεν ὁ θεὸς διὰ τοῦ πνεύματος· τὸ γὰρ πνεῦμα πάντα ἐραυνᾷ, καὶ τὰ βάθη τοῦ θεοῦ.

Paul's remarks in 2 Corinthians 3:1-18 recall Moses' experience with the Lord as he encountered the Lord and revealed to Israel at the bottom of the mountain the content of what the Lord revealed to him (Ex 34). Especially pertinent to the Exodus background regarding my thesis about God's revelation in Paul is the text's emphasis upon the Lord making himself known to Moses as YHWH (= the Lord); its mention of the veiled glory; its reference to Moses' entrance into the presence of God with an unveiled face and then speaking to the people with a veiled face; and finally the omission of a reference to the Spirit anywhere in the text. Moses went up on Mount Sinai with two tablets of stone (Ex 34:4). The Lord came down to Moses and proclaimed himself to Moses as the Lord saying: "The Lord, the Lord, the God of mercy and compassion, slow of anger, and abounding in lovingkindness and truthfulness, keeping steadfast love for thousands, lifting up iniquity and guilt and sin, but he will certainly not leave unpunished the guilty as he visits the iniquity of the fathers upon many generations after them" (Ex 34:5-7).

After Moses heard these words, he bowed in worship as he identified the one speaking to him as the Lord, as he urged the Lord to journey with his people, and as he begged the Lord to forgive the people for their sin of idolatry and to take them as his inheritance (Ex 34:8-9; cf. Ex 32– 33). The Lord promised Moses he would do great wonders among the people and for the people against the other nations, but the people must obey his law (Ex 34:10-27). Moses, as the Lord instructed, wrote the Ten Commandments on the tablets that he carried upon the mountain as the Lord renewed his covenant with his people (Ex 34:28). Then Moses came down from the mountain with the tablets of the renewed covenant in his hands, unaware that his face was radiantly shining because of his con- versation with the Lord (Ex 34:29). Aaron and the people saw Moses' glorious face and were afraid (Ex 34:30), while Moses summoned them to approach him to hear the words the Lord had spoken to him (Ex 34:31-32). After speaking to them, Moses placed a veil on his face because the people were afraid of the glory they saw shining on his face (Ex 34:33).

As Hafemann notes, Moses' veil allows God's glory to dwell with the people through the mediation of Moses without resulting in the people's judgment because of their previous idolatry (cf. Ex 32–33).[134] In this way, Moses' veil operates just as the boundary marking "fence" at the foot of Mount Sinai (Ex 19:12) and the "curtain" in front of the most holy place within the tabernacle: both the "fence" and "curtain" separated and protected God's people from his glory after they committed idolatry.[135] Hafemann continues that since Israel committed idolatry in Exodus 32 and since the Lord threatened them with destruction (cf. Ex 32–33), Moses' veiled face when addressing them was a sign of God's judgment against them while also functioning as a sign of God's mercy.[136] When Moses spoke with the Lord, he took away the veil until he left the Lord's presence (Ex 34:34). Because his face shined brightly after speaking with the Lord, Moses put the veil back on his face when speaking with the Israelites until he entered the presence of the Lord (Ex 34:35).

In 2 Corinthians 3:1-11, Paul draws on the narrative from Exodus 34. Paul explains that neither he nor other apostles of Jesus Christ need to commend themselves to the Corinthians (2 Cor 3:1) because they are the apostles' epistle of commendation, written by the apostles and sealed by the Spirit (2 Cor 3:2-3). He asserts that their confidence in the certainty of their apostolic ministry among the Corinthians is "through Christ" and "toward God" (2 Cor 3:5). The apostles were not sufficient in and of themselves (2 Cor 3:5), but their sufficiency in authentic gospel ministry in the midst of the Corinthians came from God (2 Cor 3:5), who made them sufficient to be ministers of a new covenant by means of the Spirit, not by means of Torah (2 Cor 3:6).[137] Paul acknowledges Moses' ministry of Torah came with glory (2 Cor 3:7), but the apostolic ministry of the gospel of Jesus Christ came

---

[134]For a detailed analysis of 2 Cor 3:6, see Scott J. Hafemann, *Paul, Moses, and the History of Israel: The Letter/Spirit Contrast and the Argument from Scripture in 2 Corinthians 3* (Tübingen: Mohr Siebeck, 1995), 223.

[135]Hafemann, *Paul, Moses, and the History of Israel*, 223.

[136]Hafemann, *Paul, Moses, and the History of Israel*, 224.

[137]Hafemann, *Paul, Moses, and the History of Israel*, 224. Hafemann argues that Paul's letter/Spirit contrast is not a contrast between the law and the gospel, but between Moses' old covenant ministry and Paul's new covenant ministry.

with much more glory, and even "surprising glory," in their midst because it came in the power of the Spirit (2 Cor 3:8-10). Unlike the fading glory of Moses' ministry of Torah, the glory of the apostolic gospel of Jesus Christ remains forever (2 Cor 3:11). Therefore, because of this hope, the Corinthians' eyes were not veiled nor their minds hardened (2 Cor 3:12-16). The veil remains on Israel's eyes, Paul says, "until this very day" at the reading of the old covenant (2 Cor 3:14). But if they turn to the Lord Jesus, the veil will be taken away (2 Cor 3:16). The Corinthians had turned to the Lord through Paul's apostolic gospel ministry (2 Cor 2 Cor 4:1-6).

In 2 Corinthians 3:6, drawing from Exodus 34, Paul calls his apostolic gospel ministry of the new covenant a ministry of the Spirit in contrast with calling Moses' ministry of the law a ministry of death, because the "Spirit gives life," but the law brings death. In 2 Corinthians 3:8, Paul contrasts unbelieving Israel's "hardened minds" and the "reading of the old covenant" with a veil on their hearts until they turn to the Lord (2 Cor 3:16; cf. Ex 32–34). In 2 Corinthians 3:17, Paul focuses again on the Spirit. He says, "The Lord is the Spirit." This is a difficult statement. But keeping the background of Exodus 34 in mind helps interpretation.

In Exodus 34, the text retells the story of Moses' encounter with the Lord after Israel committed idolatry (Ex 32–34). Moses' face was glorious because of his encounter with the Lord (Ex 34:29-35), but he put a veil on it to cover his glory when he left the presence of the Lord to speak with the people only to remove the veil once he entered the presence of the Lord to speak with him (Ex 34:29-35). With exception of two occurrences in 2 Corinthians 3:17-18, each time Paul uses the term κύριος ("Lord") in 2 Corinthians, he always refers to Jesus as the Lord (2 Cor 1:2-3, 14; 2:12; 4:5, 14; 5:6, 8, 11; 6:17-18; 8:5, 9, 19, 21; 10:8, 17-18; 11:17, 31; 12:1, 8; 13:10, 13). When Paul specifically refers to the Father in 2 Corinthians, he uses the terms "God" (2 Cor 1:2) or "God and Father" (2 Cor 1:2) together.[138]

---

[138]With the possible exception of Rom 9:5, Paul's word of choice for the Father is primarily θεός. With the possible exceptions of Rom 9:5 and Eph 5:5, Paul refers to Jesus as either the son or the Christ.

In 2 Corinthians 3:17, when he says, "The Lord is the Spirit," Paul identifies the Lord as the Spirit. This does not mean the Lord Jesus Christ is the Spirit, even though the Greek can be read as a standalone sentence (ὁ δὲ κύριος τὸ πνεῦμά ἐστιν) as "the Lord is the Spirit." Rather, Paul's point is the Lord whom Moses encountered at Sinai in the Exodus 32–34 narrative (not the Lord Jesus Christ) is also the Spirit.[139] That is, along with the Lord Jesus Christ (2 Cor 1:2) and God the Father (2 Cor 1:2), the Spirit is also the Lord. Or, as Paul says, "the Lord is the Spirit" (2 Cor 3:17). Paul seems to be saying more than simply the "Lord represents the Spirit" as Paul offers a "clarifying update on v. 16" to suggest "the Lord (= YHWH) of Exodus 34:34 is, in the present ear, the Spirit mentioned in 3:3, 6, 8,"[140] that the Lord's Spirit gives the people of God the ability to enter God's presence when they approach him.[141] In addition, Paul seems to be saying more than the Lord who spoke with Moses in Exodus 34 was actually the Spirit,[142] or that Paul simply interprets Exodus 34:34 to mean that this passage refers to the Spirit for the purpose of reminding the Corinthians that the Lord that empowers Paul's apostolic gospel ministry is God's Spirit.[143] Once more, Paul seems to be saying more than the verb *is* (in the sentence the "Lord is the Spirit") means the Spirit "as an indication that Paul is here interpreting Moses' paradigmatic experience in terms of the experience now being realized in the new covenant in Christ."[144] Each of these readings is possible and has an element of theological truth in them, but I am not sure whether they are correct. Instead, Paul seems to be especially making a statement about the identity of the Lord as the Spirit and about the complex identity of the Lord as he argues in defense of his new covenant ministry of the Spirit in contrast with the opponents' old covenant ministry of the law.

---

[139]Similarly Hafemann, *Paul, Moses, and the History of Israel*, 397.

[140]Murry J. Harris, *The Second Epistle to the Corinthians*, NIGTC (Grand Rapids, MI: Eerdmans, 2005), 311-12. Position first argued by James D. G. Dunn, "2 Corinthians III.17—'The Lord is the Spirit,'" *JTS* (1970): 309-20.

[141]Ralph P. Martin, *2 Corinthians*, 2nd ed., WBC 40 (Grand Rapids, MI: Zondervan, 1986), 213-14.

[142]George H. Guthrie, *2 Corinthians*, BECNT (Grand Rapids, MI: Baker, 2015), 225-26.

[143]David E. Garland, *2 Corinthians*, CSBC (Nashville: B&H, 2021), 211-12.

[144]Hafemann, *Paul, Moses, and the History of Israel*, 398-99.

Mark A. Seifrid contends Paul identifies the Lord with the Spirit while also distinguishing the Lord from the Spirit.[145] Paul gives a "Christological definition" of 2 Corinthians 3:17 in 2 Corinthians 4:1-6.[146] Seifrid further claims that in 2 Corinthians 3:17, Paul offers a theological exegesis of Exodus 34 that emphasizes the eschatological realization of the events by connecting them to the current events in Paul's time.[147] According to Seifrid, Paul is "an emissary of a new covenant of the Spirit (v. 6), the Spirit of the living God, who writes Christ upon hardened hearts (v. 3)."[148] Seifrid continues, "The Spirit given through the apostolic mission is none other than the Lord himself."[149] However, Seifrid argues, Paul clearly states that "the Lord is the Spirit."[150] Paul identifies the Lord as the Spirit to suggest that the Lord who spoke with Moses at Sinai was the Spirit about whom the Hebrew Scriptures speak and that "in speaking gives himself through the apostle to the Corinthians."[151] Paul's remarks in 2 Corinthians 3:17, Seifrid infers, recollects his comments in 1 Corinthians 2:9, 12.[152] God's Spirit reveals to God's people "the things of God" (1 Cor 2:10-11) in a similar way as humans know their own thoughts because of their own spirit.[153] God speaks both "to" and "with" his people.[154] Thus, when Paul says "the Lord is the Spirit" (2 Cor 3:17), "Paul interprets the Exodus narrative, which explains that Moses' face was shining because he had spoken *with* God on Sinai (Ex 34:29), and that Moses entered the tent of meeting in order to speak *with* the Lord (Ex 34:34)."[155] To a greater degree than Moses, those in Christ communicate with God and hear his voice in "the apostolic word that opens the Scripture to us."[156]

---

[145]Mark A. Seifrid, *2 Corinthians*, PNTC (Grand Rapids, MI: Eerdmans, 2014), 174-76.
[146]Seifrid, *2 Corinthians*, 175.
[147]Seifrid, *2 Corinthians*, 174-75.
[148]Seifrid, *2 Corinthians*, 175.
[149]Seifrid, *2 Corinthians*, 175.
[150]Seifrid, *2 Corinthians*, 175.
[151]Seifrid, *2 Corinthians*, 175.
[152]Seifrid, *2 Corinthians*, 175.
[153]Seifrid, *2 Corinthians*, 175.
[154]Seifrid, *2 Corinthians*, 175.
[155]Seifrid, *2 Corinthians*, 175.
[156]Seifrid, *2 Corinthians*, 176.

Seifrid has offered helpful insights into the meaning of this difficult sentence, but I am not sure whether he actually arrives at the point Paul is making in 2 Corinthians 3:17. I agree with Hafemann: Paul does not identify Jesus with the Spirit in 2 Corinthians 3:17 but rather insists that his new covenant ministry of and "experience of the Spirit" is on equal grounds with (and I would add is superior to!) Moses' "experience of the Spirit of YHWH" at Sinai.[157] Furthermore, Hafemann is correct when he says Paul is not making an ontological point about the Spirit in 2 Corinthians 3:17 but giving an apologetic for his ministry to the Corinthians.[158] Paul's new covenant gospel ministry "mediates the Spirit of YHWH, just as Moses mediated the glory of YHWH."[159]

Yet, in my view, the statement "the Lord is the Spirit" in 2 Corinthians 3:17 also teaches the Spirit, the emblem of Paul's new covenant ministry promised in the Hebrew Scriptures (Jer 31:31-34; Ezek 11:19-20; 36:22–37:28), shares in the "divine identity" of YHWH (= of the Lord),[160] and that his comments about the Spirit in 2 Corinthians 3:17 include an ontological statement about the identity of the Spirit, even if that is not Paul's primary point. This interpretation fits with Paul's comments in 2 Corinthians 3:18 when he says, "Where the Spirit of the Lord is, there is liberty." In 2 Corinthians 3:18, he does not refer to the Lord as the Spirit but to the Spirit that comes from the Lord, while at the same time in 2 Corinthians 3:17 he asserts, "The Lord is the Spirit." In 2 Corinthians 3:18, he says those who turn to the Lord are being transformed from one stage of glory to another stage of glory because they gaze upon the same image, namely, the image of the glory of God with an unveiled face as they look upon the image of Jesus Christ through the preaching of the gospel by the Spirit (cf. 2 Corinthians 4:1-6), just as "from the Lord of the Spirit." The phrase with the genitives (καθάπερ ἀπὸ κυρίου πνεύματος) could be taken in multiple ways. Given Paul's statement in

---

[157]Hafemann, *Paul, Moses, and the History of Israel*, 399.
[158]Hafemann, *Paul, Moses, and the History of Israel*, 399, esp. 400-407.
[159]Hafemann, *Paul, Moses, and the History of Israel*, 399.
[160]For a discussion of divine identity, see Richard Bauckham, *Jesus and the God of Israel: God Crucified and Other Studies on the New Testament's Christology of Divine Identity* (Grand Rapids, MI: Eerdmans, 2008).

2 Corinthians 3:17, that "the Lord is the Spirit," the phrase ἀπὸ κυρίου πνεύματος likely means "from the Lord, who is the Spirit."

The Lord in 2 Corinthians 3:17 includes the Spirit in 2 Corinthians 3:3, 6, and 8, but should not be limited to the Spirit. If this is correct, Paul concludes v. 18 the way he began v. 17: identifying the Lord as the Spirit. In 2 Corinthians 4:1-6, Paul identifies the gospel as the revelation of the good news of the glory of Jesus Christ (2 Cor 4:4) and refers to Jesus as the image of God the Father (2 Cor 4:4) and as the Lord (2 Cor 4:5). In 2 Corinthians 4:6, he says God the Father, who declared that light shall illuminate the darkness in Genesis 1:3, has illuminated "in our hearts for the illumination of the knowledge of the glory of God, [the Father], in the face of Jesus Christ." That is, in Christ Jesus through the preaching of the gospel by the illumination of the Lord, who is the Spirit, God the Father has removed the veil from all who turn to the Lord: Father, Son, and Spirit.

In the LXX, τὸ πνεῦμα κυρίου ("the Spirit of the Lord") occurs in the same context as a reference to the Lord (κύριος) to identify the Spirit as representing the Lord and with a clear distinction of the Spirit from the Lord (LXX Judg 3:10). Yet, when the Spirit of the Lord is present, the Lord himself is present (LXX Judg 3:10).[161] The phrase "Spirit of the Lord" in 2 Corinthians 3:18 (τὸ πνεῦμα κυρίου) is a different grammatical construction from "the Lord is the Spirit" (ὁ δὲ κύριος τὸ πνεῦμά ἐστιν) in 2 Corinthians 3:17. Yet, both communicate the exact same thing with respect to the Spirit: namely, the Lord is the Spirit too.[162]

The appropriate way to interpret Paul's statements about the Spirit in 2 Corinthians 3:17 is further complicated by his reference in 2 Corinthians 3:18 to the "glory of the Lord" (τὴν δόξαν κυρίου) and the phrase

---

[161]For additional references to τὸ πνεῦμα κυρίου, see also Judg 11:29; 13:25; 14:6, 19; 15:14; 1 Sam 10:6; 11:6; 16:13-15; 2 Sam 23:2; 1 Kings 18:12; 22:24; 2 Kings 2:16; Mic 2:7; 3:8; Is 61:1; Ezek 11:5; Wis 1:7. In LXX Ezek 37:14, the Lord says he would put his Spirit within his people (καὶ δώσω τὸ πνεῦμά μου εἰς ὑμᾶς, καὶ ζήσεσθε, καὶ θήσομαι ὑμᾶς ἐπὶ τὴν γῆν ὑμῶν, καὶ γνώσεσθε ὅτι ἐγὼ κύριος λελάληκα καὶ ποιήσω, λέγει κύριος).

[162]Paul interchangeably uses the phrases "Holy Spirit" and "the Spirit of God." For "Holy Spirit," see Rom 5:5; 14:17; 15:13, 16, 19; 1 Cor 6:19; 12:3; 2 Cor 6:6; 13:13; Eph 1:13; 1 Thess 1:5; 2 Tim 1:14; Titus 3:5. For "the Spirit of God," see Rom 8:9, 14; 1 Cor 2:11, 14; 3:16; 6:11; 12:3; 2 Cor 3:3; Eph 3:16; Phil 3:3. See also Eph 4:30 and 1 Thess 4:8 where Paul combines both phrases. These insights are from Hafemann, *Paul, Moses, and the History of Israel*, 401n211.

"from the Lord of the Spirit" (ἀπὸ κυρίου πνεύματος). Both the words "glory of the Lord" and the "Lord" draw again from the Exodus 34 narrative where Moses was unaware that his face was glorious after having been in the presence of the Lord. He put a veil on his face when talking to the people because the glory of the Lord scared them as they looked upon it (LXX Ex 34:29-30).[163] Thus, we can at least say the Lord's glory in 2 Corinthians 3 contrasts with Moses' veiled glory in Exodus 34; the Lord's glory in 2 Corinthians 3 is inseparable from Jesus and Paul's new covenant gospel ministry about him; and Paul's new covenant gospel ministry introduces and relates to the Spirit (2 Cor 3:6-16). When those who are blinded turn to the Lord Jesus, the veil is taken away (2 Cor 3:16).

In Exodus 34, Israel could not look upon the glory of the Lord as it was conveyed through Moses' face because they committed idolatry in Exodus 32. The Lord has to renew his covenant with them in Exodus 33–34 because they sinned and because Moses shattered the tablets of stone after they sinned. In 2 Corinthians 3, the glory of God is clearly revealed in the face of Jesus Christ by the power of the Spirit through the apostolic gospel ministry of the new covenant (2 Cor 3:12-18; 4:6). As to the meaning of "the Lord is the Spirit" in 2 Corinthians 3:17, the Spirit himself shares in the "divine identity of YHWH" along with the Father and the Lord Jesus Christ. LXX Judges 16:14 connects the Spirit with the "divine identity of YHWH" while distinguishing the Spirit from YHWH. The author commands "all of creation" to serve the Lord, then grounds this command in the Lord's creative word and the sending of his Spirit to create life. He concludes that no one will resist the Lord's creative voice.[164]

In 2 Corinthians 3:17-18, the Spirit is *not* an independent actor in Paul's new covenant gospel ministry; he is the Lord along with God the Father and the Lord Jesus Christ. Together, the triune God (God the Father, who

---

[163]So also Hafemann, *Paul, Moses, and the History of Israel*, 335-36; Linda Belleville, *Reflections of Glory: Paul's Polemical Use of the Moses-Doxa Tradition in 2 Corinthians*, BAC (New York: Bloomsbury, 2015).

[164]σοὶ δουλευσάτω πᾶσα ἡ κτίσις σου· ὅτι εἶπας, καὶ ἐγενήθησαν· ἀπέστειλας τὸ πνεῦμά σου, καὶ ᾠκοδόμησεν· καὶ οὐκ ἔστιν ὃς ἀντιστήσεται τῇ φωνῇ σου. LXX Jud 16:14 does not use the Greek term for the Lord. But the context suggests the Lord is the Creator because the author recalls the creation narrative of Genesis 1–2.

is the Lord, the Lord Jesus Christ, and the Spirit, who is also the Lord) grants liberty to those who see Jesus' glory to live as the transformed people of God in Christ when they turn to the triune Lord who has revealed his glory in a saving way through the Lord Jesus Christ. This liberty allows them to see the glory of God clearly and fully in the gospel of Jesus Christ and to be free to obey his commands by the Spirit (2 Cor 4:4-6). But Paul especially emphasizes the eternal and unveiled new covenant ministry of the gospel of Jesus Christ, which gives life by the Spirit. This new covenant ministry of glory and of the Spirit, which gives life, contrasts with the temporarily veiled old covenant ministry of the Torah, which brings death, for the Lord is the Spirit (cf. 2 Cor 3:1-18 with Ex 34).

The Spirit is likewise prominent in the central section of the letter in Galatians 3–4 as Paul discusses the pathway to the Abrahamic blessing is Christ, not Torah. Similarly to Paul, the Galatians "received" the Spirit by faith (cf. Gal 3:14; 4:5-6 with 1 Cor 2:12). Even though Paul does not explicitly mention the Spirit in Galatians 1:15-16, the Spirit's role in helping Paul grasp the revelation about Christ in Galatians 1:15-16 seems plausible both considering his comments about the Spirit and revelation in 1 Corinthians 2 and 2 Corinthians 3, which I enumerated above, and considering his comments about the Spirit in Galatians. In Galatians 1:15-16, when Paul says God revealed his Son "in" him, he identifies this experience as a defining moment for him when he made an epistemological shift in his thinking with respect to the good news about Jesus (Gal 1:15-16). As he says in 1 Corinthians 2:10-16, God reveals to him and to other servants of Christ the deep things of God by the Spirit and helps them understand by the Spirit the deep things of God.

The phrase ἐν ἐμοί, which I have translated as "in me," in Galatians 1:16 from the phrase ἀποκαλύψαι τὸν υἱὸν αὐτοῦ ἐν ἐμοί ("to reveal his Son in me") is an important translation for my thesis.[165] The infinitive

---

[165]Both the ESV and NRSV translate ἐν ἐμοί in Galatians 1:16 as "to me," whereas the NASB and NIV translate it as "in me." Of course, the idea of "in me" does not discount the revelation was given to Paul. Instead, the "in me" accentuates the apocalyptic nature of God's revelation to Paul: God, without being solicited, invasively broke into the present evil age, disrupted it, and revealed himself to Paul by the revelation about Jesus, his resurrected Son, in him. This

ἀποκαλύψαι ("to reveal") in Galatians 1:16 comes from the same lexical form (ἀποκαλύπω) as the verb ἀπεκάλυψεν ("he revealed") in 1 Corinthians 2:10, when Paul states God revealed spiritual things "in/to us" by the Spirit (ἡμῖν δὲ ἀπεκάλυψεν ὁ θεὸς διὰ τοῦ πνεύματος). Paul's thoughts about God's revelation in Galatians 1:16 and 1 Corinthians 2:10 seem parallel both because of his use of a similar verb and because of what the revelation of Jesus Christ does in those who receive it: namely, it transforms their thinking and their living (cf. Gal 1:11-23 with 1 Cor 2:10-16).

Paul states Christ is in believers (Gal 1:16; Col 1:27), and the Spirit dwells in believers (cf. Rom 8:11; 2 Cor 1:22). In Galatians, however, Paul explicitly connects Christ in him with God's revelation of his resurrected and crucified Son in him (Gal 1:15-16; 2:19-20). Paul also says because of Christ's death to redeem those under the law, they receive the Spirit by faith (Gal 3:13-14), and the Spirit dwells in their hearts (Gal 4:6). Jesus was appointed the Son of God with power in accordance with the Holy Spirit at the resurrection of the dead (Rom 1:4). The Spirit was active in Paul through God's revelation about the exalted Christ, compelling and convincing him by his indwelling presence and power in him that Jesus is the Son of God (Acts 9:1-22; 22:6-21).

Paul's remarks about God sending his Son in the fullness of time to redeem us and to make us adopted members of his family supports this point about Paul's experience of the Spirit on the Damascus Road and after Ananias laid hands on him (Gal 4:4-6; cf. 1:15-16; Acts 9:1-22; 22:6-21). Prior to Damascus, Paul vigorously persecuted the church of God (cf. Acts 7:58–8:3; 9:1-22; Gal 1:13-14). After God revealed his resurrected Son in Paul on the Damascus Road, he immediately preached that Jesus is the Son of God (Gal 1:15–2:10; cf. Acts 9:1-22). Because those

revelation fundamentally did something in and to him to change his entire course of action and to alter dramatically his life as God was revealing the truth of his resurrected Son, whom Paul was persecuting (cf. Acts 9; Gal 1:13-14). This revelation to and in Paul caused the churches in Judea, which only knew him as the persecutor of the church, to glorify God "in me" (ἐν ἐμοὶ) because they had heard that the former persecutor of the church was now preaching the faith that he formerly persecuted (Gal 1:23-24). This revelation of God's Son in him was the turning point in his life when Christ began to "live" in him (Gal 2:20).

in Christ are sons, God sent forth the Spirit of his Son into their hearts (Gal 4:6). God's sending of his Son to redeem "us" resulted in God sending forth the "Spirit of his Son" to dwell in our hearts because of this redemption (Gal 4:6). The Spirit was a key reason as to why Paul experienced the revelation of God's resurrected and exalted Son, Jesus, on the Damascus Road.[166] The Spirit made him aware of the fact that Jesus is the good news for the Gentiles (Gal 1:15-16) and that the Gentiles, along with Jews, could receive the Spirit by faith because of Jesus' death "for our sins" and his resurrection (Gal 1:4; 3:2-14; 4:5-6).

God's revelation of his Son in Paul was a disruptive and an apocalyptic invasion of the cosmos that changed both the cosmos and Paul's entire course of action. The Spirit was part of God's revelation of his Son to and in Paul. The revelation indwelled (filled) (Gal 1:15-16; cf. 3:2-3, 14; 4:6), enabled (helped) (Gal 2:19), energized (created life) (Gal 2:20),[167] transformed (Gal 1:15-23), and empowered (strengthened) (Gal 2:8-9) him by God's Spirit to live in obedience to the gospel of Jesus Christ and to be faithful to his mission as an apostle to the Gentiles, because the Spirit of God's Son began to dwell in him (Gal 3:14; 4:6; cf. 1:15-16). Paul realized by the Spirit this revelation in him of God's saving action in Christ was the moment "when" God invaded the present evil age to inaugurate new creation in Christ, and it was the moment "when" he became crucified with Christ, to the world (= the present evil age), and the world to him (Gal 1:15-16; 2:19-20; 6:15).

THE SPIRIT AND JUSTIFICATION BY FAITH IN CHRIST

Justification by faith is another important piece to Paul's understanding of the Spirit and God's saving action in Christ in Galatians. In the history of interpretation of Galatians, interpreters have read Galatians as a

---

[166]Philip points out that the resurrection of the dead is connected to the Spirit in certain Old Testament (Ezek 37:1-14) and Second Temple Jewish texts (Wis 16:13; 2 Macc 7:22-23; 4Q521). Cf. Philip, *Origins of Pauline Pneumatology*, 137-38.

[167]I borrow the language of energized from John M. G. Barclay. See, for example, John M. G. Barclay and Simon J. Gathercole, eds., *Divine and Human Agency in Paul and His Cultural Environment* (New York: T&T Clark, 2006).

defense of justification by faith.[168] Of course, justification by faith is an
important part of Paul's argument in the letter. Paul emphatically states
three times in Galatians 2:16 "we" are justified by faith in Christ. Justification also continues to be an explosive conversation in Pauline
scholarship:[169] scholars representing the so-called Old Perspective,[170]
New Perspective,[171] Newer Perspective,[172] Paul-within-Judaism (also
known as radical New Perspective),[173] apocalyptic Pauline perspective,[174]

---

[168]For example, see bibliography in Stephen Westerholm, *Perspectives Old and New on Paul: The
"Lutheran" Paul and His Critics* (Grand Rapids, MI: Eerdmans, 2003); John Riches, *Galatians
Through the Centuries* (Malden, MA: Wiley-Blackwell, 2013).

[169]See, for example, D. A. Carson et al., eds., *Justification and Variegated Nomism*, vol. 1, *The Complexities of Second Temple Judaism* (Grand Rapids, MI: Eerdmans, 2001); *Justification and Variegated Nomism*, vol. 2, *The Paradoxes of Paul* (Grand Rapids, MI: Eerdmans, 2004); James K. Beilby
and Paul Rhodes Eddy, *Justification: Five Views* (Downers Grove, IL: InterVarsity Press, 2011).

[170]E.g., Westerholm, *Perspectives Old and New on Paul*; Simon J. Gathercole, *Where Is Boasting?
Early Jewish Soteriology and Paul's Response in Romans 1–5* (Grand Rapids, MI: Eerdmans,
2002); Thomas R. Schreiner, *Faith Alone—The Doctrine of Justification by Faith: What the
Reformers Taught . . . and Why It Still Matters* (Grand Rapids, MI: Zondervan, 2015); Charles
Lee Irons, *The Righteousness of God: A Lexical Examination of the Covenant-Faithfulness Interpretation*, WUNT 386 (Tübingen: Mohr Siebeck, 2015). For a recent monograph that corrects
certain misrepresentations of the Reformers, see especially Stephen J. Chester, *Reading Paul
with the Reformers: Reconciling Old and New Perspectives* (Grand Rapids, MI: Eerdmans, 2017).

[171]E.g., Krister Stendahl, "The Apostle Paul and the Introspective Conscience of the West," *HTR*
(1963): 199-215; E. P. Sanders, *Paul and Palestinian Judaism: A Comparison of Patterns of Religion*
(Philadelphia: Fortress, 1977); E. P. Sanders, *Comparing Judaism and Christianity: Common
Judaism, Paul, and the Inner and the Outer in Ancient Religion* (Minneapolis: Fortress, 2016),
1-27; E. P. Sanders, *Paul, the Law, and the Jewish People* (Philadelphia: Fortress, 1983);
James D. G. Dunn, "The New Perspective on Paul," *BJRL* 65 (1983): 95-122; James D. G. Dunn,
The Theology of Paul the Apostle (Grand Rapids, MI: Eerdmans, 1998); James D. G. Dunn, *The
New Perspective on Paul*, rev. ed. (Grand Rapids, MI: Eerdmans, 2017); N. T. Wright, *The Climax
of the Covenant: Christ and the Law in Pauline Theology* (Philadelphia: Fortress, 1991);
N. T. Wright, *Paul and the Faithfulness of God*, 2 vols. (Minneapolis: Fortress, 2013).

[172]A. Andrew Das, *Paul, the Law, and the Covenant* (Peabody, MA: Hendrickson, 2001); *Galatians*
(St. Louis: Concordia, 2014).

[173]Pamela Eisenbaum, *Paul Was NOT a Christian: The Original Message of a Misunderstood Apostle*
(San Fransisco: HarperOne, 2010); Mark D. Nanos and Magnus Zetterholm, eds., *Paul Within
Judaism: Restoring the First-Century Context to the Apostle* (Minneapolis: Fortress, 2015); Mark
D. Nanos and Magnus Zetterholm, eds., *Reading Paul Within Judaism: Collections of Essays*,
vol. 1 (Eugene, OR: Cascade, 2017); Matthew Thiessen, *Paul and the Gentile Problem* (Oxford:
Oxford University Press, 2016); Paula Fredriksen, *Paul, the Pagan's Apostle* (New Haven: Yale
University Press, 2017); Gabriele Boccaccini, *Paul's Three Paths to Salvation* (Grand Rapids, MI:
Eerdmans, 2020).

[174]J. Louis Martyn, "Apocalyptic Antinomies," *NTS* 31 (1985): 410-24; J. Louis Martyn, *Galatians*,
AB (New Haven: Yale University Press, 1997); J. C. Beker, *The Triumph of God: The Essence of
Paul's Thought* (Minneapolis: Fortress, 1990); Beverly Gaventa, ed., *Apocalyptic Paul: Cosmos and
Anthropos in Romans 5-8* (Waco, TX: Baylor University Press, 2019); Douglas A. Campbell, *The
Quest for Paul's Gospel: A Suggested Strategy* (New York: T&T Clark, 2005); Douglas A. Campbell,

and the "Gift Perspective"[175] continue to debate the meaning of justification in Paul's theology.[176] Others affirm some aspects of the New Perspective thesis while denying others,[177] or are critical of both the Old and New Perspectives.[178] To be sure, the teachers in Galatia are compelling the Galatians to walk away from Paul's gospel (Gal 1:6). This would include apostasy from his teaching that Jews and Gentiles are justified by faith in Christ alone apart from the works of the law (Gal 2:16; 5:3-5). As the different readings of Galatians, discussed in the history of research above, demonstrate, it should be apparent that numerous Pauline scholars no longer read the letter primarily as a defense of justification by faith.[179]

In this section, however, my intent is not to discuss the significance of justification by faith for Paul's argument in Galatians but to make the argument that justified people walk in obedience to the gospel in step with the Spirit as proof that they are justified by faith. I also argue a faithful walk of obedience in step with the Spirit is *not* the same thing as justification by faith in Paul's soteriology in Galatians. Justification by faith and walking in the Spirit are different! Nevertheless, they are both important to Paul's soteriology in Galatians, to the point that those

---

The Deliverance of God: An Apocalyptic Rereading of Justification in Paul (Grand Rapids, MI: Eerdmans, 2009); Martinus de Boer, *Galatians* (Louisville: Westminster John Knox, 2011); Ben C. Blackwell, John K. Goodrich, and Jason Maston, eds., *Paul and the Apocalyptic Imagination* (Minneapolis: Fortress, 2017).

[175]John M. G. Barclay, *Paul and the Gift* (Grand Rapids, MI: Eerdmans, 2015). I get the phrase "Gift Perspective" from McKnight and Oropeza, eds., *Perspectives on Paul*, 22, who influenced my arrangement of the section on the different readings of Paul's soteriology.

[176]For a history of research on justification and judgment according to works in Paul's theology up to 2009, see Dane C. Ortlund, "Justification by Faith, Judged According to Works: Another Look at a Pauline Paradox," *JETS* 52, no. 2 (2009): 323-39.

[177]Chris VanLandingham, *Judgment and Justification in Early Judaism and the Apostle Paul* (Peabody, MA: Hendrickson, 2006); Bruce W. Longenecker, *The Triumph of Abraham's God: The Transformation of Identity in Galatians* (Edinburgh: T&T Clark, 1998); Michael F. Bird, *The Saving Righteousness of God: Studies on Paul, Justification and New Perspective*, PBM (Milton Keynes: Paternoster, 2007).

[178]Francis Watson, *Paul, Judaism, and the Gentiles: Beyond the New Perspective* (Grand Rapids, MI: Eerdmans, 2007); *Paul, Judaism, and the Gentiles: A Sociological Approach*, SNTSMS 56 (Cambridge: Cambridge University Press, 1986).

[179]Riches, *Galatians Through the Centuries*; Mark Nanos, ed., *The Galatians Debate: Contemporary Issues in Rhetorical and Historical Interpretation* (Grand Rapids, MI: Baker, 2002); McKnight and Oropeza, eds., *Perspectives on Paul*.

who claim to be justified by faith in Christ and yet do not walk in obedience to the gospel in step with the Spirit will not inherit the kingdom
of God since their lack of obedience will prove they never received the
gift of justification by faith, and they will therefore not pass the eschatological test on the day of judgment.[180] Still, both Jews and Gentiles
experience justification by faith in Christ alone, and those who are justified by faith in Christ alone prove this by an obedient walk in step with
the Spirit by faith in Christ alone because of God's saving action for
them in Christ. Yet, both justification by faith in Christ alone and
walking in obedience to the gospel in step with the Spirit are distinct
soteriological realities.

The forensic nature of God's saving action in Christ. Paul first discusses justification by faith in Galatians 2:16 in a context where he
records his confrontation of Peter in Galatians 2:11-14. Before certain
visitors came from Jerusalem to Antioch (Gal 2:14-21), Peter (a Jewish
Christian) constantly had table fellowship with Gentile Christians
(Gal 2:12). Once they came, however, Peter began to separate from table
fellowship with these Gentiles (Gal 2:12), and his actions led other Jewish
Christians into hypocrisy with him (Gal 2:13).

Jews and Gentiles associated in various forms of social engagement
in antiquity (cf. Joseph and Aseneth, Letter of Aristeas, the Tobiad
dynasty in Josephus). Nevertheless, Torah created specific boundaries
between Jews and Gentiles to maintain a Jewish way of life in compliance with Torah (cf. Lev 11:1-47; cf. Ex 20:1–Deut 33:29). In the Second
Temple period, certain Jewish communities created additional marks of

---

[180]For this "Pauline paradox," see Ortlund, "Justification by Faith, Judged According to Works,"
323-39. For scholarship on judgment according to works in Paul's theology after 2009, see
Kyoung-Shik Kim, *God Will Judge Each One According to Works: Judgment According to Works
and Psalm 62 in Early Judaism and the New Testament*, BZNW 178 (Berlin: de Gruyter, 2011);
Kevin W. McFadden, *Judgment According to Works in Romans: The Meaning and Function of
Divine Judgment in Paul's Most Important Letter* (Minneapolis: Fortress, 2013). See also especially
Barclay, *Paul and the Gift*, 463-71 as he comments on the difficult text of Romans 2. Recently,
see Brendan Byrne, *Paul and the Economy of Salvation: Reading from the Perspective of the Last
Judgment* (Grand Rapids, MI: Baker, 2021). Byrne argues that "the last judgment is a central ele-
ment" of Paul's "economy of salvation" within his apocalyptic framework and that Paul's
"economy of salvation" needs to be viewed from his perspective of the last judgment (1-2).

separation based on a rereading of Torah in their social contexts as dispersed Jews living in an increasingly Hellenistic society (Jub. 22:16-21; Let. Arist. 142). Jewish and Gentile table fellowship has important social implications for those who participated in these interactions (Philo, *Abr.* 107-14). One implication was that fellow Jews would have perceived Jews who participated in table fellowship with Gentiles as accepting a Gentile way of life or living as renegades against God's law (1 Macc 2:44; 3:5-6; 7:5; 9:23, 58, 69; 11:25; 14:14). This perception was problematic in the Jewish community since many Gentiles did not worship Israel's God (Jos. Asen. 8:5; 21:14-15; 4 Macc 5:2; LXX Dan 1:3-20; Jdt 10-12; esp. 12:1-4, 19; LXX Add Esth 14:17; 3 Macc 3:4-7; Jub. 22:16-10).[181] Peter's act of separation in Galatians 2:11-14 was in the vein of non-Christian Jewish separation from Gentiles (cf. Jub. 22:16-19),[182] but Peter (a Jewish Christian) separated from Gentile Christians because of fear of the so-called circumcision party (Gal 2:12),[183] not because of zeal for Torah (Gal 2:14).[184]

Paul reminds Peter his actions were hypocritical because he was not living in accordance with a strict Jewish way of life while having table fellowship with Gentiles, but Peter's behavior changed when those from James came (Gal 2:14). Some Jewish texts assert Jewish identity is a matter of natural birthright (3 Macc 1:3; 4 Macc 18:1; T. Levi 15:4; Pss. Sol. 9:9; 18:3; cf. also Rom 11:1; Phil 3:5). Whereas other Jewish texts

---

[181]Jarvis J. Williams, *Galatians*, NCC (Eugene, OR: Cascade, 2020), 50-61. See also Kent L. Yinger's contribution in the late 1990s in *Paul, Judaism, and Judgment According to Deeds*, SNTSMS 105 (Cambridge: Cambridge University Press, 1999).

[182]In Jub. 22:16-19 (second century BCE), the author ascribes these words from Isaac to Jacob: "And you also, my son, Jacob, remember my words, and keep the commandments of Abraham, your father. Separate yourself from the gentiles, and do not eat with them, and do not perform deeds like theirs. And do not become associates of theirs. Because their deeds are defiled, and all of their ways are contaminated, and despicable, and abominable. They slaughter their sacrifices to the dead, and to the demons they bow down. And they eat in tombs. And all their deeds are worthless and vain. And they have no heart to perceive, and they have no eyes to see what their deeds are, and where they wander astray, saying to the tree 'you are my god,' and to a stone 'you are my lord, and you are my savior'; and they have no heart. But (as for) you, my son, Jacob, may God Most High help you, and the God of heaven bless you. And may he turn you from their defilement, and from all their errors."

[183]Scholars disagree on the identity of this circumcision party. For my discussion, see Williams, *Galatians*, 47-61.

[184]My discussion on Gal 2:11-14 in this section summarizes material in my Galatians commentary. See especially 47-61 for additional analysis and for further primary and secondary citations.

suggest Gentiles can convert to a Jewish way of life (cf. LXX Esther 8:17),[185] Paul likewise reminds Peter that Jews are Jews by birth, and they are not sinners because of their association with Gentiles (Gal 2:15; contrast with Jub. 22:16-22).

In certain Jewish texts, although Jews unfaithful to Torah became sinners because of their disobedience to the law of Moses (cf. 1 Macc 1:11, 21, 34), other Jewish texts identify all Gentiles as sinners because they neither received the law from Sinai nor followed it (1 Sam 15:18-19; 3 Macc 2:17-18; Tob 13:6; Jub. 22:16-22; 23:23-24).[186] Additionally, those who associate with Gentiles were viewed by their fellow Jews as sinners in certain Jewish texts (cf. Jub. 22:16-19). Paul, a Jewish Christian now transformed by the Spirit, however, disagrees. He tells Peter Gentiles do not make Jews sinners by association (Gal 2:15). Then, in Galatians 2:16, Paul gives Peter the fundamental theological reason why his behavior toward fellow Gentile Christians was wrong and brought condemnation upon him: Jews and Gentiles are justified by faith in Christ apart from the works of the law.

Justification by faith in Galatians 2:16 is neither an abstract nor isolated theological discussion in Galatians. Rather, it is integral to the reason Peter's behavior toward Gentile Christians is wrong in Antioch (Gal 2:11-16). The importance of justification by faith for Paul's argument here is evident by the number of times he mentions it in 2:16. He states three times that Jews and Gentiles are justified by faith in Christ apart from works of the law.[187]

The verb Paul uses (δικαιόω) in Galatians 2:16 is often translated in English to mean "to justify." The verb occurs in numerous places in the

---

[185]Compare and contrast Paul's remarks with the following Second Temple Jewish texts: Bel 1:28; 2 Macc 9:1-17; Phil, *Spec.* 1.51; Josephus, *J.W.* 7.44. For additional Jewish texts that talk about Gentile conversion, see Terence L. Donaldson, *Judaism and the Gentiles: Jewish Patterns of Universalism (to 135 CE)* (Waco: Baylor University Press, 2008).

[186]See also Pss. Sol., 2:1-2; 4 Ezra 3:28-36; 4:23. For texts that identify a sinner as one who acts contrary to Torah, see LXX Ps 54:4; 91:8; 100:8; 124:3; 128:3; 118:53; Sir 7:16; 9:11; 1 Macc 1:34; 2:44. I make this same point in my Galatians commentary following A. Andrew Das.

[187]ἰδότες [δὲ] ὅτι οὐ **δικαιοῦται** ἄνθρωπος ἐξ ἔργων νόμου ἐὰν μὴ διὰ πίστεως Ἰησοῦ Χριστοῦ, καὶ ἡμεῖς εἰς Χριστὸν Ἰησοῦν ἐπιστεύσαμεν, ἵνα **δικαιωθῶμεν** ἐκ πίστεως Χριστοῦ καὶ οὐκ ἐξ ἔργων νόμου, ὅτι ἐξ ἔργων νόμου οὐ **δικαιωθήσεται** πᾶσα σάρξ.

LXX and in the New Testament. Recently, Boakye has argued justification in Galatians "is an expression of new life that is (1) triggered by Abrahamic faith, a faith which is (2) exemplified in the birth of Isaac as the archetypal 'son of Abraham.' The miraculous birth of Isaac is (3) the 'promise of the Spirit' in Gal 3:14b . . . the same Spirit received because of the hearing of faith (3:2) and actively experienced within the community (3:5)."[188] Boayke argues this based on Paul's use of the "introductory context of the scripture citations" in the letter.[189] Boayke would also understand justification in Galatians as "revivification."[190] According to him, justification in Galatians is "the principal soteriological term," and Paul describes it "as something divinely engineered, actualized by faith in the risen Christ and manifest in a process of revivification."[191]

Boayke understands Paul's language of justification to refer to a manifestation of "revivification" before God and that this status illuminates Paul's "transformative experience."[192] Brant Pitre, a Roman Catholic New Testament scholar, specifically argues that since Paul uses the language of justification, baptism, union with Christ, righteousness, and forgiveness of sins together in the same contexts, then each of these things must necessarily explain what justification is and that justification in Paul is both forensic and transformative/participatory.[193] However, in my view, Paul's verb for justification *never* refers to transformation in the LXX or the New Testament, and it likewise never refers to "revivification." In Romans 6:7, it refers to liberation from sin's power, but the context makes this clear that this meaning is different from the way in which Paul uses the verb in contexts when he uses the verb to contrast the right way of being justified (namely, by faith) with the wrong way of pursuing justification (namely, by works of the law).

---

[188]Peter Oakes and Andrew K. Boakye, *Rethinking Galatians: Paul's Vision of Oneness in the Living Christ* (New York: T&T Clark, 2021), 41-73, 80-105; esp. 41.

[189]Oakes and Boakye, *Rethinking Galatians*, 41-73, 80-105.

[190]Oakes and Boakye, *Rethinking Galatians*, 89.

[191]Oakes and Boakye, *Rethinking Galatians*, 89.

[192]Oakes and Boakye, *Rethinking Galatians*, 89.

[193]Brant Pitre, "The Roman Catholic Perspective on Paul," in *Perspectives on Paul: Five Views*, ed. Scot McKnight and B. J. Oropeza (Grand Rapids, MI: Baker, 2020), 25-55.

The history of interpretation of both Paul's understanding of justification and works of the law is a large body of scholarship.[194] In the LXX, δικαιόω refers to someone being in the right (LXX Gen 38:26; 44:16). In legal contexts in the LXX, δικαιόω refers to the act of not acquitting the guilty (Ex 23:7).[195] The verb also refers to a judge declaring righteous the innocent in a legal context both when humans are the ones rendering the innocent to be not guilty (LXX Ex 23:7) and when God is the Judge rendering justification to the innocent (LXX Deut 25:1; 2 Sam 15:4; 1 Kings 8:32).[196] The verb occasionally refers to the Lord as being in the right for judging the guilty when they sin (LXX Ps 50:6; Sir 18:2).[197] With the exception of three occurrences (Rom 3:5; 6:7; 1 Tim 3:16),[198] Paul's uses of δικαιόω ("to justify") always refer to God's act to δικαιόω sinners (Rom 2:13; 3:4, 20, 24, 26, 28, 30; 4:2, 5; 5:1, 9; 8:30, 33; 1 Cor 4:4; 6:11; Gal 2:16-17; 3:8, 11, 24; 5:4; Titus 3:7). Paul often explicitly states God as the grammatical subject of δικαιόω, and exclaims that God does δικαιόω on behalf of Jews and Gentiles by faith in Christ (Rom 3:22-26, 28-30; 4:4-8; 5:1-2; Gal 2:15-16; 3:8-9, 23-25). Galatians 2:16 is the first place in Galatians, and the earliest place in any of his writings, where Paul mentions δικαιόω ("to justify") by faith, and he does so in the context of table fellowship. He contrasts the concept of justification by faith with justification, not by works of the law (2:16).

Boayke's analysis of δικαιοσύνη ("righteousness") focuses on God's work in Christ to bring life from death.[199] He argues Paul uses Abraham

---

[194]For recent scholarship on works of the law in second century reception history, see Matthew J. Thomas, Paul's "Works of the Law" in the Perspective of Second Century Reception (Downers Grove, IL: InterVarsity Press, 2020). See also Westerholm, Perspectives Old and New on Paul; McKnight and Oropeza, eds., Perspectives on Paul.

[195]For recent work on God as the Judge and justifier in Paul, see James B. Prothro, Both Judge and Justifier: Biblical Legal Language and the Act of Justifying in Paul, WUNT 2/461 (Tübingen: Mohr Siebeck, 2018).

[196]See also LXX 2 Chron 6:23.

[197]Some LXX texts state that humans justify God (Sol 2:1; 3:5; 8:7, 23) or God's judgments (Sol 4:8; 8:26; 9:2).

[198]In Rom 3:5, God is justified when he judges. In context, this means his righteous judgment against sin is right. In 1 Tim 3:16, Jesus is justified in the Spirit. In context, this means Jesus was vindicated by God in his resurrection. In Rom 6:7, δικαιόω refers to the sinner's liberation from sin.

[199]Oakes and Boayke, Rethinking Galatians, 75-105.

in Galatians to highlight this life and righteousness from death idea. God gave Abraham a promise that he would give him a child (life), namely Isaac.[200] Isaac was old, and Sarah was old and barren (death).[201] God brought life to Abraham in the birth of the promised son (Isaac) from the death (barrenness) of Sarah's womb.[202] Paul identifies Isaac's birth as a birth according to the Spirit (Gal 4:29), because Isaac exemplifies both the faith of Abraham and the life that God creates as a result.[203] Paul also identifies the Spirit as the blessing of Abraham, because the Spirit is the life God created from Jesus' death similarly as Isaac was the life God created from Sarah's barrenness (death).[204]

Thus, the link between life based on faith and the death of Christ is as follows:

> God raised the crucified Christ from the dead (Gal 1:1); God calls people to trust in his life-giving power in the same way he called Abraham to. Those who respond with trust, or faith, will be true sons of Abraham (Gal 3:7-9)—that is, they will be brought into new life as Isaac was. This new life is birth according to Spirit, which, in the new age, refers to that revolutionary sphere of existence energized by the risen Christ, conveyed into the faithful by the Spirit (Gal 4:28).[205]

Boayke further supports his argument by discussing the relationship between "righteousness and life" in Galatians together with the first occurrence of justification appearing in a text about "interethnic social mixing" and transformative ethnic unity together with statements in the letter about God bringing life by faith from death through Jesus' death and resurrection (cf. Gal 1:1, 4; 2:5, 14, 19, 20; 3:11, 13, 28; 5:6, 24, 25; 6:15).[206] Therefore, Boayke concludes one must understand righteousness in Galatians as a "righteous status."[207] A righteous status in the presence

---

[200]Oakes and Boayke, *Rethinking Galatians*, 75-105.
[201]Oakes and Boayke, *Rethinking Galatians*, 75-105.
[202]Oakes and Boayke, *Rethinking Galatians*, 75-105.
[203]Oakes and Boayke, *Rethinking Galatians*, 100.
[204]Oakes and Boayke, *Rethinking Galatians*, 100.
[205]Oakes and Boayke, *Rethinking Galatians*, 101, emphasis original.
[206]Oakes and Boayke, *Rethinking Galatians*, 101.
[207]Oakes and Boayke, *Rethinking Galatians*, 101.

of God is "revivified status."[208] According to him, this "revivified status" is transformative because of the life-giving presence and power of Christ, experienced by the Spirit.

If I correctly understand Boayke's argument, he argues Paul uses a life-from-death line of argumentation to accentuate that new life in Christ is compelling. However, I disagree with his analysis of justification. Although δικαιόω ("to justify") and justification in Galatians are related to life or are part of eternal life, Paul does not describe justification as an expression of life. He never with any clarity identifies justification as transformation, and he never clearly calls justification life. The terms δικαιόω ("to justify") and δικαιοσύνη ("righteousness") are in proximity with the concept of life in the letter (Gal 2:16, 19-21; 3:11), and Paul exhorts the Galatians to walk in the Spirit (Gal 5:13–6:10). However, Paul does not define justification as life, as transformation, or as a walk by the Spirit. That is, in my view, Paul uses the verb δικαιόω and the language of justification in Galatians in a very narrow sense to state a positive verdict of "not guilty" given to Jews and Gentiles in the day of judgment by faith in Christ (Gal 2:16). This verdict has entered the present evil age right now and is true right now for those of faith because of the indwelling presence and power of the Spirit in them, because of Jesus' cross and resurrection, and because of their association with Jesus by faith (cf. Gal 1:4; 2:16; 3:1-14; esp. 3:13-14; 4:5-6; 5:6). God renders this verdict of "not guilty" on behalf of those who are united to Christ by faith because he counts them righteous in Christ (cf. Gal 3:6-8).

Paul says the law justifies (δικαιοῦται) no one and that the righteous one by faith (ὁ δίκαιος ἐκ πίστεως) "will live" (ζήσεται) in the future. The future life is yet to come, and it will be completely experienced on the day of judgment when those by faith no longer await by the Spirit the hope of righteousness by faith (Gal 5:5). Yet, the future life is already here and realized in part now within this present evil age by those who are

---

[208] Oakes and Boayke, *Rethinking Galatians*, 101-05.

righteous by faith because of the indwelling presence and power of the Spirit, for Jesus died for our sins to deliver us from the present evil age (Gal 1:4; 3:13-14; 4:5-6; 5:5), and because God raised Jesus from the dead (Gal 1:1) to inaugurate new creation (Gal 6:15). In Galatians 3:11, the righteous one by faith is the one who is justified by faith apart from the law since Paul has already established in Galatians 2:16 that one is justified by faith in Christ and not by works of the law. In Galatians 3:11-12, he does not say justification or righteousness is eternal life or transformative. He does not even say justification is an expression of eternal life or transformation. Furthermore, he does not identify righteousness as a resurrected or transformative status as he talks about justification. Rather, he says the one who is righteous by faith will live in the future (Gal 3:11-12).

Similarly, in Galatians 3:21, Paul uses δικαιοσύνη ("righteousness") and the infinitive "to make alive" (ζῳοποιῆσαι) in the same sentence to assert the law was not given to create eternal life, and that if it was, then δικαιοσύνη ("righteousness") would come by means of Torah. The verb ζῳοποιεω always refers to a divine giving of life in the New Testament and never to justification. Each time the verb ζῳοποιεω is used in the New Testament, it refers to either God or Jesus giving eternal life by means of resurrection (Jn 5:21; 6:63; Rom 8:11; 1 Cor 15:22, 36, 45; 2 Cor 3:6; Gal 3:21; 1 Pet 3:18). This eternal life may emphasize a bodily resurrection or a spiritual resurrection in context, but both are part of the eternal life that is present when this verb appears in the New Testament. That is, physical resurrection from the dead and a spiritual resurrection of the Spirit are foretastes and manifestations of eternal life, but ζῳοποιεω is neither another way of way discussing justification nor another term for "righteousness" (δικαιοσύνη) in the New Testament.

For example, in John 5:21, ζῳοποιεω refers to the Father creating life by resurrecting dead bodies and to the Son creating life by spiritually resurrecting the spiritually dead. In John 6:63, the verb refers to the Spirit creating spiritual life in those who are spiritually dead. In Romans 4:17, ζῳοποιεω refers to God resurrecting dead bodies as an analogy for the eternal life that he gives to those who are justified by faith in Christ (cf. Rom 4:1-25). In Romans 8:11, the verb refers to God's act of physically resurrecting Jesus from the dead, and Paul connects God's act of raising Jesus' body from the dead with the indwelling presence of the Spirit within believers, the same Spirit of the God who raised Jesus from the dead.[209] In 1 Corinthians 15:22, 36, 45 and 2 Corinthians 3:6, ζῳοποιεω refers to a bodily resurrection as eternal life. In 1 Peter 3:18, ζῳοποιεω refers to Jesus' bodily resurrection from the dead as being raised to eternal life.

Likewise, in Galatians 3:21, with the verb ζῳοποιεω, Paul's point is the law does not create eternal life (or resurrection) in the lives of God's people. In this context, the law does not perform the transformative work of the Spirit. This can only be received by faith and only dwells in those who are sons of God because of Jesus' death for our sins to deliver us from this present evil age (Gal 1:4) and to redeem us from the curse of the law. We receive the Spirit by faith (Gal 3:13-14) in our hearts as adopted sons whom Christ has redeemed (Gal 4:5-6). The one who receives a righteous status before God by faith (= justification) because of his association with Christ instead of the law "will" receive eternal life (Gal 3:11), and those who are righteous/justified by faith have already in fact begun to taste this eternal life now by the indwelling presence and power of the Spirit (cf. Gal 3:2–4:31; 5:13–6:10).

However, Paul does not call this life justification in Galatians. Justification is the status given, declared, reckoned, and imputed to the one who has faith in Jesus; it is God's act of declaring sinners to be in the right in Christ by faith. Justification is not another way for Paul to talk about the life that the justified will inherit and that they have already begun to participate in right now by faith. Justification is a forensic declaration of "not guilty" on behalf of those to whom God credits Christ's righteousness and thereby grants them the status of not guilty, without condemnation, in his presence (Gal 3:6; cf. Rom 4:1-25; 8:1). He says very clearly: "because no one is justified in the law before God, it is evident that the righteous one [= the justified one] by faith will live" (Gal 3:11)

---

[209]εἰ δὲ τὸ πνεῦμα τοῦ ἐγείραντος τὸν Ἰησοῦν ἐκ νεκρῶν οἰκεῖ ἐν ὑμῖν, ὁ ἐγείρας Χριστὸν ἐκ νεκρῶν ζῳοποιήσει καὶ τὰ θνητὰ σώματα ὑμῶν διὰ τοῦ ἐνοικοῦντος αὐτοῦ πνεύματος ἐν ὑμῖν.

(brackets mine). The righteous one/the justified one by faith shall live because this one has been justified by faith in the resurrected Christ apart from works of the law (Gal 2:16-21; 3:6-12; cf. 1:1).

In multiple Second Temple Jewish texts, the authors connect the concepts of "righteousness" and entrance into "life."[210] In Galatians 3:11-12, Paul likewise places the concepts of righteousness and life in proximity in the text as he describes God's saving action in Christ apart from the works of the law. He neither equates righteousness and life as either one and the same thing or as one expression of the other, nor does he identify righteousness as life. Instead, Paul intends to say in context that the law does not cancel the promises God gave to Abraham and his offspring when it entered salvation history. The promises came directly from God to Abraham and his offspring, whereas the law came from God to a mediating angel, to Moses, and then to the people of God (cf. Gal 3:1-21a). That is (γὰρ in Gal 3:21b), if the law overrides the promises to Abraham and actually gives the life that it promises to the people of God if they obey the law (cf. Gal 3:11 with Lev 18:5) instead of by means of the promises to Abraham to be realized by faith in Christ, who is the seed of Abraham, then righteousness (= a righteous status before God/justification) would indeed come by means of the law. Consequently, the law would be contrary to the promises given to Abraham, to whom and through whom God gave promises to bless the nations through him and his offspring. God gave Abraham these promises prior to and apart from the giving of the law (cf. Gal 3:1–4:31 with Gen 12; 15; 17). If righteousness/justification comes by law, then Christ died in vain (Gal 2:21).

The law does not give eternal life, although it promised long life in the land in the Mosaic covenant if the people of God obeyed it (Lev 18:5). Yet, those who are justified by faith in Christ receive eternal life and

---

[210]Cf. 1 En. 1:8-9; 39:6-7; 48:7; 58:2-3; 62:13-16; 91:12-13; 94:1-4; 99:10; 103:3; 104:1-6; Apocalypse Zephaniah 3:6-7; 4 Ezra 8:33, 48-52; 2 Bar. 21:12; 24:1; 44:7-15; 51:1-16; Apocalypse of Abraham 13:10-14; Testament of Asher 5:2; Testament of Abraham 11:10 (A); Jub. 30:20; LAB 51:5; Pss. Sol. 9:4-5; 12:6; 13:11; 14:1-4; 9-10; 15:6-13; 1 QS, IV 6-8; 1QH XV, 14-18.

inherit the blessing of Abraham (Gal 3:6-9). According to Paul, righteousness and life are not the same thing, but the righteous one (the
justified one) by faith experiences eternal life in the present and will
inherit eternal life in the future (cf. Gal 2:16–3:14; 6:8). Those who are
righteous by faith have the "already" aspect of eternal life by the
indwelling presence and power of the Spirit, and a status of righteousness
imputed to them by faith is the pathway to the not-yet aspect of the life
promised in the law apart from association with the law (Gal 3:10-14).
Paul explicitly says in Galatians 6:8 the one who sows in the Spirit will
reap the reward of eternal life in the future.

Paul's remarks in Galatians 2:16 with the verb δικαιόω are helpful
here. There he uses the verb for justification, but he does not associate
this verb with the language of life or eternal life. His message is Jews and
Gentiles in Christ receive God's eschatological verdict of "not guilty"
right now in this present evil age and will receive it in the future by faith
in Christ apart from anyone identifying with the Mosaic covenant or
living a Jewish way of life in accordance with Jewish works of Torah.

As I argued above, δικαιόω most often refers to a forensic/legal
verdict on behalf of the innocent (LXX Deut 25:1; 2 Sam 15:4;
1 Kings 8:31-32; Prov 17:15; Is 5:23). In Galatians 2:16, Paul categorically
excludes works of the Jewish law from playing any role in that verdict.
In Galatians 2:17, Paul connects the verdict of justification with those
who are seeking justification because they are found as sinners. These
works of law in Galatians 2:16 refer to the stipulations outlined in the
Mosaic covenant (cf. Gal 2:16; 3:2, 5, 10 with Ex 20:1–Deut 34:12).[211] Paul
asserts that with force justification comes ἐκ πίστεως Χριστοῦ,[212] which
I argue below means "faith in Christ." God's verdict of justification is
fundamentally an eschatological forensic declaration that has invaded
this present evil age and that God renders on behalf of Jews and Gentiles
by faith in, and in association with, Christ. This is accomplished by

---

[211]For a history of reception of the phrase in the second century, see Thomas, Paul's "Works of
the Law."
[212]Cf. also Paul's uses in Rom 3:21-22; 5:1-2; Gal 2:15-16; 3:21-22, 26-27.

Jesus' resurrection (Gal 1:1) and his death "for our sins to deliver us from the present evil age" (Gal 1:4) and to "redeem us from the curse of the law by becoming a curse for us" (Gal 3:13).

For example,[213] first, in Galatians 3:6, Paul uses a cognate noun δικαιοσύνη ("righteousness") to describe a status reckoned to Abraham by faith: "just as Abraham believed God, and it was reckoned to him as righteousness."[214] Boayke states this status is a "righteous status" and refers to a "revivified status."[215] Yet, the noun δικαιοσύνη ("righteousness") appears in LXX Genesis 15:6, where God restates the promise of the universal blessing of the nations in and through Abraham from Genesis 12:1-3. When Paul says God reckoned Abraham as righteous because he believed God's promise, this is another way of saying God justified Abraham before him because he believed God's promise. Both Paul (Gal 2:16, 21) and James (Jas 2:21-23) easily move from using the noun δικαιοσύνη ("righteousness") and the verb δικαιόω ("to justify") to describe Abraham's status before God, and to describe those who have a faith like Abraham's.

Second, Paul contrasts the right way of justification (by faith) with the wrong way of justification or attaining righteousness (by works of law) in Galatians 2:16, 21 (cf. 1 QS X and 4QMMT). Paul forcefully asserts God declares Jews and Gentiles to be innocent by faith instead of by works. One of the greatest differences between Paul's discussion of justification and justification in the LXX is Paul says those whom God declares not guilty are guilty, spiritual slaves under a curse because of sin and because of the law prior to when God declares them to be in the right (Gal 2:17; 3:10, 19; 4:1-10, 21-25).

---

[213]With some modifications, my discussion of justification summarizes material from my Galatians commentary. See especially 64-86 for further discussion and for the citations of both primary and secondary literature.

[214]Καθὼς Ἀβραὰμ ἐπίστευσεν τῷ θεῷ, καὶ ἐλογίσθη αὐτῷ εἰς δικαιοσύνην. An important Pauline phrase in the justification debates in Paul is δικαιοσύνη θεοῦ (Rom 1:17; 3:21; 2 Cor 5:21). In Galatians, Paul uses the noun δικαιοσύνη (Gal 2:21; 3:6, 21; 5:5), but not the phrase δικαιοσύνη θεοῦ. For an examination of the righteousness of God, see Irons, *Righteousness of God*. He forcefully argues against the covenant-faithfulness interpretation and defends a traditional understanding of the phrase.

[215]Oakes and Boayke, *Rethinking Galatians*, 101.

In the LXX, only the innocent ones receive acquittal, and they play a role in their acquittal by doing what is right (e.g., LXX Gen 38:26; 44:16). Paul's point, however, in Galatians 2:17 seems to be Christ is not a minister of sin, but Jews were found to be sinners as they were seeking to be justified by faith in Christ. In fact, according to Paul, Jews and Gentiles are enslaved to the present evil age and under sin, under the curse of the law, under slavery, under the elementary principles of the world, and under the seductive power of the flesh prior to their justification by faith when God declares them not guilty by faith in Christ (Gal 3:10; 3:15–4:8; 5:17, 19-21; 6:9). Their slavery within the present evil age is the reason they need to be justified by faith in Christ, have Christ's righteousness counted in their favor and reckoned to their account (Gal 2:16; 3:6), and emancipated from the present evil age (Gal 1:4; 3:10-14). Jesus' death for "our sins" delivers Jews and Gentiles from the present evil age because he became a curse for us (Gal 3:13; 4:6). Jesus' death (and resurrection) provides the liberation those under the curse of the present evil age need to participate in the cosmic liberation accomplished by Jesus' death and resurrection. Jews and Gentiles personally participate in God's cosmic liberation (i.e., new creation [Gal 6:15]) from the present evil age (Gal 1:4) by being justified by God by faith in Jesus Christ, who died and was resurrected to accomplish vertical, horizontal, and cosmic redemption.

Contrary to those who read Paul only in apocalyptic terms, justification in Galatians specifically and only refers to the exoneration of individual Jews and Gentiles by faith in Jesus Christ (Gal 2:16-17; 3:12; 5:4). Paul only refers to the justification of Jews and Gentiles by faith in Galatians (Gal 2:16). He never clearly refers to the justification of the cosmos in the letter, but to the liberation of sinners from the present evil age (Gal 1:4) and to the liberation of the cosmos with the language of new creation (Gal 6:15; cf. Rom 8:18-30).

In Romans 6:7, Paul states the one who has died with Christ "is liberated" from sin with a form of the verb δικαιόω ("for the one who died is liberated from sin").[216] The context of this statement in Romans 6 supports the notion that Paul uses the verb there to affirm liberation from sin's power (cf. Rom 8:19-26). Those who experience eternal life in Christ are liberated from the power of sin and walk in the newness of this eternal life by subjecting themselves to be slaves of righteousness instead of slaves to the power of the flesh and sin because they have died with Christ in baptism and have been raised to walk with him in the newness of eternal life (Rom 6:1-23). According to Paul in Galatians, individuals are justified by faith, liberated from the present evil age, and liberated from the bondage of the present evil age as they participate in cosmic renewal by faith in Christ (Gal 1:4; 2:16; 3:1–6:15). Paul argues in Galatians the creation is liberated and renewed (Gal 6:15), but he never calls this liberation justification. In Galatians, he only applies justification to the individuals who place faith in Christ (Gal 2:16-17, 21; 3:12; 5:4-5).

Third, justification "by faith" is the antithesis of justification "by works of the law." In Galatians, faith is closely associated with an obedient walk in the power of the Spirit (Gal 3:1-29; 5:13–6:10), but it is not identified as obedience in the Spirit. Faith relates to both cognitively embracing facts about Jesus and showing one's loyalty and allegiance to those facts by faithfully following Jesus.[217] Paul never reduces faith to mere cognition. In Galatians, faith relates to one's loyalty, faithfulness, and commitment to God's saving action in Jesus Christ (Gal 1:23; 2:16, 20; 3:2, 5, 7-9, 11-12, 14, 22-26; 5:5-6, 22; 6:10). One's loyalty to Christ transfers believers into the new age as they are empowered by the Spirit and delivered from the present evil age (Gal 3:2-5; 5:13–6:10). Those with faith follow Jesus faithfully until the end of the age so that they will inherit the kingdom of God (Gal 5:16–6:10), but Paul does not call this transferal from one age to the other justification. Justification in

---

[216] ὁ γὰρ ἀποθανὼν δεδικαίωται ἀπὸ τῆς ἁμαρτίας.

[217] For recent work on faith in Paul, see Teresa Morgan, *Roman Faith and Christian Faith: Pistis and Fides in the Early Roman Empire and Early Churches* (New York: Oxford University Press, 2013); Nijay K. Gupta, *Paul and the Language of Faith* (Grand Rapids, MI: Eerdmans, 2020); Kevin W. McFadden, *Faith in the Son of God: The Place of Christ-Oriented Faith Within Pauline Theology* (Wheaton: Crossway, 2021).

Galatians is *only* forensic and *never* transformative or a term of transfer, while Paul's *soteriology*[218] has both forensic (justification) and transformative (walking in the Spirit) elements to it.[219] In Galatians, a faithful walk of obedience in step with the transformation of the Spirit proves that one is justified by faith since justified Jews and Gentiles walk in obedience in the power of the Spirit (Gal 5:16–6:10). Paul *never* says in Galatians that a walk of obedience to the gospel in step with the Spirit justifies Jews and Gentiles in the judgment. Rather, he insists justification is only by faith in Christ (Gal 2:16-17; 3:10-14; 5:5).

Interpreters have traditionally argued for "faith in Christ" or "the faithfulness of Christ" as the proper translation of ἐκ πίστεως Χριστοῦ.[220] Recent scholarship suggests both "faith in Christ" and "the faithfulness of Christ" are Paul's intention in Romans, while emphasizing Christ's faith/faithfulness is the emphasis as we participate in his faith and faithfulness by personal faith.[221] In a recent monograph on Galatians, Peter Oakes argues neither "faith in Christ" nor "the faithfulness of Christ" captures the meaning of the phrase.[222] Instead, according to Oakes, the best one can say from the evidence in the letter is faith is a relational term in Galatians, and it refers to "participation." The phrase ἐκ πίστεως Χριστοῦ speaks to the manner by which righteousness comes to Jews and Gentiles in Galatians 2:16.[223] To be specific, Oakes argues the genitival phrase ἐκ πίστεως Χριστοῦ that primarily

---

[218]Paul's soteriology includes justification but should not be reduced only to justification. As Thomas R. Schreiner, a strong exegete and laborious defender of the traditional Protestant understanding of justification in Paul's theology, makes abundantly clear in his *Pauline Theology*, justification is not the center of Paul's theology. See Thomas Schreiner, *Paul, Apostle of God's Glory in Christ: A Pauline Theology*, 2nd ed. (Downers Grove, IL: InterVarsity Press, 2020), 4. Soteriology is an important category in Paul's theology in Galatians that includes justification by faith alone and many other theological truths. I am currently writing a Pauline soteriology in which I will comprehensively discuss Paul's soteriology in all thirteen of his letters.

[219]Contra a Catholic view. For example, see Pitre, "Roman Catholic Perspective on Paul," 25-55.

[220]For a summary of the debate up to 2009, see Michael F. Bird and Preston M. Sprinkle, eds., *The Faith of Jesus Christ* (Milton Keynes, UK: Paternoster, 2009).

[221]Morna D. Hooker, "Another Look at *Pistis Christou*," *Scottish Journal of Theology* 69 (2016): 46-62.

[222]Oakes and Boakye, *Rethinking Galatians*, 36-37.

[223]Oakes and Boakye, *Rethinking Galatians*, 37.

refers to a present relationship with the resurrected Christ instead of one's personal belief in the benefits of the past event of Jesus' death and resurrection.[224] He says: "Trust in Christ's cross is part of relating to the living Christ, but the centre is the relationship itself."[225]

I recently argued that a choice between "faith in Christ" and "the faithfulness of Christ" may be a matter of emphasis. That is, Paul may simply intend to emphasize "faith in Christ" as the way Jews and Gentiles experience justification instead of emphasizing that Jews and Gentiles experience justification because of Jesus' faithfulness. Both positions would affirm God is faithful. The latter view accentuates it. In my view, Paul seems to emphasize "faith in Christ" with both the phrase ἐκ πίστεως Χριστοῦ and the sentence ἡμεῖς εἰς Χριστὸν Ἰησοῦν ἐπιστεύσαμεν ("we believed in Christ Jesus") in Galatians 2:16 to highlight that God justifies Jews and Gentiles "by faith in Christ" apart from any association with Torah observance and apart from one's ethnic (either Jewish or Gentile) identity. My reading affirms that Paul's soteriology has participatory elements since an individual participates in God's saving action in Christ by faith in Christ, while I also reject the idea that justification is participatory in a transformative sense. Furthermore, my reading of ἐκ πίστεως Χριστοῦ assumes a *relationship* with Christ since the justified ones are justified by their relationship with Christ by faith because they are united to him by faith (Gal 1:22; 2:4).[226]

For example, (1) Paul pits believing/faith against doing works of the law in Galatians 2:16–3:10. He does so in the context of arguing the Galatians received the Spirit by responding in faith to the message of the gospel instead of by performing works of the Torah (Gal 3:1-5). (2) Paul asserts no one is justified in the law since the law curses those who identify with it (Gal 3:10) and since the law promises life only to those who obey it (Gal 3:11; cf. Lev 18:5). However, since those under the law are accursed, justification by the law and life by means of the law are

---

[224]Oakes and Boakye, *Rethinking Galatians*, 37.
[225]Oakes and Boakye, *Rethinking Galatians*, 37.
[226]Oakes and Boakye, *Rethinking Galatians*, 29.

impossible achievements (Gal 3:10-12). (3) Paul argues Jesus redeemed Jews and Gentiles from the curse of the law so that both groups would receive the blessing of Abraham, namely the Spirit, by faith, just as Abraham believed God, and God reckoned his faith to him as righteousness (Gal 3:6). (4) Paul uses the verb ἐπίστευσεν ("he believed") in Galatians 3:6 to describe why Abraham was reckoned as righteous instead of using the noun πίστις ("faith"). This verb in Galatians 3:6 is the same verb Paul uses in Galatians 2:16 to refer to believing in Christ (ἡμεῖς εἰς Χριστὸν Ἰησοῦν ἐπιστεύσαμεν). Thus, in Galatians, ἐκ πίστεως Χριστοῦ ("by faith in Christ") appears to be another way of saying ἡμεῖς εἰς Χριστὸν Ἰησοῦν ἐπιστεύσαμεν ("we believed in Christ Jesus"). (5) The law places all under its power and jurisdiction under slavery until Christ would come to justify them by faith (Gal 3:15–4:7). (6) Christ freed Jews and Gentiles, who have faith, from slavery to the law and to the present evil age and grants them the life-giving Spirit (Gal 4:31–6:10).

Fourth, in Galatians, Paul discusses justification as both a present reality we experience by faith and a future hope for which we wait by the Spirit by faith. In Galatians 2:16, he states Jews and Gentiles are justified by faith in Christ with a present-tense verb (δικαιοῦται), with a subjunctive verb (δικαιωθῶμεν), and with a future-tensive verb (δικαιωθήσεται). One can read these tenses as timeless verbs in a gnomic sense (especially the subjunctive). However, since Paul states in Galatians 5:5 that we await δικαιοσύνη ("righteousness") by faith by the Spirit, at least the present and the future tenses should be pressed in Galatians 2:16. If this is correct, justification in Galatians is already here now in this present evil age by faith in Jesus Christ, which the indwelling presence of the Spirit in the believer and the empowerment of the Spirit in a life of obedience support (Gal 3:2-14; 4:6–6:10). Still, justification will not be fully realized until the day of judgment. In Galatians, justification is both a present reality (Gal 2:16) and a future hope Jews and Gentiles await on the day of judgment by faith in the power of the Spirit as they walk in step with the Spirit (Gal 5:5). Nevertheless, this future hope has invaded this present evil age right now by faith in Christ (Gal 2:16-17).

Paul's talk of a present and future inheritance in the letter supports this reading (Gal 3:29; 4:1, 7; 5:21).

Fifth, in Galatians, the reason Jews and Gentiles are justified by faith in Christ is because of Jesus' death for their sins to deliver them from the present evil age and from the curse of the law (Gal 1:4; 3:1, 13). Jesus' death for sins, his resurrection from the dead, and faith in Jesus are part of God's saving action in Christ. To believe in Jesus and to be justified by faith reckons the status of the justified as righteous in Christ; they are not righteous by works of the law (Gal 2:16; 3:6, 8, 11; 5:4) or by works in general. The status of the justified in Christ changes in the present evil age before God only because they are seeking to be justified by faith in Christ (Gal 2:17). The status of the justified before God now will be proven true in the day of judgment only because of the indwelling presence of the Spirit, which the justified receive by faith (Gal 3:14) because of Jesus' death for their sins (Gal 3:13-14; 4:5-6). The Spirit is the emblem and signpost of faith throughout the present evil age because of God's saving action for them in Christ (Gal 5:5). The Spirit causes the justified to live in step with the verdict that God has pronounced in this present evil age in their favor by faith in Christ, and that he will pronounce on the day of judgment when the justified stand in his presence and are judged according to their works because of their faith in Christ at the end of history. They will prove God's justifying verdict of "not guilty" right now in the present evil age to be true by their daily walk even as the present evil age continues to triumph.[227]

The Spirit and Salvation History

Certain trends of Pauline scholarship tend to make the mistake of adopting an either-or reading of the letter to the Galatians. From the so-called Old Perspective, New Perspective, Apocalyptic, Anti-imperial, and Paul-within-Judaism readings of the letter, there are scholars who have not allowed for nuance and complexity in understanding Galatians

---

[227]For further discussion of imputation, see also Brian J. Vickers, *Jesus' Blood and Righteousness: Paul's Theology of Imputation* (Wheaton, IL: Crossway, 2006).

and the soteriology therein.[228] Space does not allow me to engage each
of the above perspectives. For my purposes here, I simply argued above
that Paul describes God's saving action in Christ in Galatians as apocalyptic and forensic. In what follows, I argue he also presents God's
saving action in Christ for Jews and Gentiles and for the cosmos in
salvation-historical language.

Salvation history and God's saving action in Christ. In Galatians,
Paul weaves together an apocalyptic, forensic, and salvation-historical
soteriology.[229] In Galatians 3:15–4:7,[230] Paul makes a careful argument
about the slavery under which the law places everyone. He argues with
force the law promised life (Gal 3:12), but it was never intended to be the
pathway to life (Gal 3:21). Rather, the law was given "on account of transgressions" as a temporary guardian until the moment in time when Jesus,
the seed of Abraham, would come so that we would be justified by faith
in Christ (Gal 3:19-24). Now that Jesus has come, neither Jewish nor
Gentile Christians need a guardian (Gal 3:25). "By faith, we are all God's
sons in Christ Jesus" (Gal 3:26) since we put on Christ in baptism
(Gal 3:27). The result is Jewish and Gentile Christ followers share in the
Abrahamic blessing as Jewish and Gentile Christ followers (Gal 3:28).
Neither ethnicity nor social status grants Jews and Gentiles the blessing
of Abraham or excludes them from it (Gal 3:28).

Paul reiterates the temporary nature and function of the law in history
in Galatians 4:1-7. He describes the life of Jews (and Gentiles too) under
the law's power as analogous to a child under a pedagogue (Gal 4:1-2).
This child, Paul says, is similar to a slave until he reaches the age of
maturity as the rightful heir (Gal 4:2). The child's father sets the proper
age of maturity (Gal 4:2). Paul applies the analogy to life under the law.
He says, "In the same way, we ourselves were enslaved under the

---

[228]For a summary of Paul's recent interpreters, see Wright, *Paul and His Recent Interpreters*. For
the Paul within Judaism view, see Mark D. Nanos and Magnus Zetterholm, eds., *Paul Within
Judaism: Restoring the First-Century Context to the Apostle* (Minneapolis: Fortress, 2015).

[229]For an early argument for salvation history in New Testament scholarship, see Oscar Cullmann,
Salvation in History (New York: Harper & Row, 1967).

[230]For my analysis of these verses, see Williams, *Galatians*, 112-34.

elementary principles of the world when we were infants" (Gal 4:3). In context, the time of infancy to which Paul refers is the time prior to the coming of Christ when Jews (and Gentiles) were under the law (Gal 3:15–4:7). But, Paul says, "when the fullness of time came," God himself sent his Son to become a Jew and to live under the power of the law so that "he would redeem those under the law" (Gal 4:4-5). The phrase "fullness of time" refers to the specific moment in history, appointed by God, when God determined to invade and disrupt the present evil age by sending his Son to die for our sins (Gal 1:4), to deliver us from the present evil age (Gal 1:4), to justify us by faith (Gal 2:16), to redeem us from the law's curse (Gal 3:13; 4:4-5), to give us his Spirit and the fruit of the Spirit in which to walk (Gal 3:14; 4:6; 5:16–6:10), to give us freedom (Gal 5:1, 13), and to begin the process of cosmic restoration and new creation (Gal 6:15).

Paul uses much temporal language in Galatians 3:23–4:7 to support the salvation-historical nature of God's saving action in Christ in Galatians. Paul says, "Before faith came" (Πρὸ τοῦ δὲ ἐλθεῖν τὴν πίστιν), those under the law were held in bondage as slaves (Gal 3:23). Those under the law were also "imprisoned until faith in Christ was revealed" (εἰς τὴν μέλλουσαν πίστιν ἀποκαλυφθῆναι) (Gal 3:23). The law was a pedagogue "until Christ" came (εἰς Χριστόν) (Gal 3:24). "But after faith came" (ἐλθούσης δὲ τῆς πίστεως) (Gal 3:25), those under the law were no longer slaves under the law (Gal 3:25). "As long as the heir is an infant" (ἐφ᾽ ὅσον χρόνον ὁ κληρονόμος νήπιός ἐστιν) (Gal 4:1), he did not differ from the slave (Gal 4:1). The pedagogue ruled over the child "until the set time of the father" (ἄχρι τῆς προθεσμίας τοῦ πατρός) (Gal 4:2). "When" Jews and Gentiles were infants enslaved under the law and under the elementary principles of the world (ὅτε ἦμεν νήπιοι πὸ τὰ στοιχεῖα τοῦ κόσμου ἤμεθα δεδουλωμένοι), they were kept in temporary custody by the guardian of the law (Gal 4:3). But "when the fullness of time came" (ὅτε δὲ ἦλθεν τὸ πλήρωμα τοῦ χρόνου) (Gal 4:4), God sent his Son to be a Jewish man under the same power of the Jewish law to redeem Jews and Gentiles to make them sons and heirs who have his Spirit (Gal 4:4-7). Thus, Paul describes God's saving action in Christ as salvation-historical. The moment

God acted in history to send his Son to accomplish God's vertical, horizontal, and cosmic saving action in Christ was the moment he likewise disrupted and invaded the lives of Jews and Gentiles by faith by means of the indwelling presence and power of the Spirit for all who are justified by faith and the moment he began the process of cosmic renewal (Gal 6:15).

CONCLUSION

In this chapter, I argued the foundational reason the Galatians received the Spirit, experienced personal agency and ethical transformation, and participated in eternal life is because of God's vertical, horizontal, and cosmic saving action in Christ for Jews, Gentiles, and for the cosmos (Gal 1:1, 4; 3:1-14). Paul articulates God's saving action in Christ for Jews and Gentiles and for the cosmos with apocalyptic language (e.g., Gal 1:4, 15-16; 5:16-26; 6:15), with forensic language (Gal 2:16; 3:6-8; 5:5), and with salvation-historical language (Gal 4:5-6).

4

Justified by Faith and Walking in Step with the Spirit

In this chapter, I argue those justified by faith in Christ alone *can*, *will*, and *must* walk in step with the Spirit to inherit the kingdom of God and eternal life. The concept of soteriology is complex in Paul's theology. The kingdom of God is only one aspect of his soteriology in Galatians.

Galatians 5:21 is Paul's only explicit reference to the kingdom of God in the letter, and Galatians 6:8-9 is his last reference to the concept of eternal life. This chapter sets my thesis in the context of Paul's remarks about the Spirit, the cross, the resurrection, and the authority of his gospel ministry in Galatians. God's saving action in Christ grants deliverance to those justified by faith and gives Spirit-empowered personal agency and ethical transformation in Christ to the justified. This personal agency and ethical transformation prove Jews and Gentiles have been justified by faith in Christ alone right now in this present evil age, guarantee they will be justified by faith on the day of judgment, and prove they will participate in the future inheritance of the kingdom of God in the age to come.

The Spirit and Walking in Obedience as the Justified

Awaiting the hope of righteousness by faith by the Spirit. In chapter three, I discussed justification by faith in Galatians. I argued Paul describes justification by faith in Christ in Galatians as God's already-not-yet forensic declaration of "not guilty" upon sinners who unite themselves to Jesus by faith. I also argued that God reckons (imputes) the guilty to be righteous in Christ because of Jesus' death for our sins and his victorious resurrection from the dead and because God reckoned and counted those by faith as not guilty on the basis of what God in Christ has done for them (Gal 1:1, 14; 2:16; 3:6-8; 3:10-13; 5:4-5). My intention here is not to repeat my discussion of justification from the previous chapter. Instead, I simply point out the relationship between the Spirit, obedience, present justification, the future hope of justification, and eternal life.

Justification by faith occurs the first time in Galatians in 2:16-17. As Paul rebukes Peter in Antioch for his hypocrisy toward the Gentiles (Gal 2:11-15), he emphasizes Jews and Gentiles are justified by faith in Christ apart from Torah observance (Gal 2:16-21). In chapter three, justification by faith occurs again beside Paul's discussion about the Spirit (Gal 3:2-14). Its occurrence here begins the central section of the letter, which I think consists of Galatians 3:1-6:10. Based on the number of references to the Spirit in Galatians (Gal 3:2-3, 5, 14; 4:6, 29; 5:5, 16-18, 22, 25; 6:1, 8) in comparison to Paul's references to justification by faith (Gal 3:8, 11, 24; 5:4), Paul's main purpose in chapter three seems to be to remind the Galatians they received the Spirit by faith, not by works of the law, instead of simply defending justification by faith. Justification by faith is an important piece of the central section of the letter, but Paul is not only or even primarily engaged in the central section of this letter in an apologetic for justification by faith. To the contrary, he reminds the Galatians how they received the Spirit: namely, by faith. He also reminds the Galatians they participate in justification by faith. Faith is perhaps the central concept in the central section of the letter.

In Galatians 3:1, Paul begins the central section of the letter calling the Galatians "foolish" because although he publicly proclaimed the crucifixion of Christ to them, the teachers duped (at least some of) them with their distorted gospel. In Galatians 3:2-5, Paul frames the section around the question of how they received the Spirit and began their journey of faith. He asks the same question in multiple ways in

Galatians 3:2-5: Did you experience the blessing of the Spirit by works of the law or by faith? In Galatians 3:2, he states, "I only desire to learn this thing from all of you" (τοῦτο μόνον θέλω μαθεῖν ἀφ᾽ ὑμῶν): how did you receive the Spirit, how did you begin your journey of faith, and how are you being brought to full completion (transformation?) on that journey: by works of the law or by the Spirit by faith?[1] The importance of the phrase "only this" (τοῦτο μόνον) is instructive for how the Galatians would have heard the rest of the letter. This statement anticipates Galatians 5:13–6:10, where Paul gives the Galatians a series of exhortations to walk in step with the Spirit. His questions in Galatians 3:2-5 anticipate his remarks to the Galatians in 5:13–6:10 that the Spirit gives them everything they need to live in step with the Spirit and to live a life pleasing to God as Gentiles, for they have already begun to participate by faith in God's vertical, horizontal, and cosmic saving action in Christ in the present evil age by the Spirit.

The first thing Paul mentions after his question in Galatians 3:2 is a question about how they received the Spirit (Gal 3:3). Paul eventually asks the Galatians whether God supplied to them the Spirit and worked supernatural miracles in their midst by works of the law or by their hearing of the gospel that required a response of faith (Gal 3:5).[2] Paul's remarks that the Galatians received the Spirit by faith apart from works of the law are different from statements in Jewish sources that pre-date Paul.

The author of Jubilees states Israel will disobey his law and ordinances as they go the way of the Gentiles, worship their gods, violate his laws, and suffer his judgment as a result (Jub. 1:7-18). Moses prays for God's mercy for Israel, asking God not to forsake Israel but to create an upright Spirit within the people so that they would return to him and not go the way of the Gentiles (Jub. 1:19-21). The author records the Lord's response to Moses' prayer in Jubilees 1:22-25:

---

[1] ἐξ ἔργων νόμου τὸ πνεῦμα ἐλάβετε ἢ ἐξ ἀκοῆς πίστεως; οὕτως ἀνόητοί ἐστε, ἐναρξάμενοι πνεύματι νῦν σαρκὶ ἐπιτελεῖσθε.
[2] ὁ οὖν ἐπιχορηγῶν ὑμῖν τὸ πνεῦμα καὶ ἐνεργῶν δυνάμεις ἐν ὑμῖν, ἐξ ἔργων νόμου ἢ ἐξ ἀκοῆς πίστεως.

I know their contrariness and their thoughts and their stubbornness. And they will not obey until they acknowledge their sin and the sins of their fathers. But after this they will return to me in all uprighteousness and with all of (their) heart and soul. And I shall cut off the foreskin of their heart and the foreskin of the heart of their descendants. And I shall create for them a holy spirit, and I shall purify them so that they will not turn away from following me from that day and forever. And their souls will cleave to me and to all my commandments. And they will do my commandments. And I shall be a father to them, and they will be sons to me. And they will all be called "sons of the living God." And every angel and spirit will know and acknowledge that they are my sons and I am their father in uprightness and righteousness. And I shall love them.[3]

In response to Moses' request that the Lord would create in Israel an upright spirit of obedience within the people (Jub. 1:19-21), the author records the Lord saying the foregoing. First, the people must acknowledge their sins and the sins of their fathers with their entire hearts. Second, only after the first step, he would "create for them a holy spirit" so that they would keep his commandments (Jub. 1:22-25). Israel's experience of a "holy spirit" (which likely refers to a transformed human spirit) occurs after their repentance and their obedience to the law and its ordinances (Jub. 1:22-25).

In Galatians 3:6, however, Paul asserts the Galatians received the Spirit and had supernatural experiences of the Spirit by faith apart from obedience to the law with the example of Abraham (Gal 3:6). Just as Abraham believed God and his faith was reckoned to him as righteousness, so also the Galatians believed God's saving action in Christ (= the gospel). God, consequently, blessed them (with the Spirit) (cf. Gal 3:6 with Gal 3:14). In Galatians 3:6-14, Paul's discussion of faith intersects with his comments about the Spirit. His conclusion from his comments in Galatians 3:2-6 is "those from faith are the sons of Abraham" (Gal 3:7). The teachers

---

[3]Unless otherwise indicated, all translations of the Pseudepigrapha come from James H. Charlesworth.

in Galatia likely explained to these Gentile Christians works of the law were the pathway to membership within the Abrahamic family, to receiving the blessing of Abraham, and to experiencing the life promised in Torah (cf. Gal 3:10-29). Paul takes up the theme of Abraham, the Abrahamic blessing, and eternal life in Galatians 3:7-14 to emphasize these things are realized by means of the justification of Jews and Gentiles by faith because of God's saving action for them in Christ.

In the Old Testament, God promised Abraham land, seed, and a universal blessing (Gen 12:1-3; 15:1-5). Leviticus 18:5 promises life in the land and participation in life in the age to come if the people of God obeyed Torah to receive the life that it promises (cf. also Deut 27–28). Second Temple Jewish authors apply the promise of life in the law afresh in their specific social locations (e.g., Bar 3:14–4:37). If Israel obeys Torah, the Lord blesses them (e.g., T. Levi 13:1-5; T. Jud. 26:1; 4 Ezra 7:88-101).[4] Fourth Maccabees 17:12 connects faithful obedience to Torah even in the context of suffering for God's law with eternal life. Second Temple Jewish authors also apply the temporal promise of life in the land from Leviticus 18:5 to eternal life in the age to come (Pss. Sol. 14:1-10; 2 Bar. 24:1; 48:19, 22, 24; 51:3-7). Other Second Temple texts present Abraham as the ideal Jew who kept Torah before it was inscribed on tablets of stone (Jub. 11:16-17; 12:2-8, 16-24; 15:3; 23:10; 24:11; T. Lev 9:1-14; T. Benj. 10:4; 2 Bar. 57:1-3). In at least one Jewish text, a Jewish author declares God reckoned Abraham as righteous because of his faithfulness (1 Macc 2:52). Sirach 44:19-21 is instructive for the relationship between God's blessing of Abraham and his obedience to God's law:

> Abraham was the great father of a multitude of nations, and no one has been found like him in glory. He kept the law of the Most High, and entered into a covenant with him; he certified the covenant in his flesh, and when he was tested he proved faithful. Therefore, the Lord assured him with an oath that the nations would be blessed through his offspring; that he would make him as numerous as the dust of the earth, and exalt

---

[4]See also T. Dan 5:1; T. Ash. 6:3; Let. Aris. 127.

his offspring like the stars, and give them an inheritance from sea to sea and from the Euphrates to the ends of the earth.[5]

Sirach says Abraham was "the father of a multitude of nations." "No one" was comparable to him "in glory." He kept God's law and, consequently, "entered into a covenant with him." He received circumcision as a sign of the covenant with God; he was faithful to God's test, and, as a result, "the Lord assured him with an oath" that the nations of the earth would experience a blessing through Abraham's offspring, that he would receive many descendants, and that he would receive a Promised Land (Sir 44:19-21).

Other Jewish texts clearly associate eternal life with the keeping of the law. In the Syriac Apocalypse of 2 Baruch, the author says the righteous go before the Lord without fear because they have stored up for themselves treasuries of good works. The righteous are those who obey the law (2 Bar. 14:12). Those who prove themselves to be righteous in accordance with the law will be transformed in glory and receive the promise of eternal life (2 Bar. 51:3). These statements should be understood within the frame of God's grace in these Jewish texts since the righteous will not be saved apart from God's grace (2 Bar. 77:6-7; 78:7; 84:10-11).[6] Still, final salvation and transformation are connected to Torah observance.

Similar to the Second Temple Jewish texts I cite above, Paul understands the law promises life, for he cites Leviticus 18:5 in Galatians 3:12 to make this very point.[7] However, in contrast to the above Jewish texts, Paul does not think life comes through obedience to the law (cf. Gal 3:21). In Galatians 5:25, he says in an if-then sentence that the Spirit gives life and that we should live by the Spirit, who is the source of life: "If we

---

[5]Unless otherwise indicated, all translations of the Apocrypha are from the New Revised Standard Version.

[6]See Brendan Byrne, *Paul and the Economy of Salvation: Reading from the Perspective of the Last Judgment* (Grand Rapids, MI: Baker, 2021), 24-25.

[7]For the reception of Lev 18:5 in early Judaism and in Paul, see Preston M. Sprinkle, *Law and Life: The Interpretation of Leviticus 18:5 in Early Judaism and in Paul*, WUNT 241 (Tübingen: Mohr Siebeck, 2008). For discussion of Paul's hermeneutic of faith, see Francis Watson, *Paul and the Hermeneutics of Faith* (New York: T&T Clark, 2015).

live by the Spirit, let us also conduct our daily lives by the Spirit"
(cf. Gal 5:16-26).[8] Additionally, Paul interprets the Abrahamic blessing
and the promise of life in a soteriological way. He conflates the concepts
of the Abrahamic blessing, the promise of inheritance, and the promise
of life together to communicate they are both accomplished in God's
saving action in Christ and realized in the distribution of the Spirit to
Jews and Gentiles who are justified by faith in Christ.

For example, in Galatians 3:8, Paul asserts because the Scripture
foresaw that God would justify the families (τὰ ἔθνη) of the earth by
faith, it preached as good news in advance to Abraham that all the families of the earth would be blessed in him.[9] Paul's language of blessing
the families of the earth (τὰ ἔθνη) here is important (ἐνευλογηθήσονται
ἐν σοὶ πάντα τὰ ἔθνη) (Gal 3:8; cf. LXX 12:3; 18:18). He interprets the
blessing of Abraham to be fulfilled in the justification of the τὰ ἔθνη
(families of the earth consisting of both Jews and Gentiles) by faith in
Christ, the true seed of Abraham (Gal 3:16), not in the keeping of the law
(contra Sir 44:19-21).[10] In Galatians 3:8 (cf. LXX Gen 12:3), Paul likewise
says the Scripture both foresaw this justification of the Gentiles and
preached this justification to Abraham as the good news (= gospel).[11]

In Galatians 3:9, Paul says, "Therefore, those from faith are blessed with
faithful Abraham" (ὥστε οἱ ἐκ πίστεως εὐλογοῦνται σὺν τῷ πιστῷ Ἀβραάμ).
That is, those who are justified by faith receive the blessing of Abraham the
same way as faithful Abraham: by faith. Then, in Galatians 3:10-12, Paul
states the law brings a curse against all under its jurisdiction (Gal 3:10);
no one is justified by or receives eternal life by works of the law (Gal 3:11),
but only by faith (Gal 3:12), because those under the law are under a curse

---

[8]John R. Levison points out that in certain Second Temple Jewish texts, the Spirit relates to life and that the Spirit is life. E.g., Levinson, *The Spirit in First-Century Judaism* (Leiden: Brill, 2002), 56-77.

[9]προϊδοῦσα δὲ ἡ γραφὴ ὅτι ἐκ πίστεως δικαιοῖ τὰ ἔθνη ὁ θεός, προευηγγελίσατο τῷ Ἀβραὰμ ὅτι ἐνευλογηθήσονται ἐν σοὶ πάντα τὰ ἔθνη.

[10]For a recent analysis of τὰ ἔθνη and Gentile Christian identity, see Terence L. Donaldson, *Gentile Christian Identity from Cornelius to Constantine: The Nations, the Parting of the Ways, and Roman Imperial Ideology* (Grand Rapids, MI: Eerdmans 2020).

[11]προϊδοῦσα δὲ ἡ γραφὴ ὅτι ἐκ πίστεως δικαιοῖ τὰ ἔθνη ὁ θεός, προευηγγελίσατο τῷ Ἀβραὰμ ὅτι ἐνευλογηθήσονται ἐν σοὶ πάντα τὰ ἔθνη.

(Gal 3:10, 12). But Christ redeemed Jews and Gentiles from Torah's curse in that he himself became identified with the curse of the law for them in his life and in his death (Gal 3:13; cf. Deut 21:23). Christ redeemed us from Torah's curse, Paul says, "so that the blessing of Abraham would come to the families of the earth, so that we would receive the promise of the Spirit through faith" (Gal 3:14). Interpreters disagree on the proper way to translate Galatians 3:14 because of the two purpose clauses. In my view, Paul identifies "the blessing of Abraham" as "the promise, which is the Spirit" (Gal 3:14), and the second purpose clause epexegetically explains the first.

In Galatians 3:7-14, Paul squeezes together the reception of the Spirit by faith (Gal 3:2-6), justification by faith (Gal 3:6-8), the blessing of Abraham (Gal 3:9, 14), and the promise of the Spirit (Gal 3:14) into one tight argument. This suggests Paul understands the blessing of Abraham to be fulfilled in the soteriological blessings given to Jews and Gentiles by faith in Christ because of God's saving action for them in Christ and because Jesus is the true promised seed of Abraham (Gal 3:16). God neither talked to Abraham about justification by faith nor did he promise him the Spirit in Genesis (cf. Gen 12:1–25:8). Paul seems to suggest Gentile reception of the Spirit by faith (Gal 3:2-5, 14) proves all of God's redemptive promises to Abraham have been realized in God's saving action for Jews and Gentiles and for the world in Christ. Evidence of this fulfillment is the justification of Jews and Gentiles by faith and their mutual reception of and experience of the Spirit by faith (Gal 3:2-14; 4:6). In Galatians 6:15, Paul's comments on new creation suggest he understands God's promise of land to Abraham to be realized in the new heavens and the new earth (cf. Is 65:17-25). As I argue later in this book, the indwelling presence of the Spirit (Gal 4:6) and a faithful pattern of obedience in step with the Spirit are the emblem and signpost in this present evil age that God fulfills all of his redemptive promises via his saving action in Christ for justified Jews and justified Gentiles and for the world (Gal 5:5, 16-26; 6:1-9; cf. Deut 30:1-10; Jer 31:31-33; Ezek 36–37, 40–48).

In Galatians 4:21-31, Paul's argument focuses on the freedom of the new covenant versus the slavery of the old covenant. Those under the law without faith in Christ are children of slavery, and those in Christ by faith are children of the free Jerusalem from above (cf. Is 54:1). Paul identifies those in Christ as promised children analogous to Isaac (Gal 4:28). He identifies those under the law as children of the flesh, just like Ishmael, and those of faith in Christ as children of the free woman, just like Isaac (Gal 4:31). He says Isaac was born "according to the Spirit" (Gal 4:29). Since he links those in Christ with the promised child, Isaac, and since he links Isaac with the Spirit, Paul's primary point is likely those with faith in Christ are the promised children because they have the Spirit. In Galatians 4:29, Paul refers to the Spirit to identify those justified by faith in Christ, the true seed of Abraham, as the true children of Abraham.

In Galatians 5:1-4, Paul clearly states for the first time in the letter circumcision is the issue to which the teachers were compelling the Galatians to turn. Circumcision would have appeared attractive to the Galatians since they were Gentiles and since circumcision was the sign of the Abrahamic covenant (cf. Gen 17). Circumcision eventually becomes folded within the Mosaic covenant (Lev 12:3). In at least one text in Josephus, two Jews disagree over whether circumcision is a prerequisite for a Gentile proselyte to Judaism. One Jew said a Gentile could become a proselyte without circumcision if he keeps other aspects of the law, while another Jew informs that same Gentile that one cannot keep the law without being circumcised since circumcision is the sign of godliness; thus, he compels the Gentile to be circumcised, and this Gentile gives in to his compulsion (Josephus, *Ant.* 20.33-46).

As more than one scholar has pointed out, in the Greco-Roman world, there are examples of Gentiles mocking Jews because of circumcision (Horace, *Sat.* 1.9.68-74; Petronius, *Satyrica* 68.8; 102.14; Martial, *Epigrams* 7.30, 55, 82; 11.94).[12] In the Second Temple period, Jews fought against Gentile invaders who compelled them to stop practicing circumcision by force (1 Macc 1:48, 60-63; 2:46; 2 Macc 6:10; 4 Macc 4:25; Josephus, *Ant.* 12.253-56; *J.W.* 1.34). LXX Esther 8:17 says Gentiles

---

[12]Cf. also Juvenal, *Sat.* 14.99; Tacitus, *Hist.* 5.2. See also my Williams, *Galatians*, 41-44 for citations of relevant secondary literature.

received the mark of circumcision because they feared the God of the Jews. In Jubilees, circumcision is soteriological in that it provides deliverance from the Lord's wrath: "The sons of Beliar" will not circumcise their children, resulting in the Lord's wrath upon Israel if they neglect circumcision and make themselves like the Gentiles (Jub. 15:34). If Israel neglects circumcision, God will not forgive their sins (Jub. 15:33), for circumcision is an eternal law, the neglect of which would result in eternal destruction (Jub. 15:25-34). God even created the angels as circumcised creatures (Jub. 15:27).[13]

Paul seeks to deter the Galatians away from the teachers' message about the necessity of circumcision for Gentile Christians, for it is a distorted message that only leads to a curse (Gal 1:6-9; 3:10-11). Paul warns if they receive circumcision, they would be obligated to do everything the law said (Gal 5:3). They would be entitled to keep every single aspect of the law and adopt entirely a Jewish way of life (cf. Deut 27–28 with Gal 5:3). He reiterates the severity of their prospective turn from Christ to the law by saying those who seek justification by the law instead of by faith in Christ will become severed from Christ and will fall from the grace of the gospel (Gal 5:4).

In Galatians 5:5, Paul offers a reason for the premises in Galatians 5:3-4: "for we by the Spirit by faith await the hope of righteousness" (ἡμεῖς γὰρ πνεύματι ἐκ πίστεως ἐλπίδα δικαιοσύνης ἀπεκδεχόμεθα). Here Paul links the Spirit (πνεύματι), faith (ἐκ πίστεως), and the hope of righteousness/ justification (ἐλπίδα δικαιοσύνης) as an inseparable chain. He also states righteousness is a future hope (ἐλπίδα δικαιοσύνης), for which we await (ἀπεκδεχόμεθα). This one statement brings together comments I argued in the previous chapter about justification in Galatians 2:16: justification is both a present reality and a future hope realized by faith. The hope of justification by faith is certain because of Jesus' death for our sins and his resurrection from the dead (Gal 1:1, 4; 3:10-14; 4:5-6), and because the justified receive the Spirit by faith because of God's saving action for them

---

[13]For a discussion on circumcision, see Williams, *Galatians*, 41-44.

in Christ (Gal 1:4; 3:2-5, 13-14; 4:5-6; 5:5). The justified ones begin their experience of the Spirit by faith (Gal 3:3), and they continue their completion and transformation in the Spirit by faith (Gal 3:3) as they await their future justification by walking in step with the Spirit by faith (Gal 5:5; cf. 5:13–6:10; esp. 5:16, 18, 25). The Spirit enables those in Christ to await the hope of righteousness (i.e., future participation in the age to come) by faith (Gal 5:5) because they received the Spirit by faith (Gal 3:2-5, 13-14; 4:5-6) and because the Spirit dwells in their hearts by faith as part of God's saving action in Christ (Gal 1:4; 3:13-14; 4:5-7).

Walking in step with the Spirit and living by the Spirit. In Galatians 5:13–6:10, Paul commands the Galatians to walk in step with the Spirit, and he mentions the grave consequences of disobedience. As John M. G. Barclay states, the primary emphasis in Galatians 5:13–6:10 is the dynamics of community life and "social practice."[14] Since Paul directly warns the Christian community in Galatia if they walk according to the flesh they will not inherit the kingdom of God (Gal 5:19-20), they could possibly lose all of God's saving benefits in Christ if they fail to obey the gospel.[15] But this does not mean Paul argues in Galatians 5:13–6:10 that eternal life is based on human effort.[16]

In Galatians 5:13, Paul reminds the Galatians they were effectually called into freedom to participate in God's saving action in Christ (cf. Gal 1:6; 5:8).[17] This calling liberates the Galatians from the bondage of the present evil age (Gal 1:4, 6; 4:21–5:1), but they must not use their freedom as an occasion to gratify the flesh (Gal 5:13-21). Flesh in Galatians 5:13, and in the rest of the section, primarily refers to a power or

---

[14]John M. G. Barclay, *Paul and the Gift* (Grand Rapids, MI: Eerdmans, 2015), 425. Citing Todd Wilson (*The Curse of the Law and the Crisis in Galatia* [Tübingen: Mohr Siebeck, 2007], 7), Barclay (424) observes that most scholars now agree that the dynamics of community life discussed in Gal 5:13-6:10 is "integral" to Paul's gospel in Galatia.

[15]Barclay, *Paul and the Gift*, 440.

[16]Against Chris VanLandingham, *Judgment and Justification in Early Judaism and the Apostle Paul* (Peabody, MA: Hendrickson, 2006), 205-10. He specifically focuses on Gal 5:16–6:10.

[17]For texts where Paul uses the Greek verb translated as "to call" to refer to an effectual calling to faith in Christ that results in a heart transformation, see Rom 4:17; 8:30; 9:7, 12, 24-26; 1 Cor 1:9; 7:15, 17-18, 20-22, 24; 1 Cor 15:9; Gal 1:6, 15; 5:8, 13; Eph 4:1, 4; Col 3:15; 1 Thess 2:12; 4:7; 5:24; 2 Thess 2:14; 1 Tim 6:12; 2 Tim 1:9.

realm characterized by immoral behavior contrary to the Spirit.[18] This power manifests itself in the present evil age by means of various individual works that manifest themselves in social vices that flow from the fleshly realm (Gal 5:19-20).

In Galatians 1:4, Paul begins the letter asserting Jesus died to liberate the Galatians from the realm and power of the present evil age (Gal 1:4). He later says "we" were slaves to the elementary principles of the world prior to God sending his Son to redeem those under the law (Gal 4:3-7). He warns them that if the Galatians turn away from his gospel, then they would become enslaved all over again to the elementary principles of the world in a similar way as they were enslaved when they did not know God (Gal 4:8-9).

The flesh-and-Spirit antithesis in Galatians is both a reference to the old age and to the old covenant. More specifically, this antithesis represents the two different realms or powers. The old age represents the power of slavery and oppression to sin and to all earthly and demonic forces of evil, but the Spirit represents the new age and freedom in Christ (Gal 3:15–4:31). These two realms that represent two different and opposing powers are also personal agents. The Spirit represents God's divine action in Christ and the flesh represents a competing and inferior divine agent that enslaves the human agent to the present evil age. Paul says the flesh and Spirit have a desire and a will; the desires and wills of both oppose the desires and wills of each other, and they both demand the loyalty of all human agents and the cosmos (cf. Gal 5:17-26 with Gal 1:4; 4:3, 9).

The age and power of the flesh contrast with and strongly oppose the freedom and life represented in the new age of the Spirit inaugurated by Christ (Gal 1:1, 4; 3:12-13, 21; 5:1-26). The Spirit refers to the Holy Spirit and to the realm of new creation in which all those with faith in Christ have already begun to participate now in this present evil age because of God's saving action in Christ (Gal 1:4; 3:13–5:1; 6:15). God liberated the Galatians from slavery to the flesh through Christ and the Spirit to be slaves of one another in love (Gal 5:14). In love, the Galatians walk in

---

[18]Gal 5:16-17, 19, 24.

step with the Spirit (Gal 5:16), are led by the Spirit (Gal 5:18), live by the Spirit (Gal 5:25), and fulfill the entire intent of the Mosaic law (to love God and neighbor as self as they bear one another's burdens) by the Spirit by faith in Christ, not by doing works of the law (Gal 5:14; 6:2; cf. Lev 19:18). The Galatians manifest this new life and freedom in Christ when they love God and avoid backbiting one another, refrain from being cruel to one another, and refuse to hurt one another in the power of the flesh with selfish rivalry, slanders, lies, divisions, and various forms of enmities and immoralities (Gal 5:15-20).

God's saving action in Christ for Jews and Gentiles to liberate them from the power of the present evil age is the reason Paul commands the Galatians in 5:13–6:10 to perform the deeds of the Spirit. In fact, Paul commands the Galatians to use their freedom in Christ to be slaves of one another in love (Gal 5:13-14). If the Galatians walk in step with the Spirit, they certainly will not fulfill the lust of the flesh (Gal 5:16). This point seems obvious later in the text because Paul says "flesh and Spirit" have nothing in common with one another; they are opposed to each other (Gal 5:17). The flesh is part of the present evil age, represents a realm of enslavement to the present evil age and an age of enslavement under the principalities and elementary principles of the cosmos, and is characterized by behavior contrary to the Spirit (Gal 1:4; 4:3, 9). The Spirit represents the Holy Spirit, the realm of the new age inaugurated by Christ because of God's saving action in Jesus and characterized by behavior in step with the Spirit (Gal 1:1, 4; 3:13-5:1; 6:15). Since those who have been justified by faith have already begun to participate in God's saving action in Christ in this present evil age and since their reception of the Spirit by faith is part of God's saving action in Christ (Gal 2:16; 3:13-14; 4:5-6), then it follows that justified people who have the Spirit will faithfully walk in obedience in step with the Spirit, and they will certainly not live in compliance within the present evil age or within the realm of enslavement to the flesh.

Barclay has argued in detail that grace in Paul's theology should be "reconfigured" as a gift analogous to the practice of gift-giving in the ancient world.[19] Barclay points out ancient gifts were socially binding and mutually obligated the gift-giver to the recipient, and the recipient to the giver, in a reciprocal relationship.[20] While noting similarities between Paul and his ancient contemporaries, Barclay argues Paul "perfects" (accentuates) the gift of Christ in Galatians as an "incongruous gift," which is "a gift given to unworthy recipients without regard for their worth."[21] Commenting on Galatians 5:13–6:10, Barclay states because of the incongruity of the gift of Christ to the Galatians and their reception of that gift by faith, the gift of Christ "neither reflects nor endorses criteria of value operative" in Galatia.[22] Instead, in Christ Jesus, the "community of the new creation" in the churches of Galatia is free "to follow its own systems of values, unconstrained by the dominant systems of cultural capital" as they live by faith and follow their new standard of living in Christ (Gal 5:6; 6:15-16).[23] This new standard of living is given to them by the Spirit, who comes to the Galatians because of the gift of Christ. In my view, since God's saving action in Christ for Jews and Gentiles is an "incongruous gift," no human agent in Christ is perfect or without boundaries. Perfection awaits the day of consummation. Still, the justified ones by faith in Christ, who in fact are the *only* ones who have been delivered from the present evil age, have the moral capacity as free moral agents in Christ to walk in step with the Spirit as the appropriate response to the gift of Christ and no longer be enslaved to the oppressive power of the flesh (Gal 5:1, 13, 16).

To be clear, free moral agency has boundaries, restrictions, and limitations. God's saving action in Christ liberates by the Spirit those who were enslaved to and oppressed by the law, sin's power, and the demonic forces of evil controlled by sin. That liberation enables the liberated to choose life in Christ since the Spirit makes them alive (cf. Gal 3:21; 5:25). Yet, those who have been liberated by God's saving action in Christ to

---

[19]Barclay, *Paul and the Gift*, 1-574.
[20]Barclay, *Paul and the Gift*, 1-78.
[21]Barclay, *Paul and the Gift*, 351-446.
[22]Barclay, *Paul and the Gift*, 423.
[23]Barclay, *Paul and the Gift*, 423.

be free moral and personal agents are not beyond having their ability to choose controlled by God and Christ, superior divine agents, or by sin and everything within the present evil age. So, the justified who have the Spirit have the moral capacity to make a real and viable choice to choose life in Christ (Gal 5:13–6:10) or to choose the way of destruction apart from Christ if they desire and consequently forfeit all the saving benefits given to them in Christ by the Spirit (cf. Gal 1:6-9; 5:2-7, 21; 6:8-10).

However, their personal agency to choose is not without limitations. The Galatians are either enslaved to the flesh or liberated by the Spirit to be slaves of one another in love (Gal 5:13-26). Yet, if they choose life in Christ and the path of the Spirit, they will receive the inheritance of eternal life (Gal 5:13–6:10). If they choose the way of the flesh, they will receive eschatological destruction (Gal 5:21; 6:8-10). These two paths are freely theirs to take, and the promises of life and judgment therein impinge upon the freedom of these free justified agents, serving as motivations for them to choose the right path to receive the reward that Christ's death purchased for them. The Spirit fills, energizes, empowers, transforms, and strengthens them to walk in obedience to the gospel in step with the Spirit.[24] The justified *can* walk in the Spirit. They *must* walk in the Spirit, and they *will* walk in the Spirit. The warning they will fall short of the kingdom if they fail to walk in step with the Spirit is a motivation and a means by which they will obey the Spirit and prove their justified status in this present evil age and in the day of judgment.

If the Galatians choose the way of the Spirit, they will certainly not walk in step with the power of the flesh (Gal 5:13, 16). Moreover, the

---

[24]Discussions of agency in Pauline theology are plentiful in the secondary literature. For a few examples, see John M. G. Barclay and Simon J. Gathercole, eds., *Divine and Human Agency in Paul and His Cultural Enviornment* (New York: T&T Clark, 2006); Jason Maston, *Divine and Human Agency in Second Temple Judaism and Paul: A Comparative Study*, WUNT 297 (Tübingen: Mohr Siebeck, 2010); Preston M. Sprinkle, *Paul and Judaism Revisited: A Study of Divine and Human Agency in Salvation* (Downers Grove, IL: InterVarsity Press, 2013); Kyle B. Wells, *Grace and Agency in Paul and Second Temple Judaism: Interpreting the Transformation of the Heart*, NovTSup 157 (Leiden: Brill, 2015). My view of agency in Galatians agrees with Barclay's "non-contrastive transcendent" model whereby God's action surrounds human action and is the cause of human agency, the Creator of human agency, and defines the boundaries of human agency. Barclay and Gathercole, eds., *Divine and Human Agency*, 7.

justified ones *must* walk in step with the Spirit and choose not to practice the desires of the flesh, for flesh and Spirit have nothing in common; they are two entirely different realms of opposing hostility (Gal 5:16-20). Their choice to obey the Spirit manifests itself in a consistent pattern of behavior developed as a rhythm of life over time through a faith in Christ that works through love in real social relations in the community.[25] Since faith works through love (Gal 5:6), since love is part of the fruit of the Spirit (Gal 5:22), and since Jesus modeled this selfless sacrificial love for the community by dying for the sins of Jews and Gentiles, then one's faith in Christ should not be reduced to one's private and personal relationship with Christ.[26] Faith is both personal and communal.[27] However, those who choose to walk in the flesh and fail to exercise this faith through love in right communal relations by disrupting the unity of the community with the deeds of the flesh (Gal 5:19-20) while claiming to possess the Spirit will not inherit God's kingdom (Gal 5:21).

Paul uses the phrase "kingdom of God" elsewhere in his letters (Rom 14:17; 1 Cor 4:20; 6:10; 15:24, 50 ["kingdom to God" with a dative of possession in 1 Cor 15:24];[28] Gal 5:21; Eph 5:5; Col 4:11; 2 Thess 1:5). In Colossians 1:14, he refers to the "kingdom of God's beloved Son." There Paul associates the kingdom of God's Son with God the Father's deliverance of those whom Christ has redeemed (i.e., provided forgiveness of sins) and reconciled by his blood (Col 1:13-14, 20), and with the Father's deliverance of the redeemed from the sovereignty of the rulers of darkness and his transferring of them into the rule and reign of the Son's kingdom (Col 1:14). His kingdom reigns over all earthly and demonic kingdoms in the heavens and on the earth, and Jesus is preeminent over all kingdoms in heaven and on the earth, demonic and human, as the beloved Son (Col 1:15-20).

---

[25]Barclay, *Paul and the Gift*, 430.
[26]Barclay, *Paul and the Gift*, 430.
[27]Barclay, *Paul and the Gift*, 430.
[28]τὴν βασιλείαν τῷ θεῷ.

The phrase "kingdom of God" occurs only once in Galatians in 5:21. There Paul speaks of the kingdom of God as a future inheritance. He further states the kingdom of God is an inheritance the Galatians would forfeit in the future in the age to come if they do not walk in the Spirit now in the present evil age (οἱ τὰ τοιαῦτα πράσσοντες βασιλείαν θεοῦ οὐ κληρονομήσουσιν, "those who practice such things will not inherit the kingdom of God") (cf. Gal 5:21 with 5:16-26).

In 1 Corinthians 6:9-10, Paul says the Corinthians believers will fail to inherit the kingdom of God if they lack the necessary ethical transformation now in the present evil age: "Do you not know that the unrighteous will not inherit the kingdom of God?" (οὐκ οἴδατε ὅτι ἄδικοι θεοῦ βασιλείαν οὐ κληρονομήσουσιν). Paul explains the unrighteous are not those who fail to do works of the law, but they are those who misuse their moral agency, lack ethical transformation, and practice vices unbefitting of those who identify with Christ: "Do not be deceived! Neither the sexually immoral, nor idolators, adulterers, effeminate homosexual males, male homosexuals, thieves, greedy or covetous people, drunkards, slanderers, or swindlers will inherit the kingdom of God."[29]

In 1 Corinthians 6:11, Paul says some of the Corinthians were lacking ethical transformation prior to their faith in Christ as they committed those specific acts of unrighteousness that he outlines in 1 Corinthians 6:9. However, he reminds the Corinthians in 6:11 they were washed, sanctified (= set apart to be wholly devoted to God), and "justified in the name of the Lord Jesus Christ and in the Spirit of our God."[30] In 1 Corinthians 15:50, he mentions the future inheritance with an aorist infinitive (κληρονομῆσαι) and a present indicative (κληρονομεῖ) in the context of the future resurrection of the dead. He says "flesh and blood"

---

[29]μὴ πλανᾶσθε· οὔτε πόρνοι οὔτε εἰδωλολάτραι οὔτε μοιχοὶ οὔτε μαλακοὶ οὔτε ἀρσενοκοῖται οὔτε κλέπται οὔτε πλεονέκται, οὐ μέθυσοι, οὐ λοίδοροι, οὐχ ἅρπαγες βασιλείαν θεοῦ κληρονομήσουσιν.

[30]καὶ ταῦτά τινες ἦτε· ἀλλ᾽ ἀπελούσασθε, ἀλλ᾽ ἡγιάσθητε, ἀλλ᾽ ἐδικαιώθητε ἐν τῷ ὀνόματι τοῦ κυρίου Ἰησοῦ Χριστοῦ καὶ ἐν τῷ πνεύματι τοῦ θεοῦ ἡμῶν. For Paul's other references to the Spirit in the Corinthian correspondence in connection with eternal life, see 1 Cor 2:4, 10-14; 3:16; 4:21; 12:3; 2 Cor 3:6, 17-18; 13:13.

is not able to inherit the kingdom of God, and corruption cannot inherit immortality.[31]

"Flesh" in 1 Corinthians likely does not have the same cosmic flavor as it does in Galatians 5:16-26 (cf. 1 Cor 1:26, 29; 5:5; 6:16; 7:28; 10:18; 15:39, 50; 2 Cor 1:17; 4:11; 5:16; 7:1, 5; 10:2-3; 11:18; 12:7). However, more than once Paul does refer to "this age" and to "this world" in ways that reflect his point about two opposing ages in Galatians. In 1 Corinthians 1:20, Paul asks where the "debater of this age" is in the context of critiquing the "wisdom of the world" as foolish (1 Cor 1:21). In 1 Corinthians 2:6-8, as he argues his preaching was by the power of the Spirit instead of by earthly wisdom, Paul says "we" do not speak about the perfect things by means of the "wisdom of this age or by the rulers of this age who are fading away," but "we" speak God's wisdom by means of a mystery, which "none of the rulers of this age has known." If they would have known this wisdom, they would not have crucified Jesus (1 Cor 2:8). In 1 Corinthians 3:18, Paul says those who think they are wise "in this age" must become fools. That is, they must embrace the message of the cross, which is foolishness to those who perish but the power of God for those who are being saved (1 Cor 1:18). In 1 Corinthians 2:12, Paul contrasts the "spirit of the world" with the "Spirit of God," stating believers received "the Spirit of God" and not the "spirit of the world." In 1 Corinthians 3:19-20, Paul argues that no one should boast in humans because "the wisdom of this world is foolish" (esp. 1 Cor 3:19).[32]

When Paul refers to "flesh and blood" in 1 Corinthians 15:50, he at least means only those who experience a comprehensive resurrection from the dead and inherit a resurrection body of immortality will inherit the kingdom of God. Only those who are redeemed to live contrary to unrighteousness and who in fact live contrary to unrighteousness will participate in this bodily resurrection from the dead in the age to come

---

[31]Τοῦτο δέ φημι, ἀδελφοί, ὅτι σὰρξ καὶ αἷμα βασιλείαν θεοῦ κληρονομῆσαι οὐ δύναται οὐδὲ ἡ φθορὰ τὴν ἀφθαρσίαν κληρονομεῖ.

[32]For additional occurrences of κόσμος in 1 Corinthians, see 1 Cor 4:9, 13; 5:10; 6:2; 7:31, 33-34; 8:4; 11:32; 14:10.

(cf. 1 Cor 6:9-10). In Ephesians 5:5, Paul states those lacking ethical transformation have no inheritance in the kingdom of Christ and of God.[33]
In Galatians 5:21, Paul's reference to the Galatians' forfeiture of a future
inheritance should be interpreted in connection with his comments
about inheritance and promise in Galatians 3:18: "for if the inheritance
is by means of law, then it is no longer by means of promise. But God
gifted Abraham through a promise."[34]

Most of the time, Paul uses the noun promise (ἐπαγγελία) to refer to
specific promises given to Abraham (Rom 4:13-14, 16, 20; 9:4, 8-9; 15:8;
2 Cor 1:20; 7:1; Gal 3:14, 16-18, 21-22, 29; 4:23, 28; Eph 1:13; 2:12; 3:6; 6:2).
He argues these promises are fulfilled in God's saving action in Christ
(cf. Gal 3:1–4:31). On a couple of occasions, Paul employs the term
"promise" to refer to eternal life in Jesus Christ (1 Tim 4:8; 2 Tim 1:1). In
his letters, inheritance refers to different aspects of eternal life. He either
specifically calls the Spirit the deposit, seal, or realization of the inheritance of eternal life (Gal 3:18; Eph 1:14) or he more generally says the
Spirit points to the promise of the future inheritance of eternal life, of
which those in Christ will participate in the age to come (Eph 1:18; 5:5;
Col 3:24).

In Galatians, the noun "inheritance" (κληρονομία) occurs only once
(Gal 3:18), while Paul uses the verb "to inherit" (κληρονομέω) twice
(Gal 4:30; 5:21).[35] Of the many times Paul uses the term "promise" in his
letters, eight occur in Galatians 3 and two in Galatians 4. Paul brings the
concepts of promise and inheritance together into one soteriological
argument in Galatians 3–4 to highlight the Galatians had already begun
to experience full membership in the Abrahamic blessing in this present
evil age by faith in Christ and by the Spirit prior to Paul writing to them
and prior to the opponents irritating them with their distorted false

---

[33]τοῦτο γὰρ ἴστε γινώσκοντες, ὅτι πᾶς πόρνος ἢ ἀκάθαρτος ἢ πλεονέκτης, ὅ ἐστιν εἰδωλολάτρης,
οὐκ ἔχει κληρονομίαν ἐν τῇ βασιλείᾳ τοῦ Χριστοῦ καὶ θεοῦ.

[34]εἰ γὰρ ἐκ νόμου ἡ κληρονομία, οὐκέτι ἐξ ἐπαγγελίας· τῷ δὲ Ἀβραὰμ δι' ἐπαγγελίας
κεχάρισται ὁ θεός.

[35]He uses κληρονομήσει ("he will inherit") in Gal 4:30 and κληρονομήσουσιν ("they will inherit")
in Gal 5:21. Both are future tenses.

gospel (cf. Gal 1:6-9). Because of God's saving action for them and the cosmos in Christ, and because of their participation in God's saving action by faith, the Galatians were legitimate children of Abraham by faith in Christ, not by works of the law (Gal 3:14, 16-18, 21-22, 29; 4:23, 28). Evidence of their membership into the family of Abraham is the Spirit's work in their midst (Gal 3:2-5, 13; 4:5-6).

In Galatians 3:1–4:31, Paul's basic argument is the Galatians received the blessing of Abraham and the promise of Abraham, which is the Spirit, by faith (Gal 3:2-14), not by works of the law (Gal 3:10-14). Earlier in Galatians, Paul refers to the families of the earth experiencing the blessing of Abraham as he defines the Abrahamic blessing to be the reception of the Spirit by faith (Gal 3:14). As I argued earlier, God did not promise the Spirit to Abraham in the Genesis narrative (Gen 12:1–25:8). Paul instead interprets the promises to Abraham to be realized for the multiethnic families of the earth and for the cosmos through God's saving action in Christ and by the distribution of the Spirit to them by faith (Gal 3:2-14). The Spirit is the emblem in Jews and Gentiles and the signpost for the entire cosmos that Jews and Gentiles are justified by faith and that creation's renewal has already begun in the present evil age as the justified ones walk in step with the Spirit because of both their and the world's co-crucifixion with Christ (Gal 3:2–6:15). Jewish and Gentile reception of the Spirit by faith is the evidence God has fulfilled all of his redemptive promises to Abraham, as Jews and Gentiles are justified by faith (Gal 2:16), are reconciled to one another as they live in a new community marked by love (Gal 2:11-14; 5:6; 5:13–6:10), and as they participate in cosmic renewal (Gal 6:15). This is so because of God's saving action for Jews and Gentiles and for the cosmos in Christ as Christ has delivered them, and the entire creation (Gal 4:8-10; 6:15), from the present evil age (Gal 1:4).

Therefore, those who are justified by faith in Christ *can*, *must*, and *will* walk in step with the Spirit and not conduct themselves in accordance with the flesh, because they have already begun to participate in eternal life now in this present evil age. However, they will not participate in the future inheritance of the kingdom of God (= God's comprehensive rule in Christ over the entire creation), which is one aspect of life in Christ, if they choose to walk in the flesh now instead of walking in step with the Spirit (Gal 2:16–5:21). Those who walk in the flesh now show they are still enslaved to the present evil age and are under the curse and slavery of the law, under the power of sin, and under the power of the present evil age (Gal 3:15–4:7). Those who walk in the flesh and by no means walk in step with the Spirit are counted among those who are still subject to a yoke of slavery (Gal 5:1) and for whom Christ's death will not profit in the eschatological judgment (Gal 5:2, 8-9). These are obligated to perfectly keep the entire law (Gal 5:3). They are severed from Christ (Gal 5:4), and they have fallen from grace (Gal 5:4), even as they may claim to have been justified by faith in Christ, because they do not wait for the hope of righteousness by walking in step with the Spirit by faith (Gal 5:5, 16). But if the Galatians walk in the Spirit in this present evil age, choose to avoid the desires of the flesh, and pursue the desires of the Spirit, they will inherit the kingdom of God because they cannot do whatever they want (Gal 5:17, 21).

A real ethical choice is set before the justified ones in Galatia, but they cannot do whatever they want and expect to participate in eternal life in the age to come. In the light of God's saving action in Christ for Jews and Gentiles and for the cosmos, Paul states in no uncertain terms the only reasonable option for the Galatians is to walk in step with the Spirit if they want to inherit the kingdom of God (Gal 5:16-21). There are two *real* choices before them, but there is only one *viable* moral option before them that leads to inheriting the kingdom of God. Their viable option is the choice to walk in step with the Spirit because the Galatians have been justified by faith in Christ and because they have been made alive by the Spirit by faith in Christ because of God's saving action in and for them and the cosmos (Gal 3:13-14; 4:6; 21; 5:16, 21, 25; 6:15). However, if the Galatians choose the way of the flesh, they will be akin to Ishmael, who was not the promised child, as he did not inherit the promise of Abraham with the free woman and her son.

As a matter of clarification, the Galatians can either choose the way of the Spirit or the way of the flesh if they want. They in fact were liberated in Christ to have the moral capacity and the personal agency to choose one path or the other, the way of life or the way of the curse (cf. Gal 1:6-9 and 2:11 with 5:1, 13). Otherwise, Paul's shock that at least some of the Galatians were turning so quickly from God who called them in Christ to the distorted message and turning to this distorted gospel is pointless (Gal 1:6-7). Prior to their experience of the Spirit and participation in God's saving action in Christ, the Galatians were enslaved to the present evil age and to all its seductive powers (Gal 1:4; 3:15–4:31). They only had the ability to choose the path of slavery when they did not know God (Gal 4:8-10). Once they participated in God's saving action in Christ by faith as they were delivered from the present evil age (Gal 1:4), redeemed from the curse of the law (Gal 3:13), came to know God, and came to be known by God (Gal 4:8-11), the Spirit began to indwell their hearts to begin the work of transforming, enabling, empowering, and energizing the Galatians to walk in step with the Spirit as an expression of the eternal life that they had already experienced and participated in by faith in Christ now in this present evil age (Gal 1:4; 3:13-14; 3:15–5:1, 13). The Spirit did not liberate the Galatians so that they could gratify the flesh or do whatever they wanted whenever they wanted (Gal 5:13-26). The Spirit liberated them to conduct themselves daily in step with the Spirit (Gal 3:14; 4:3, 6-7; 5:16, 18, 25).

The way of the Spirit is the only way that leads to life (Gal 6:8-9). The way of the flesh is the only way that leads to eschatological destruction (Gal 6:8). Since God has acted in Christ to deliver the justified ones in Galatia from the present evil age and from the curse of the law so that they would have the Spirit (Gal 1:4; 3:13-14; 4:5-6), the Galatians must conduct their everyday rhythms of life in step with the way of the Spirit in order to inherit the kingdom of God (Gal 5:16–6:10; esp. 5:21), for they received life by the Spirit when they crucified the flesh with its passions and desires at the moment of participating in God's saving action in Christ by faith (Gal 5:24-25; cf. 2:19-21). The law will not give the Galatians life (Gal 3:21). Pursuing the lust of the flesh will not give the Galatians life (Gal 5:16-21; 6:8-9). Only the Spirit gives life (Gal 5:25), and the Spirit comes to Jews and Gentiles only by faith in Christ (Gal 3:2-5) because Jesus died for their sins to deliver them from the present evil age (Gal 1:4) and to deliver them from the curse of the law (Gal 3:13) so that they would receive the Spirit by faith in Christ (Gal 3:14; 4:5-6). The life that Paul lived in his human existence on a daily basis when he was crucified to the world and died with Christ and to the law was a life that he lived by faith in Christ because of the life he received from God by the Spirit by faith in Christ (Gal 1:15-16; 3:21; 5:25). That life in Christ was the source of righteousness (justification) and the life-giving power of the Spirit that comes by Christ himself living in Paul by the Spirit (Gal 2:19-21; 3:13-14; 4:5-6). This is the same life for which God in Christ has acted on behalf of the Galatians, the reason for which he has acted to deliver and redeem the Galatians (Gal 1:4; 3:13-14; 4:5-7), and the reason they are so foolish for contemplating a turn away from his vertical, horizontal, and cosmic saving action in Christ (Gal 3:1, 3; cf. 1:6-9).

As I argued earlier, God's saving action in Christ includes freedom and liberation for the justified from everything associated with the present evil age (Gal 5:1; cf. also Gal 1:4; 3:13–5:13). This freedom from the present evil age and from the curse of the law does not result in slavery to the power of the flesh (Gal 5:13) but in freedom to be enslaved to love one another and therefore to fulfill the entire law of Christ (Gal 5:14; 6:2). The Spirit produces fruit in those justified by faith in Christ because of God's invasive disruption of the cosmos in Christ and because of his death for their sins to deliver Jews and Gentiles from the present evil age and from the curse of the law (Gal 1:4; 3:13-14; 4:6; 5:16–6:10).

Paul states Jesus died on the cross to "deliver us from the present evil age" and "redeem us from the law's curse" with the result that "we" receive the Abrahamic blessing of the Spirit by faith (Gal 3:13-14). God's saving action for Jews and Gentiles through Christ's death and the Galatians' experience of this salvation by faith in Christ was also the moment in history when the Galatians were adopted into God's family as sons (Gal 4:5-7). God "sent the Spirit of his Son" into the hearts of Christ-following Jews and Gentiles (Gal 4:6). His Son's Spirit cries out to God as Father on behalf of those whom the Son has redeemed (Gal 4:6). The Spirit's work in them through Christ's redemption for them proves Jews and Gentiles, once enslaved to the law and to the present evil age (Gal 3:15–4:11), are now free sons and heirs of Abraham's inheritance through God (Gal 4:7–5:1, 13). The Spirit's work in Jews and Gentiles through Christ, then, proves God's deliverance of the entire creation has now broken into this present evil age in Christ (Gal 3:13-14). The distribution of the Spirit to Jews and Gentiles,[36] who are justified by faith in Christ[37] and who attest to their justification by faith by walking in the Spirit, reveals they have received the blessing of Abraham, which is the Spirit (Gal 2:16; 3:6-14; 5:2-5), and that they are signposts and emblems of the fact that God's saving action in Christ has now begun in the present evil age to renew the cosmos (Gal 6:15).

The Spirit indwells (cf. Gal 3:2, 5, 14; 4:6), transforms (Gal 3:3), empowers (Gal 3:21; 5:25; 6:8; cf. 6:15), and leads (Gal 5:5, 18, 22, 25; 6:1) Christ-following Jews and Gentiles in the assemblies of Galatia to walk in the Spirit and to live contrary to the flesh and the present evil age. Through Christ's redemption of the Galatians from the curse of the law by his death and resurrection (Gal 1:1, 4; 3:13-14), the Spirit frees the Galatians to choose to live by the Spirit in the present evil age (Gal 5:16-26) as he gives them the fruit of the Spirit upon their participation in Christ by faith (Gal 5:22). As a result, those in Christ triumphantly oppose the flesh and the present evil age as they walk in the Spirit while they live in the present evil age (Gal 5:16-26). Because of God's saving action in Christ, the Galatians had already both conquered the flesh's power and the present evil age (Gal 1:1, 4, 15-16; 2:11–6:10), and they and the creation had already begun to participate in the renewal of creation because of God's vertical, horizontal, and cosmic saving action in Christ.

Paul commands the Galatians as those justified by faith in Christ to walk in the Spirit to inherit eternal life (Gal 5:21) because God has defini-tively acted in Christ "to deliver us" and the cosmos from the present

---

[36]For the eschatological endowment of the Sprit upon Gentiles in Second Temple Judaism, see Finny Philip, *The Origins of Pauline Pneumatology*, WUNT 194 (Tübingen: Mohr Siebeck, 2005), 81-120.

[37]I argue for this reading of the genitive in the exegetical sections.

evil age (Gal 1:4; 6:15) so that we would participate in eternal life now by faith in Christ in this present evil age and in the age to come (Gal 2:16–3:29). The age to come has already broken into the present evil age by the indwelling presence and power of the Spirit (Gal 1:4; 3:14; 4:5-6; 5:16-26). The evidence of the breaking-in of the age to come now is that those who participate in Christ by faith walk in the Spirit, and they prove that God in Christ has already begun the process of cosmic renewal by their obedient walk in the Spirit (Gal 3:1–6:15). Those in Christ must walk in the Spirit to inherit eternal life because walking in the Spirit is a manifestation of the life that God has already given to all who are justified by faith in Christ and who await the "hope of righteousness by faith by the Spirit" (Gal 2:16–3:14; 5:5–6:10). The future certainty of eternal life is realized and manifested now by the Spirit in and through Jewish and Gentile Christ followers as they walk a path of obedience in the power of the Spirit, in community with one another as slaves of love, in the assemblies of Christ, and in society because of the freedom they have in Christ by faith (Gal 5:13–6:10).

Paul warns the Galatians their failure to walk in step with the Spirit in obedience to the gospel would result in their falling short of inheriting the kingdom of God (Gal 5:16, 21). He asserts "we" await future righteousness (= justification) by faith "by the Spirit" (Gal 5:6). On the contrary, those who walk in accordance with circumcised flesh and the Mosaic covenant will not benefit from Christ's death in the judgment, will sever themselves from Christ, will obligate themselves to keep the entire law to gain life, will subject themselves to both the apostolic and the Deuteronomic curse of the law, and will fall short of God's saving action in Christ (Gal 1:8-9; 3:10; 5:2-5). In Paul's view in Galatians, Christ-following Jews and Gentiles walk in freedom in obedience to the gospel in the power of the Spirit because of God's saving action *for* and *in* them through Christ, and because of his liberation of creation from the present evil age. Thus, their walk of obedience is the *proof* of God's saving action for them in Christ and for the cosmos through Christ, and it is necessary for those justified by faith to inherit the kingdom of God

(Gal 5:19-21). Since the Galatians received life by the Spirit, they *must* also conduct their daily lives in step with the Spirit (5:16, 21, 24, 25).

To be clear, in Paul's view, the Galatians' walk of obedience in step with the Spirit is neither the *ground* of their inheritance of the kingdom of God in Christ nor the *result of* their inheritance of the kingdom of God in Christ. Both of these preceding ideas are contrary to Paul's soteriological argument in Galatians.[38] Rather, Paul's point to the Galatians is because of God's saving action in Christ for Jews and Gentiles and for the world, an obedient walk in the power of the Spirit is both the *necessary proof* now, and will be the *necessary proof* in the day of judgment in the future, that Jews and Gentiles have already begun to participate now in this present evil age in God's saving action in Christ. An obedient walk in the Spirit is necessary, for God requires this walk before those who have already participated now by faith in God's saving action in Christ in Galatia would inherit the kingdom of God and the not-yet aspect of eternal life in the day of judgment in the future in the age to come (Gal 5:16–6:10; esp. 6:8-9).[39] Obedience is both *part of* and the *expression of* eternal life in Christ, neither the *cause of* nor the *result of* eternal life in Christ.[40] This obedience is necessary both now and in the day of judgment. This is a reason Paul says the Galatians will not inherit the kingdom of God if they walk in accordance with the flesh (5:16-20), and this is a reason Paul also says the Galatians must sow in the Spirit,

---

[38]For a similar point, see Victor Paul Furnish, *Theology and Ethics in Paul* (Louisville: Westminster John Knox, 2009), 226. I nuance some things differently from Furnish in my discussion of the Spirit, ethical transformation, and eternal life. Furnish's comment occurs in a discussion of the indicative and the imperative in Paul's theology, not in a discussion about the Spirit.

[39]Judgment according to works is an important piece to soteriology in the New Testament. See Mt 3:8-10; 7:16-21; 12:37; Rom 2:6-7; 1 Cor 3:13-15; Jas 2:14-21; Jude 15; Rev 2:2, 5-6, 19, 26; 3:1-2, 8, 15; 9:20; 14:13; 16:11; 20:12-13; 22:12. For a few examples of judgment according to works in Second Temple Judaism, see Sir 16:12; 35:24; 4 Ezra 14:35; Wis 1:9; 4:20; 1 En 1:7, 9; 9:3; 10:6, 12; 13:1; 14:4; 16:1; 19:1; 22:4, 8, 10-11, 13; 25:4; 27:2-4; 45:6; 47:2; 50:4; 54:6; 59:1; 60:6, 25; 61:9; 62:3; 63:8, 12; 65:10; 66:1; 67:10, 13; 69:1; 81:4; 91:7; 91:12; 91:14; 94:9; 95:2; 98:8, 10; 99:15; 100:4; 2 Bar 54:14; Jub 21:4.

[40]A similar point in Barclay (*Paul and the Gift*, 429-30). Barclay says: "Practice and behavior are not simply the consequence of this new 'life': they are its expression" (429). He continues: "The indicative of 'life' is a statement not of *status*, divorceable from practice, but of *existence*, whose reality is necessarily evidenced in practice. That life is not humanly generated (it derives from the Spirit), but it is humanly expressed, and it can hardly be said to be real without such expression" (429-30).

not in the flesh, to reap eternal life; otherwise, they would reap eternal destruction (Gal 6:8-10).

The Galatians' walk of obedience in step with the Spirit is one aspect of God's saving action in Christ that Jews and Gentiles receive right now because Jesus died for their sins to deliver them from the present evil age (Gal 1:4) and to give them the Spirit, which is the blessing of Abraham, by faith (Gal 3:13-14; 4:6). God's saving action in Christ brings freedom and liberation by the Spirit right now (Gal 3:2–5:1; 5:13–6:10). As Paul says in 2 Corinthians 3:17: "The Lord is the Spirit, and where the Spirit of the Lord is, there is freedom" (ὁ δὲ κύριος τὸ πνεῦμά ἐστιν οὗ δὲ τὸ πνεῦμα κυρίου, ἐλευθερία). In Galatians, Paul discusses this freedom as deliverance from the power of the present evil because they have received the Spirit by faith and because Jesus died for their sins (Gal 1:14; 2:16; 3:13-14; 4:5-7). In fact, the reception of the Spirit by faith and the Spirit's transformative work in the Galatians is part of the soteriological life the Galatians received by faith in Christ because of God's saving action for them in Christ through Jesus' death and resurrection (Gal 1:4; 3:13-14; 4:5-6; 5:25).

To state the matter plainly, those Galatian Christ followers who walk in the Spirit in obedience to the gospel in the present evil age participated in eternal life in the present evil age and will inherit the kingdom of God in the age to come. They have already participated in eternal life right now in the present evil age by the Spirit because Jesus died for their sins to deliver them from the present evil age and from the curse of the law to give them the Spirit (Gal 1:4; 3:13-14; 4:5-6). They live (i.e., they have eternal life) by the Spirit (Gal 5:25), not by the law (Gal 3:21),[41] because of God's saving action for them in Christ. The Spirit's presence in and among the Galatian Christ followers was both *part* of and the *proof* of God's saving action *for* and *in* them in Christ.[42]

---

[41]Numerous Jews texts state that life comes from the law (Lev 18:5; Sir 17:11; 45:5; 2 Macc 7:9; Bar 4:11; 4 Ezra 14:30; Pss Sol 14:2).

[42](a) Both individuals and the cosmos have already begun to participate in new creation because of God's saving action in and for them in Christ, a saving action including both individual Jews and Gentiles with faith in Christ and the entire creation. (b) God in Christ has acted to

The Spirit indwells (fills) (cf. Gal 3:2, 3, 5, 14; 4:6), transforms (Gal 3:3), energizes (creates/gives life) (Gal 3:21; 5:25; 6:8; cf. 6:15), and enables, empowers, strengthens, and helps (Gal 5:5, 18, 22, 25; 6:1) Christ-following Jews and Gentiles in the assemblies of Galatia to walk in the Spirit and to walk contrary to the flesh and the present evil age as they continue to live in the present evil age, and as the present evil age continues to triumph. The flesh represents the old age, and the Spirit represents the new age inaugurated by Christ's cross and resurrection. As a result of these opposing ages and powers, Paul argues the Galatians are not free to do whatever they want (Gal 5:17). They are free in Christ to choose between the age of the flesh or the Spirit (Gal 5:16-26). If they choose to walk in the realm of the flesh, they will not inherit the kingdom. If they sow in the Spirit, they will reap eternal life (Gal 6:8). If they sow in the flesh, they will reap eternal destruction (Gal 6:8). Paul compels the Galatians to use their liberated personal agency and choose life daily by walking in step with the Spirit because they both already have and will receive eternal life if they walk in step with the Spirit because of God's saving action for them and the cosmos in Christ. Everyone justified by faith in Christ has received the Spirit *can*, *must*, and *will* walk in the Spirit and therefore will inherit the kingdom of God because they have already begun to participate in God's saving action right now in the present evil age by faith in Christ. But if those who claim the status of the justified do not walk in the Spirit, they will not inherit the kingdom of God.[43]

CONCLUSION

In this chapter, I argued those Galatians justified by faith in Christ *can*, *will*, and *must* walk in step with the Spirit to inherit the kingdom of God. Galatians 5:21 is Paul's only explicit reference to the kingdom of God in the letter. This chapter set my argument in the context of Paul's remarks

---

inaugurate new creation. Both (a) and (b) are parts of the Abrahamic blessing in which the Galatians participated by faith in Christ and through which the entire creation is renewed and transformed because of God's saving action *in* and *for* them and *for* the cosmos in Christ.

[43]My view of judgment according to works contrasts with a Catholic view. See, for example, Pitre, "Roman Catholic Perspective on Paul," 25-55, esp. 46-49.

about the Spirit, the cross, the resurrection, and the authority of his gospel in the letter. God's saving action in Christ for Jews and Gentiles via his invasive and disruptive act of sending his Son to deliver Jews and Gentiles from the present evil age was an act that granted to those justified by faith with Spirit-energized, Spirit-empowered, Spirit-transformed, and Spirit-enabling personal agency and ethical transformation in Christ. This personal agency and ethical transformation prove Jews and Gentiles have been justified by faith right now in this present evil age and guarantee they will be justified by faith on the day of judgment and participate in the future inheritance of the kingdom of God in the age to come.

5

The Spirit and Eternal Life

In this chapter, I bring together the arguments in the exegetical sections of chapters three and four. I set Paul's comments about the Spirit, personal agency, ethical transformation, and eternal life in those chapters in the context of his argument in the letter. This chapter argues Paul is anxious and deeply concerned about the Galatians' situation because they are in danger of making a choice to walk away from his gospel to embrace Torah. He fears perhaps he has labored among the Galatians in vain since they are turning so quickly from his gospel to another so-called gospel. Only his gospel gives to them the Spirit and leads to eternal life by faith by the Spirit because of Jesus' death for sins and his resurrection.

This chapter offers a reading of the letter that gives the Spirit a more privileged role in Paul's argument than other readings in the history of interpretation. If my arguments in chapters three and four were correct, then Paul's fear over the Galatians' situation and his polemical efforts to persuade them from turning away from his gospel arise because he fears some of the Galatians may not have life in Christ. He reminds them they experience life by faith by the Spirit as they received the Spirit by faith. Since they are turning so quickly from the gospel he preached to them, Paul therefore worries some of the Galatians will choose the wrong path and not inherit the kingdom of God. If they choose the way of the flesh instead of the way of the Spirit, then they certainly do not have any of the soteriological blessings for which Jesus died and was resurrected. They will not inherit the kingdom of God since a walk in step with the

Spirit is the proof of their present participation in God's vertical, horizontal, and cosmic saving action in Christ for Jews and Gentiles by faith and for the cosmos.

A DEFENSE OF THE AUTHORITY OF PAUL'S APOSTOLIC GOSPEL MINISTRY

In Galatians 1–2, Paul defends the authority of his apostolic gospel ministry by grounding it in Jesus' victorious resurrection and his death for our sins (Gal 1:1, 4). In Galatians 1:1, he asserts his apostleship and gospel come from Jesus Christ and God the Father, who raised him from the dead. In Galatians 1:4, Paul says Jesus "gave himself for our sins to deliver us from the present evil age." In Galatians 1:15-16, Paul describes his apostolic gospel ministry as a prophetic call for which he was set apart from his mother's womb (cf. LXX Is 49:1; Jer 1:5).

As I argued in earlier chapters, Paul states Jesus redeemed us from the law's curse via his crucifixion so that we would receive the Spirit by faith (Gal 3:13-14; 4:5-6). Paul's apostolic gospel ministry is centered on God's vertical, horizontal, and cosmic saving action in Jesus' death "for our sins" and resurrection (Gal 1:1, 4; 2:11-21; 3:10-14; 6:15). Jesus' death "for our sins" and resurrection introduce the Spirit into the hearts of Jews and Gentiles by faith (Gal 1:1, 4; 3:13-14; 4:5-6). Paul's apostolic gospel ministry is the only pathway for the Galatians to have access to the Spirit (cf. also 1 Cor 2 and 2 Cor 3). So, he must defend his apostolic gospel ministry with force to the Galatians and against the teachers in Galatia who are seeking to lead the Galatians away to their distorted message that will neither give them the Spirit nor lead them to life in the Spirit in this life or in the age to come (cf. Gal 3:10-14, 21; 5:21, 25).

An autobiographical defense of Paul's gospel. Paul continues his defense of his apostolic gospel ministry in the body of the letter. He first expresses his shock that the Galatians are making a turn "so quickly from the one who called them by the grace of Christ to another gospel" (Gal 1:6). God is the one who calls the Galatians into the grace of Christ since Paul connects this calling here to the "grace of Christ" (Gal 1:6) and since he connects the concept of calling later to the Galatians' freedom in Christ (Gal 5:1, 13). The Galatians' turn away from their calling is shocking to Paul because there is no other gospel that leads to life in the Spirit (cf. Gal 1:7, 15-16, 23 with 2:19-21; 3:10-14); there are only distortions of the gospel that lead to destruction (cf. Gal 1:8-9). Paul makes this latter point clear when he says those who preach another gospel to the Galatians besides the one that he preached to them are accursed (Gal 1:8-9). This apostolic curse makes sense because Paul's gospel focused on Jesus' death and resurrection, and God's vertical, horizontal, and cosmic saving action in Christ, whose signpost and emblem are the Spirit (cf. Gal 3:1–4:31).

Paul's references to the gospel in Galatians 1:8-9 are important for my thesis regarding the relationship between the Spirit, personal agency, ethical transformation, and eternal life in Galatians. Paul connects his apostolic ministry to the gospel he preached, which centers on Jesus' resurrection and death for our sins (Gal 1:1, 4). He says in Galatians 1:7 the troublemakers preach "another gospel" (εἰς ἕτερον εὐαγγέλιον), which is a distortion of the "gospel of Christ" (μεταστρέψαι τὸ εὐαγγέλιον τοῦ Χριστοῦ). He states in Galatians 1:11-12, "The gospel that was announced by him as good news" came not to him from a person but through a revelation about Jesus Christ.[1] Paul's focus on the gospel and his apostolic gospel ministry are the main reasons I have persisted thus far in this chapter to refer to Paul's apostolic gospel ministry. His verbs for gospel in Galatians 1:8 (εὐαγγελίζηται; εὐηγγελισάμεθα) and Galatians 1:9 (εὐαγγελίζεται), the noun for gospel (εὐαγγέλιον) in Galatians 1:11; 2:2, and 5, and his message in the central section of the letter in chapters three and four—that the Galatians experienced the Spirit by faith apart from works of the law—suggest that if the Galatians embrace the teachers' distorted message, which leads only to a curse (Gal 1:8-9; 3:10), they reject his gospel, which is the only good news that leads to life (cf. Gal 3:10-14). This is one reason Paul emphasizes earlier he received

---

[1] γνωρίζω γὰρ ὑμῖν, ἀδελφοί, τὸ εὐαγγέλιον τὸ εὐαγγελισθὲν ὑπ' ἐμοῦ ὅτι οὐκ ἔστιν κατὰ ἄνθρωπον· οὐδὲ γὰρ ἐγὼ παρὰ ἀνθρώπου παρέλαβον αὐτὸ οὔτε ἐδιδάχθην ἀλλὰ δι' ἀποκαλύψεως Ἰησοῦ Χριστοῦ.

the good news about Jesus as a revelation from God (Gal 1:11, 15-16). He announced Jesus as the good news among the Gentiles in Galatia and beyond when God revealed this good news in and to him (Gal 1:15-16). Therefore, if the Galatians walk away from Paul's gospel, they walk away from God's saving action in Christ, of which the Spirit is the sign and emblem of their participation in eternal life by faith now in this present evil age and in the age to come (cf. Gal 3:1–6:10; 6:15-16).

Paul's gospel about Jesus in Galatians is the announcement that God has fulfilled all his redemptive promises for Jews and Gentiles and for the world in Christ. Paul states God revealed this gospel to him on the Damascus Road when he was violently persecuting the church of God (Gal 1:11-16). Paul says God was pleased "to reveal his Son in him so that I would announce him as the good news among the Gentiles" (Gal 1:15-16). Jesus is the good news in Galatians 1:11 and Galatians 1:16 (ἵνα εὐαγγελίζωμαι αὐτὸν). Paul announced Jesus as the good news "among the Gentiles" (ἐν τοῖς ἔθνεσιν). Jesus is good news for both Jews (Gal 2:1-21) and Gentiles (Gal 1:15-16) because Paul's message about Jesus leads to life in the Spirit (Gal 3:13-14, 21; 5:21, 2-23, 25). The message of Torah on this side of the cross, Paul says, only leads to an eschatological anathema at the end of the age (Gal 1:8-9) and a curse in the present evil age and in the age to come (Gal 3:10). The gospel of Jesus Christ leads Gentiles and Jews to the pathway of life by faith, not works of Torah (Gal 3:10-14, 21). One reason Jesus is good news for the Gentiles is because God's saving action for Jews and Gentiles in Christ is the pathway to the Spirit (Gal 3:13-14; 4:5-6), and the Spirit gives life (Gal 5:25; cf. 3:21). The Spirit is the signpost and emblem in those with faith in Christ that God has fulfilled all his redemptive promises in Christ for Jews and Gentiles and for the world (Gal 3:2-5, 13-14; 4:29; 5:16, 18, 25; 6:15-16).

Recent scholarship demonstrates the book of Isaiah influenced Paul's argument in Galatians.[2] Isaiah mentions the Spirit in connection with the righteous one (= the Messiah) who would come and bring right-eousness and salvation to God's people (LXX Is 11:2-4). The Lord puts

---

[2]Matthew S. Harmon, *She Must and Shall Go Free: Paul's Isaianic Gospel in Galatians* (Berlin: De Gruyter, 2010).

his Spirit upon his servant (= Messiah) (LXX Is 42:1). Isaiah connects the Spirit with the offspring of the people of God (LXX Is 44:3). In LXX Isaiah 61:1, Isaiah connects the same verb for announcing the good news (εὐαγγελίσασθαι) with the Messiah and the Spirit as Paul uses to refer to Jesus, the Messiah and Son of God (εὐαγγελίζω) (cf. LXX Is 61:1 with Gal 1:8-9, 16).

Isaiah refers to the Spirit of the Lord resting upon the Messiah to preach the gospel to those who are oppressed (LXX Is 61:1): "The Spirit of the Lord is upon me, because of whom he has anointed me. He has sent me to announce good news to the poor, to heal those who are crushed in the heart, to preach to the captive forgiveness and sight to the blind."[3] In Luke's Gospel, Jesus says he fulfills this prophecy from Isaiah in his ministry (Lk 4:18-19). In Galatians 1:16, Paul announces Jesus as the good news (ἵνα εὐαγγελίζωμαι αὐτὸν). He calls Jesus the Christ on multiple occasions in Galatians (Gal 1:1, 3, 6-7, 10, 12, 22; 2:4, 16-17, 19; 3:1, 13-14, 16, 22, 24, 26-29; 4:14, 19; 5:1-2, 4, 6, 24; 6:2, 12, 14, 18). Paul identifies the gospel of Jesus Christ as the faith that he formerly attempted to destroy (Gal 1:23). However, because of God's saving action in Christ and Paul's participation in it by faith, Paul preached this faith as the good news among the Gentiles (εὐαγγελίζεται τὴν πίστιν) (Gal 1:23; cf. Gal 1:15-16). Consequently, the churches in Judea that likewise believed the gospel of Jesus that he now preached glorified God in Paul (Gal 1:24). Paul's announcement of good news about Jesus, the Christ and Son of God, is good news because God fulfills his redemptive promises for Jews and Gentiles and for the world in his Spirit-anointed Messiah and Son, who gives the Spirit of new creation to Jews and Gentiles (Gal 3:13-14; 4:5-6) and who likewise recreates the world (Gal 6:15). The result is they have already begun to participate now in God's saving action in Christ by faith in Christ (Gal 3:2–4:7).

The Galatians were foolish for contemplating a turn away from this good news since Jesus was publicly preached to them as having been

---

[3]Πνεῦμα κυρίου ἐπ᾽ ἐμέ, οὗ εἵνεκεν ἔχρισέν με εὐαγγελίσασθαι πτωχοῖς ἀπέσταλκέν με, ἰάσασθαι τοὺς συντετριμμένους τῇ καρδίᾳ, κηρύξαι αἰχμαλώτοις ἄφεσιν καὶ τυφλοῖς ἀνάβλεψιν.

crucified (Gal 3:1) and since they began their journey in the Spirit by faith instead of by Torah works (Gal 3:2-5). He implies they are foolish for thinking they can continue their journey in God's saving action in Christ in the flesh, although they began in their participation in it by the Spirit (Gal 3:3). In Galatians 3:13, he says the Christ redeemed Jews and Gentiles from the law's curse so that they would receive the Spirit by faith (cf. Gal 4:6). According to Paul's gospel in Galatians, Jesus is good news for Jews and Gentiles, not Torah (Gal 1:15-16), and the pillars of the church in Jerusalem gave him the right hand of fellowship in his gospel ministry to the Jews, confirming it was good news for the Gentiles and for Jews (Gal 2:1-10).

One reason Jesus is good news for the Gentiles is because God's saving action for Jews and Gentiles in Christ is the pathway to the Spirit, who is the signpost of and the emblem that God has fulfilled all his redemptive promises in Christ and for the world (Gal 3:14; 4:6). This gospel is the good news that compels Jews and Gentiles to walk in a straightforward manner in the truth of the gospel about Jesus with one another without compelling Gentiles to live in a Jewish way of life and without shaming Jews for living like Gentiles (Gal 2:11-15). Boayke rightly argues the "truth of the gospel" in Galatians 2:5 and Galatians 2:14 indicates "the inconsequence of ethnic categorisation for those in Christ."[4] However, the truth of the gospel specifically relates to God's vertical, horizontal, and cosmic saving action in Christ. Therefore, the truth of the gospel is neither about Jewish identity nor Gentile identity, neither about circumcision nor uncircumcision, but about Jew and Gentile unity and new creation in Christ (Gal 2:11–3:29; 6:15). The truth of the gospel is about God's saving action in Christ to fulfill all his vertical, horizontal, and cosmic promises in Christ for Jews and Gentiles and for the world, a part of which is the irrelevance of one's ethnic designation in Christ in terms of determining one's status within, and one's ability to participate in, God's saving action in Christ. This good news about the truth of the gospel justifies Jews and Gentiles (as Jews and Gentiles) by faith as people from both

---

[4]Boayke, *Death and Life*, 100.

groups are crucified with Christ (Gal 2:19-20), and as they live their lives
by faith in God's Son, who loved and gave himself for them (Gal 2:20).
Both groups in Christ by faith receive life in the Spirit (Gal 5:25).

EXPERIENCES IN THE SPIRIT AND SCRIPTURAL CITATIONS
AS A DEFENSE OF PAUL'S GOSPEL

Paul appeals to the Galatians' experiences in the Spirit and to Scripture to
support the authority of his apostolic gospel ministry.[5] He calls the Galatians "foolish" for falling under the spell of the troublemakers (Gal 3:1).
The troublemakers likely preached the law as the means of receiving the
blessing of Abraham (cf. Gal 1:7 with Gal 3:14; 4:6; 5:2-4), and the Galatians
became cast under their spell (Gal 3:1). Paul appeals to the Galatians' own
experience in the Spirit to support the authority of his apostolic gospel
ministry and to remind them they received and experienced the Spirit by
faith apart from works of the law (Gal 3:2-3). He preached the gospel of
the crucified and resurrected Christ to them as the good news (Gal 1:1, 4,
9, 16) that gave the Galatians the Spirit as the signpost and emblem of
God's saving action in Christ so that they would walk in step with the
Spirit and bear witness to the rule of new creation (Gal 3:14; 4:6; 5:16–6:10;
6:15-16). Paul suggests their faith is itself part of God's saving action in
Christ, not simply a personal cognitive act to believe. Faith in Galatians is
on the side of God's saving action in Christ, whereas works of the law is
on the side of human agency and the present evil age (cf. Gal 2:16; 3:10-14).[6]

Earlier in Galatians 1:23, Paul says he preached as good news the faith
that he once formerly attempted to destroy (εὐαγγελίζεται τὴν πίστιν ἥν
ποτε ἐπόρθει). Faith (τὴν πίστιν) is the object of the verb εὐαγγελίζεται
("to announce as the good news") in Galatians 1:23. In Paul's first references to the Spirit in the central section in chapter 3, he discusses the
Spirit in the context of faith (cf. Gal 3:1-14). He asks the Galatians

---

[5]Francis Watson, *Paul and the Hermeneutics of Faith*, 2nd ed. (New York: T&T Clark, 2015). For
Paul's use of Scripture in Galatians 1-2, see Roy E. Ciampa, *The Presence and Function of Scripture
in Galatians 1 and 2*, WUNT 102 (Tübingen: Mohr Siebeck, 1998).

[6]For a similar point, see Preston M. Sprinkle's monograph, *Law and Life: The Interpretation of
Leviticus 18:5 in Early Judaism and in Paul*, WUNT 241 (Tübingen: Mohr Siebeck, 2008).

whether they received the Spirit "by a hearing that requires the response of faith" (ἐξ ἀκοῆς πίστεως) or by Torah works (Gal 3:2; cf. Rom 10:14-18). He then asks them whether God supplied them with the Spirit and performed miracles in their midst by Torah works or "by the hearing that requires a response of faith" (ἐξ ἀκοῆς πίστεως).

Paul's first mention of the term *faith* in the letter occurs in Galatians 1:23. There the noun is a synonym for the gospel since Paul places it as the direct object of the verb εὐαγγελίζεται ("he preaches as good news the faith") and since Paul places Jesus as the direct object of the same verb in Galatians 1:16 (εὐαγγελίζωμαι αὐτὸν; "I announce him as the good news"). Paul's remarks about the gospel in Galatians 1:11 support this latter point. In Galatians 1:11, Paul makes the noun "gospel" (εὐαγγέλιον) the direct object of the verb "to make known" (Γνωρίζω) and describes the noun εὐαγγέλιον ("gospel") with a participial form of the verb "to announce as good news" (τὸ εὐαγγελισθὲν). Thus Paul "makes known the gospel that he announced as good news" (Gal 1:11); God "revealed his Son in him so that he would announce him as the good news among the Gentiles" (Gal 1:15-16), and Paul "announced as good news the faith that he formerly tried to destroy" (Gal 1:23). When Paul announced Jesus as good news, he was announcing every soteriological blessing fulfilled in him and given to Jews and Gentiles through him as the content of that good news (cf. Gal 3:1–6:10), and he was announcing the gospel and the faith about Jesus as the good news.

Paul's use of faith in Galatians 1:23 supports the notion that faith has different layers to it. Of course, there is a personal and cognitive component to it, which Paul supports by his comments on justification by faith (Gal 2:16-17; 3:12; 5:4), his appeal to Abraham's personal faith (Gal 3:6) as an example that faith is both personal and cognitive, and by asserting those who are justified by faith participate in the blessing of Abraham (Gal 3:6-14; cf. also Gal 3:15–4:31). Paul's use of the phrase ἐξ ἀκοῆς πίστεως ("by a hearing that requires the response of faith") in Romans 10:13-18 supports this. There Paul explains those who hear the gospel and believe by faith will be saved.

However, πίστις ("faith") does not merely refer to a personal or cognitive experience.[7] Paul uses πίστις in Galatians 5:22 to mean faithfulness. The occurrence of πίστις in Galatians 5:22 is in the context of Paul's exhortations to walk in step with the Spirit in obedience to the gospel. Faith and obedience are not the same thing in Galatians, but faith and faithfulness go hand in hand in the letter. Those who have faith will demonstrate faithfulness by walking in obedience in step with the Spirit (Gal 5:16–6:10). Still, my basic point here is that Paul's use of πίστις in Galatians 1:23 suggests faith in this verse is another way of talking about the gospel and specifically about the confession of faith required by the gospel. Paul's preaching of the faith as the good news means he preached Jesus as the good news so that those who receive it by faith are those who participate in every soteriological blessing by a personal response of faith to God's saving action in Christ.

The Galatians received the blessing of Abraham and became children of God the same way that Abraham was counted righteous: namely, by faith (Gal 3:3-9), not by works of the law (Gal 3:10-14). The law leads to a curse (Gal 3:10; cf. Deut 27:26), but Paul's gospel leads to life in the Spirit (Gal 3:13-14; 4:6; 5:16-26; esp. Gal 5:25). This life in the Spirit brings freedom from slavery under the law, under sin, under the present evil age, and under the elementary principles of the world (Gal 3:15–6:10). The Galatians experienced this freedom by the Spirit because the Spirit is the emblem and signpost of their status of sons, heirs, and children of God in Christ (Gal 4:3-7, 21-31; 5:1, 13). The law promises life to those who obey (cf. Gal 3:12 with Lev 18:5; Deut 27–28), but it neither gives them the life it promises nor the ability to obey the law to achieve the life it promises. As Paul says, the law does not give life (Gal 3:21). Rather, it only promises to reward those with life who obey its stipulations (cf. Gal 3:12 with Lev 18:5; Deut 27–28). In this present evil age, however, the law only places those under its power under a curse and under slavery (Gal 3:10; 4:1-27).

---

[7]For examples of recent work on faith, see Teresa Morgan, *Roman Faith an Christian Faith: Pistis and Fides in the Early Roman Empire and Early Churches* (Oxford: Oxford University Press, 2015); Nijay K. Gupta, *Paul and the Language of Faith* (Grand Rapids, MI: Eerdmans, 2020); Kevin McFadden, *Faith in the Son of God: The Place of Christ-Oriented Faith Within Pauline Theology* (Wheaton, IL: Crossway, 2021).

The Spirit gives life (Gal 5:25; cf. Gal 3:21). The life of the Spirit is the emblem and the signpost that those who participate in God's saving action in Christ by faith have already begun to participate in eternal life right now in this present evil age. That is, the presence of the Spirit in the lives of those with faith in Christ is the realization of the life promised in the law but never given by the law (Gal 4:21-31). Those in Christ are children of freedom (Gal 4:31). Christ has freed those who have participated in God's saving action in him by faith to be free (Gal 5:1, 13). God has freed them to stand firm in freedom and to by no means subject themselves to slavery within the present evil age again (cf. Gal 5:1 with Gal 1:14; 3:1–4:31). They are free to live in the freedom of the eternal life God has accomplished for Jews and Gentiles and by means of his vertical, horizontal, and cosmic saving action in Christ for Jews and Gentiles and for the cosmos.

THE SPIRIT AND ETERNAL LIFE

Paul has forcefully argued throughout the letter that his gospel leads to life, but the law leads to a curse (Gal 3:10-14). His gospel is the announcement that God has fulfilled all his redemptive promises for Jews and Gentiles and for the cosmos in Christ. As I argued above and in the earlier chapters, Paul's gospel must be both cognitively affirmed and experientially obeyed. In fact, Paul knows no concept of faith void of either cognition, volition, or obedience to his gospel. He holds these ideas together in his apostolic gospel ministry. In Paul's view in Galatians, faith is present only when obedience in the power of the Spirit is present, and faith in God's saving action in Christ is realized in Jews and Gentiles only when obedience is present. Once more, the Spirit is active and present in the people of faith only when they have a genuine experience of faith that holds together cognition and obedience. An affirmation of facts in the gospel without the presence of a daily walk of faithful living in step in the Spirit in obedience to the gospel proves one does not have the Spirit and therefore lacks faith and participation in God's vertical, horizontal, and cosmic saving action in Christ.

For example, after telling the Galatians they have freedom in Christ because they have begun their journey of faith by the Spirit (Gal 3:1–4:31), Paul commands them to stand firm in the freedom they received by faith when they received the Spirit by faith (cf. Gal 5:1 with Gal 3:2-4, 6). He later says because they were called out of slavery to the present evil age into the realm of freedom (Gal 5:13; cf. Gal 1:4; 3:15–4:31), they should not use their freedom as an occasion to walk in the power of the flesh (Gal 5:13). Instead, their freedom in Christ now enslaves them to love one another (Gal 5:13). When they love one another and their neighbors as themselves, they fulfill the entire Torah since the Torah can be summarized as love for God and love for neighbor (Gal 5:14; cf. Lev 19:18). This love manifests itself by means of walking in the Spirit and by no means fulfilling the lust of the flesh (Gal 5:16), and this love is modeled after Jesus' selfless sacrificial love for Jews and Gentiles (Gal 2:20). They must walk in the Spirit if they desire to inherit the kingdom of God and eternal life since flesh and Spirit have nothing in common with one another (Gal 5:16–6:10).

The Galatians *must not* devour one another (Gal 5:15), be arrogant toward one another, or irritate one another (Gal 5:26) because they have crucified the flesh with its passions and desires (Gal 5:24). Rather, since they received life by the Spirit by faith (Gal 3:14; 4:6; 5:25) and since they were led by the Spirit (Gal 5:18), they *must* also daily conduct themselves in step with the Spirit (Gal 5:25; cf. Gal 5:16). They must not practice vices contrary to the Spirit (Gal 5:16-21). They must humbly and wisely restore with compassion the brothers or sisters who fall into transgression and thereby fulfill Christ's entire law, which is the law of love (Gal 6:1-4; cf. Gal 5:14). The Galatians must share all good things with those who teach them the word (Gal 6:5).

They must not mock God (Gal 6:7). They must sow in the Spirit to reap eternal life and avoid sowing to the flesh because they will reap eternal destruction (Gal 6:8). They must not grow weary in doing what is good to all people, especially to those within the household of faith (Gal 6:9-10). They must daily conduct themselves by the standard of new creation if they want to participate in soteriological peace and mercy that will only come upon the people of God who conduct themselves as participants in God's vertical, horizontal, and cosmic new creation in Christ (Gal 6:15-16). The standard of new creation is Paul's apostolic gospel that focuses on Jesus' death and resurrection and that gives to them the Spirit as the signpost and emblem that new creation has begun vertically, horizontally, and cosmically for those in Christ. Walking in the Spirit is *part of* God's saving action in Christ. That is, God's saving action in Christ justifies (forensic) and transforms by the Spirit those who are in Christ. Those who walk in the Spirit are the very ones who are justified, already have eternal life; they will walk in the Spirit to inherit the kingdom of God, and they must walk in the Spirit to inherit the kingdom of God (Gal 5:16–6:10). Therefore, Paul commands the Galatians to walk in the Spirit and not fulfill the lust of the flesh; he commands them to conduct themselves daily by the Spirit since they received life by the Spirit because of God's vertical, horizontal, and cosmic saving action in Christ (Gal 5:16, 25).

CONCLUSION

In this chapter, I brought together the arguments in chapters three and four. I set Paul's comments about the Spirit, personal agency, ethical transformation, and eternal life in the context of his argument in the letter to support that Paul is anxious and deeply concerned about the Galatians' situation because they are contemplating a turn away from his gospel, which gives to them the Spirit and life by faith, to embrace Torah, which leads to a curse and does not give them life in the Spirit. This chapter offered a reading of the letter that gives the Spirit a prominent role in Paul's argument. If my arguments in chapters three and four are correct, then Paul's anxiety over the Galatians and his strong rhetoric to persuade them from turning away from his gospel arise because he fears some of them do not have life by the Spirit, which is the blessing of Abraham, and therefore fears they will not inherit the kingdom of God. If they lack the Spirit, then they certainly do not have any of the soteriological blessings for which Jesus died and was resurrected, since the Spirit dwelling in the Galatians and a walk in step with the Spirit are the emblem and signpost that they have already begun to participate in God's vertical, horizontal, and cosmic saving action in Christ for Jews and Gentiles and for the cosmos right now in this present evil age.

6

The Spirit and Ethical Transformation

In this chapter, I reflect on the Spirit and ethical transformation according to Paul's argument in Galatians. This chapter makes the point that it is wrong to separate the Spirit, eternal life, personal agency, and ethical transformation from Paul's soteriology in Galatians. Rather, these things in Galatians are interconnected and are part of God's saving action in Christ for Jews and Gentiles and for the cosmos. In fact, Paul teaches in Galatians that the Spirit, personal agency, and ethical transformation are soteriological since followers of Christ experience eternal life, a liberated personal agency, and ethical transformation by the presence and power of the Spirit in them by faith in Christ because of God's saving action in Christ for Jews and Gentiles and for the cosmos. The Spirit in them, personal agency, and ethical transformation are aspects of the eternal life those in Christ experience by faith in Christ by the Spirit because he died "for our sins to deliver us from the present evil age" (Gal 1:4), from the curse of the law (Gal 3:13), and to give us the Spirit by faith (Gal 3:14; 4:5-6) because God raised him from the dead (Gal 1:1). This chapter also offers practical thoughts for spiritual formation as I connect the exegetical and theological analysis of chapters three and four to a theological ethic of social discourse in the public square and to social action.

REITERATING THE ARGUMENT

In this monograph, I argued Paul describes God's saving action in Christ in Galatians as vertical, horizontal, and cosmic for Jews and Gentiles and for the cosmos, and his saving action in Christ is the reason Paul commands the Galatians to walk in the Spirit, the reason they can walk in the Spirit, the reason they have life in the Spirit, and the reason they must walk in the Spirit in order to participate in eternal life now in the present evil age and to inherit the kingdom of God in the age to come. My thesis emphasized five primary points about the Spirit, personal agency, ethical transformation, and eternal life in Galatians that I argued throughout the exegetical chapters. First, God's vertical, horizontal, and cosmic saving action in Christ for Jews and Gentiles and for the cosmos is the foundational reason the Galatians received the Spirit by faith (cf. Gal 3:1-14; 4:5-6). Second, because of God's saving action in Christ for Jews and Gentiles and for the cosmos, the Galatians were delivered from the present evil age and from the curse of the law by the Spirit because Jesus died for their sins so that they would be free moral and personal agents and so that they could and would choose to walk in the Spirit and not gratify the lust of the flesh (Gal 1:4; 3:13-14; 4:5-6; 5:1; 5:13–6:10). Third, only those Galatian Christ followers who walk in the Spirit in obedience to the gospel in the present evil age have already participated and certainly would participate in eternal life in the present evil age and inherit the kingdom of God in the age to come (Gal 5:21; 6:8-9). Fourth, the Spirit's presence in and among the Galatian Christ followers was both the result of and proof of God's saving action *for* and *in* them in Christ. Fifth, the Spirit indwells (fills) (cf. Gal 3:2, 3, 5, 14; 4:6), transforms (Gal 3:3), energizes (creates/gives life) (Gal 3:21; 5:25; 6:8; cf. 6:15), and enables, empowers, strengthens, and helps (Gal 5:5, 18, 22, 25; 6:1) Christ-following Jews and Gentiles in the assemblies of Galatia to walk in the Spirit, contrary to the flesh, and contrary to the present evil age as they continue to live in the present evil age, and as the present evil age continues to triumph.

To support my thesis, I offered the following arguments. First, God revealed in Paul that Jesus is the good news to be preached "among the Gentiles" (Gal 1:15-16). Second, through Christ's death and resurrection (Gal 1:1, 4), God delivers by faith Jewish and Gentile sinners "from the present evil age" and "from the curse of the law" (Gal 1:1, 4; 2:16; 3:13-14; 4:5-6). Third, Paul states Jesus died on the cross to "deliver us from the present evil age" and "redeem us from the law's curse" with the result that "we" receive the Abrahamic blessing of the Spirit (Gal 3:13-14). Fourth, the Spirit indwells (fills) (cf. Gal 3:2, 5, 14; 4:6), transforms (Gal 3:3), energizes (creates/gives life) (Gal 3:21; 5:25; 6:8; cf. Gal 6:15), enables, empowers, strengthens, and helps (Gal 5:5, 18, 22, 25; 6:1) Christ-following Jews and Gentiles in the assemblies of Galatia to walk in the Spirit and to live contrary to the flesh and the present evil age. Fifth, those in Christ must walk in the Spirit to inherit eternal life (Gal 5:21) because God has definitively acted in Christ "to deliver us" and the cosmos from the present evil age (Gal 1:4; 6:15) so that we would participate in eternal life now by faith in Christ in this present evil age and in the age to come (Gal 2:16–3:29). Sixth, Paul warns the Galatians their failure to walk in the Spirit in obedience to the gospel would result in their falling short of inheriting the kingdom of God (Gal 5:16, 21).

Throughout the book, I have tried to be clear that in Paul's view, the Galatians' obedient walk in the Spirit is not the fundamental ground of their experience of eternal life or the result *of* their inheritance of the kingdom of God in Christ. I have argued both these preceding ideas are contrary to Paul's soteriology in Galatians. Rather, I have argued Paul suggests that because of God's saving action in Christ for Jews and Gentiles and for the world through Christ, a faithful walk of obedience in the power of the Spirit is both the *necessary proof* that Jews and Gentiles have already begun to participate now in this present evil age in God's saving action in Christ and what God requires for those who receive the gift of eternal life before those who have already participated by faith in God's saving action in Christ in Galatia would inherit the kingdom of God. God's saving action in Christ provides Jews and Gentiles with the personal agency to choose a pattern of life in step with the Spirit, and they can, will, and must choose the path of the Spirit that leads to life to inherit the kingdom of God, because they received life by the Spirit by faith (Gal 5:25; 6:8-9).

To state the point plainly here: Paul holds God's salvation of the Galatians in Christ together in a soteriological tension (not contradiction!) because he presents walking in the Spirit and life in the Spirit to be part of God's already but not yet saving action in Christ for Jews and Gentiles in Galatians (Gal 5:16–6:10). The Galatians' ability to choose freely to walk in obedience by the Spirit is one aspect of God's saving action in Christ, since Jesus died for their sins to deliver them from the present evil age (Gal 1:4) and to give them the Spirit (Gal 3:13-14; 4:5-6). The Spirit is the blessing of Abraham, they received by faith alone in Christ alone (Gal 3:13-14; 4:6), to liberate them from slavery to sin's power and to make them sons of God and sons of Abraham by the Spirit (Gal 3:10–5:13). Because of God's saving action in Christ for them, those with faith in Christ *can*, *must*, and *will* walk in obedience in step with the Spirit to receive eternal life since they have already begun to participate in eternal life now in this present evil age by faith in Christ, proven by the indwelling presence and power of the Spirit in their lives; those who walk in the Spirit will participate in the kingdom of God in the age to come by faith in Christ since they already have life by the Spirit. Jesus delivered them from the present evil age and gave them the Spirit by faith (Gal 1:4; 3:13-14; 4:5-6). As a result, they have life right now in this present evil age by faith; they will live in step with the Spirit because of that life and prove they have already received life by faith, and they will inherit the kingdom of God in the age to come by faith.

The Necessity of Obedience for Eternal Life in Paul's Soteriology in Galatians

Contemporary interpretations of ethics in Galatians run the risk of being much more sophisticated, creative, clever, and nuanced than Paul himself ever intended to be in Galatians in his ethical discourse.

Throughout the monograph, my argument has tried to demonstrate a close connection between Paul's statements about the *is* (God's saving action in Christ) and the *ought* (how Christians should live). In chapters three through five, I argued Paul does not neatly present theology or soteriology as an indicative in Galatians and then ethics as imperatives that flow from his earlier indicatives. Readers of Paul must do this to systematize his thinking into distinct theological categories, but the indicative-imperative paradigm, though still alive and well in certain readings of Paul, is a modern scholarly creation of which Paul himself does not even conceive in Galatians.

A better approach is to understand Paul's soteriology in Galatians as the good news about Jesus Christ, in whom God has fulfilled all his redemptive promises for Jews and Gentiles and for the cosmos. His soteriology in Galatians has within it both the *is* or the indicative (what God has done for Jews and Gentiles and for the world in Christ) and the *ought* or the imperative (how Jews and Gentiles in Christ should live in step with the Spirit in obedience to Christ) because of God's saving action in Christ. However, in my reading, Paul does not bifurcate theology from ethics, but his ethics are robustly theological in Galatians because his imperatives are grounded in God's saving action in Christ. Paul's gospel in Galatians announces Jesus died (Gal 1:4) for our sins and was resurrected from the dead (Gal 1:1) to deliver Jews and Gentiles from the present evil age (Gal 1:4); Jews and Gentiles as justified by faith alone in Christ alone (Gal 2:16); Jesus' death (and resurrection) as the pathway to receiving the Spirit and the life-giving power of the Spirit (Gal 1:1, 14; 3:2-5, 14; 4:6; 5:13–6:10); and Jesus as the means to new creation (Gal 6:15). Paul even states in Galatians he preached the gospel emphasizing these things to them. He says, "I am saying again to you, just as I said to you beforehand, that those who practice these things [i.e., the lust of the flesh] will not inherit the kingdom of God" (Gal 5:21; cf. Gal 5:16-21). This statement suggests that when Paul preached the gospel to the Galatians, once they believed, he exhorted them to walk in step with the Spirit.

In other letters, he commands his churches to walk in a manner worthy of the gospel (cf. Phil 1:27), which is another way of saying to work out your salvation by obeying the gospel because of God's saving action in Christ (cf. Phil 2:12-13). He articulates his gospel ministry focused on the "obedience of faith" among the Gentiles (Rom 1:5). He warns that since their salvation from God's wrath is closer than when they first believed, they must put off the deeds of darkness by behaving decently in the light (Rom 14:11-13). They must put on the Lord Jesus Christ and not gratify the desires of the flesh (Rom 14:14). He commands the Corinthians to cast out the incestuous fellow from their midst with the hope that maybe he would repent and be saved in the day of judgment (1 Cor 5:1-13). He tells the Ephesians that God made them alive together with Christ, when they were dead in trespasses and sin, to walk in the good works in which God prepared them to walk (Eph 2:1-10).

In Ephesians 4:17–5:20, Paul commands the Ephesians to walk in a manner worthy of their calling or they would not have an inheritance in the kingdom of God and Christ. He tells the Thessalonians they received his gospel in the power of the Spirit, imitated the apostles' conduct, and became an example to all to imitate Christ (1 Thess 1:4-10). He reminds them that when he preached the gospel of God to them, he also urged them to live lives worthy of the God who has effectually called them into his kingdom (1 Thess 2:7-12). Paul's gospel proclamation to the Thessalonians included exhortations about how to live holy lives to please God (1 Thess 4:1-2), because it is God's will for them to be morally upright and to abstain from all forms of immorality (1 Thess 4:2-8). Paul warns them that if they practice immorality, the Lord will punish them with eschatological judgment (1 Thess 4:6) because God called his people in Christ through the preaching of the gospel about Jesus to be pure and to live holy lives (1 Thess 4:7). However, if anyone rejects this instruction in the gospel, he rejects the very God who gives them the Holy Spirit (1 Thess 4:8).

To clarify, Paul articulates a difference in Galatians, and in his other letters, between justification by faith and walking in the Spirit. I went to great lengths in the preceding chapters to show a few of those differences. To make the point clear here: those who are justified by faith in Christ alone (i.e., those to whom God imputes Christ's perfect righteousness by faith in Christ and counts them as not guilty) can, will, and must walk in the Spirit to inherit the kingdom of God (cf. Gal 2:16–6:10). The point here is that different parts of Paul's soteriology, both justification by faith and walking in the Spirit, are part of God's saving action in Christ in Galatians. I argued Paul manifests the proof of justification by faith in the lives of the justified in this present evil age through a faithful walk of obedience in step with the behavioral qualities created within them by the Spirit. Justification by faith is proven in this present evil age only by a walk of obedience in step with the Spirit; living in step with the Spirit is part of God's saving action in Christ, and only those who are justified by faith and obey the gospel in step with the Spirit will inherit the kingdom of God. Otherwise, Paul's comments about the real possibility the Galatians will not inherit the kingdom of God if they walk away from Jesus and if they refuse to walk in obedience to the gospel in step with the Spirit make absolutely no sense in the letter (cf. Gal 2:16-21; 3:2-14; 5:3–6:10).

God's saving action in Christ gives those who have participated in this salvation by faith the personal agency to consciously experience justification by faith and to freely choose to live in step with the Spirit since the Spirit gives life and freedom (Gal 2:16-21; 3:2–4:31; 5:1, 13; 5:25). Paul's gospel creates eternal life in the lives of those who receive his gospel by faith so that those justified by faith alone will walk by the Spirit, live by the Spirit, and inherit the kingdom of God by sowing in the Spirit (Gal 2:16; 3:14; 5:5, 16-26; 6:8-9). In Galatians, Paul argues God's saving action in Christ for Jews and Gentiles and for the cosmos restores personal agency and effects ethical transformation because of the life given by the Spirit. This is made possible by Jesus' resurrection and his death for our sins to deliver us from the present evil age (Gal 1:4) and to deliver us from the curse of the law (Gal 3:13-14). God delivers us in Christ so that we would receive all of God's redemptive promises, realized because of Christ and internalized in us by the reception of the Spirit by faith (Gal 3:2-14; 4:5-6). Therefore, since we have life by the Spirit, Christians must daily walk in step in the power and realm of the Spirit. We can, must, and will reveal that we participate in God's vertical, horizontal, and cosmic saving action in Christ within the present evil age as we live in step with the Spirit so that we will inherit the kingdom of God.

PERSONAL AGENCY, CONTEMPORARY RACIAL AND ETHNIC DISCOURSE, AND THE ETHICS OF SOCIAL ORDER IN THE PUBLIC SQUARE

There are many areas of contemporary ethical discourse to which one could apply my thesis, my arguments, and my exegetical and theological reflections in this monograph. Here I apply them to personal agency, contemporary racial and ethnic discourse in the public square, and to "social order."[1] There is much conversation about personal agency in the contemporary race conversation and in discussions about social action. Popular talking points in the media or other areas of public discourse often use the phrase personal agency as being synonymous with a so-called bootstrapping work ethic to the neglect of recognizing the very real systemic social factors that limit the ability of certain people in certain communities to flourish, even as they exercise personal agency and work hard.[2] Certainly, personal agency and personal responsibility are important. In my view, although not everyone in the world has equal opportunities, everyone has personal agency to choose, even while their options might be limited because of their social contexts or unquestionable systemic oppression that exists in certain parts of the world. Furthermore, there are many who fail to exercise their personal agency and circumvent making responsible, personal social choices, which only make their difficult situations even more difficult. Even still, with God's

---

[1] By social order, I mean walking in step with the Spirit in society by working out one's faith by love for God and love for neighbor as oneself. I borrow the phrase "social order" from the Baptist Faith & Message 2000 Article XV.

[2] These systemic factors are not necessarily racial, but may simply be related to geographic, religious, tribal, linguistic, ethnic, and social statues.

help, hard work, good personal choices, personal responsibility, the right opportunities, and the right resources, those with limited options have and can overcome even the most difficult circumstances.

However, in Galatians, personal agency is not about one's own personal bootstrapping work ethic; it is connected to God's saving action in Christ. Personal agency in Galatians refers to the Spirit's ability, because of Christ's death and resurrection and because of God's saving action in Christ, to liberate Jews and Gentiles in Christ so that they are now free in Christ to be slaves of love toward one another and to love their neighbors as themselves. That is, personal agency, as Paul discusses it in Galatians, is for the service of love for God, Christ, and others in the power of the Spirit as Christians love God, Christ, and one another, love their neighbors as themselves, and bear one another's burdens (Gal 5:13–6:2). Paul's various imperatives in Galatians support the premise that personal agency is to be used in service of love for God and for one another to build one another up, not as a weapon to gratify the flesh (Gal 5:13-14), which would include one's boasting in a so-called bootstrapping work ethic.

A closer look at personal agency in Galatians. Paul's use of imperatives in the central section of the letter gives insight into his conception of personal agency in Christ. In Galatians 3:7, Paul commands the Galatians to know ("you know"; γινώσκετε) that those from faith are sons of Abraham. In Galatians 4:12, he commands the Galatians to become (Γίνεσθε) as he is. In Galatians 5:1, he says because Christ has freed us (Τῇ ἐλευθερίᾳ ἡμᾶς Χριστὸς ἠλευθέρωσεν), "you all stand firm" (στήκετε) and "do not be subject again to a yoke of slavery" (μὴ πάλιν ζυγῷ δουλείας ἐνέχεσθε). In Galatians 5:13, he commands the Galatians to use their freedom as occasion to be slaves of one another in love (διὰ τῆς ἀγάπης δουλεύετε ἀλλήλοις) because the whole Mosaic law is fulfilled in love (Gal 5:14; cf. Lev 19:18). In Galatians 5:15-16, he commands the Galatians to "beware" (βλέπετε) and to "walk in the Spirit" (πνεύματι περιπατεῖτε). In Galatians 6:2, he commands the Galatians to "restore" (καταρτίζετε) a brother or sister who falls into a certain transgression with compassion by means of the Spirit and to "bear the burdens of one another" (Ἀλλήλων τὰ βάρη βαστάζετε) and so fulfill Christ's law. In Galatians 6:7, he commands the Galatians not to be deceived (Μὴ πλανᾶσθε) because God will not be mocked.[3]

Each of the above imperatives appeals to the Galatians' personal agency that God both gave to them and liberated them by means of his saving action in Christ so that they would consider their status as sons of Abraham in Christ, and so that they would use their freedom in Christ to serve one another in love and to love their neighbors as themselves. Personal agency is given to the Galatians in Christ so that they would walk in the Spirit and serve others,[4] not so that they can bootstrap their way to a higher class of spiritual and social hierarchy to the neglect of their neighbors (cf. Gal 3:28). Because Paul's concept of personal agency is grounded in God's saving action in Christ for Jews and Gentiles and for the world, his understanding of personal agency is very relevant to the ethics of contemporary racial and ethnic discourse in the public square and to other aspects of social engagement.

Public discourse about race, ethnicity, and the social order. The social constructs of race and ethnicity are complex, and there are important conversations related to their similarities and their differences in the ancient world and in the modern world. For my purposes here, however, I simply acknowledge a distinction between the concept of ethnicity in Galatians and the concept of race in the complex US context.[5] Ethnicity in Galatians and in the contemporary US context are not exactly correlative to one another. However, as I have argued elsewhere, ethnicity in the contemporary world is more akin to ethnicity in Galatians than to the modern construct of race. In Galatians, the concept

---

[3]Grant Buchanan makes a similar point in "Identity and Agency in Galatians 5-6," *ABR* 68 (2020): 54-66, esp. 59-62.

[4]See also the second person plural verbs in the letter that speak to the Galatians' personal agency (Gal 1:6, 9, 13; 3:2-4, 7, 26-29; 4:6, 8-10, 12-15, 17, 21, 28; 5:1-2, 4, 7, 10, 13, 15-18; 6:1-2, 7, 11). An important second persona plural verb is in Gal 5:16. Paul says: "walk in the Spirit" (πνεύματι περιπατεῖτε), and, if they do, "you shall by no means fulfill the lust of the flesh" (καὶ ἐπιθυμίαν σαρκὸς οὐ μὴ τελέσητε).

[5]For a discussion of key terms and a bibliography, see Jarvis J. Williams, *Redemptive Kingdom Diversity: A Biblical Theology of the People of God* (Grand Rapids, MI: Baker, 2021), 4-8, 12-14, 152-73.

of ethnicity relates to cultures, values, dialects, patterns of life, geography, and so on. It has absolutely nothing to do with the color of one's skin. In Galatians, Jews are a diverse ethnicity, and Gentiles consist of several diverse ethnicities. Both Jews and Gentiles may have had dark skin, light skin, and a shade of skin in between. The color of one's skin did not determine Jewish identity, but Torah and being born of the seed of Abraham and David did. Likewise, the color of one's skin did not make one a Gentile, but one's birth outside of the seed of David and Abraham, in addition to diverse cultural and geographic factors, gave one a specific Gentile identity. One could, for example, be a Jew whether he was born in Egypt or in Jerusalem, and whether one was a Greek speaking Jew or an Aramaic speaking Jew. Likewise, one was a Gentile whether he was born in Rome or Africa, spoke Latin or Greek.

As many sociologists and historians have noted, race, on the other hand, is a biological fiction but a social reality in the complex colonial and US contexts. The historical origins of the concept of race and racism in the colonies and the US have to do with racial hierarchy within the human race.[6] In this sense, our modern notion of race in the colonies and in US history has no parallel in Galatians or in the entire Bible.

The point that many have incontrovertibly made for years, but one that far too few people still understand, is that while there are different ethnicities within the one human race, there are not any different racial

---

[6]For work on the construction of race in the Protestant Atlantic world and its impact on certain aspects of Protestant Christianity, see Colin Kidd, *The Forging of Races in the Protestant Atlantic World: Race and Scripture in the Protestant Atlantic World, 1600-2000* (Cambridge: Cambridge University Press, 2009). For work on the construction of race in the colonies and in the US, its function, and its impact on certain expressions of American Christianity, see also Michael O. Emerson and Christian Smith, *Divided by Faith: Evangelical Religion and the Problem of Race in America* (Oxford: Oxford University Press, 2001); Richard A. Bailey, *Race and Redemption in Puritan New England, Religion in America* (New York: Oxford University Press, 2011); Rebecca Anne Goetz, *The Baptism of Early Virginia: How Christianity Created Race* (Baltimore: Johns Hopkins University Press, 2012); Carolyn Renee Dupont, *Mississippi Praying Southern White Evangelicals and the Civil Rights Movement, 1945-1975* (New York: New York University Press, 2015); Mary Beth Swetnam Matthews, *Doctrine and Race: African American Evangelicals and Fundamentalism Between the Wars* (Tuscaloosa: University of Alabama Press, 2017); Donald G. Mathews, *At the Altar of Lynching: Burning Sam Hose in the American South*, Cambridge Studies on the American South (Cambridge: Cambridge University Press, 2017); Richard Rothstein, *The Color of Law: A Forgotten History of How Our Government Segregated America* (New York: Liveright, 2017).

204 THE SPIRIT, ETHICS, AND ETERNAL LIFE

groups of humans within the human race on the basis of biological superiority and inferiority. There is only one race of people, namely, humans, but there are different ethnicities of people within the same human race and within the same ethnicity and with different colors of skin within the one ethnically diverse human race. However, one's skin color has nothing to do with one's ethnicity. There are dark-skinned African Americans and dark-skinned Dominicans, and there are light-skinned African Americans and dark-skinned Anglo-Americans. The concept of race that identifies people as Black or White and that forces people to choose one of these two racial groups or another is a social invention created and developed in the colonies in the 1600s that then took on a life of its own in the US. God created one human race with many different ethnicities, but human beings created different racial groups of people within the one human race. As a result, the US has been sadly reaping the fruit of this transgression since the 1600s.[7] An African immigrant and friend of mine made this point to me in a very powerful way in personal conversation. He said, "when I lived in Africa, I was a human being, but when I came to America, I was told by Americans that I was Black." That proves the point I am making in a powerful way. God creates humans in his image, but then humans arbitrarily created the social fiction of racial groups within the one human race and forced (and continue to force) humans into a specific artificial racial box because of this social construct.

Ethnicity has nothing to do with race or skin color. In Paul's day, there were light-skinned Gentiles and dark-skinned Gentiles, but they were all Gentiles. There were Roman Gentiles, Cretan Gentiles, Greek Gentiles, Ephesian Gentiles, and so on, with different or the same color of skin. My point is not that stereotyping groups of people based on skin color and other biological perceptions was absent in the ancient world.[8]

---

[7]See sources cited in note above.
[8]For examples from primary ancient texts, see Rebecca F. Kennedy, C. Snydor Roy, and Max L. Goldman, eds., *Race and Ethnicity in the Classical World: An Anthology of Primary Sources in Translation* (Indianapolis: Hackett Publishing Company, 2013).

Instead, my point is these stereotypes were not based on a contemporary colonial and US understanding of race. The kind of racial construction developed in the colonies and then in the US was a new thing and unique to its context in the colonies and in the US. One's skin color did not make one a Jew or a Gentile in the Mediterranean world. There were Jews in Jerusalem, Egyptian Jews, Hellenistic Jews, and so on. Yet, they were all Jews. So, there is not a direct one-to-one correlation between what Paul says about Jewish and Gentile identities in Galatians and the more recent concept and invention of the idea of race and the notion that different races of people exist within the one human race.[9]

Nevertheless, Galatians 2:11-14 is a helpful text in the discussion about the ethics of contemporary racial and ethnic discourse in the public square and provides some theological resources to help Christians establish a Christian ethic of "social order" in the contemporary public square.[10]

In Galatians 2:11-14,[11] Paul explicitly builds upon the Jew-Gentile distinction he creates in the letter to emphasize their unity in Christ by faith apart from works of the law because of God's saving action in Christ. In Galatians 2:14, he states Jewish Christians should not compel the τὰ ἔθνη to become Jews (Gal 2:14). In Galatians 2:12, the term τῶν ἐθνῶν ("of the Gentiles"), the phrase τοὺς ἐκ περιτομῆς ("those from the circumcision"), and his reference to Peter (a Jew) gives a non-Jewish reference to τὰ ἔθνη ("Gentiles") in Galatians 2:11-14. The terms Ἰουδαῖος ("Jew/Judean") (Gal 2:14), ἐθνικῶς ("Gentile manner of life") (Gal 2:14), Ἰουδαϊκῶς

---

[9]To see my view worked out from Genesis through Revelation and applied to contemporary racial and ethnic discourse, see Jarvis J. Williams, *Redemptive Kingdom Diversity: A Biblical Theology of the People of God* (Grand Rapids, MI: Baker, 2021).

[10]Material in the above discussion comes from my co-authored essay with Trey Moss, "All Nations as Integral Component of World Mission Strategy," in *World Mission: Theology, Strategy, and Current Issues* (Bellingham, WA: Lexham, 2019), 131-48. Material used here with permission. For recent work on Gentile identity, see Terence L. Donaldson, *Gentile Christian Identity from Cornelius to Constantine: The Nations, the Parting of the Ways, and Roman Imperial Ideology* (Grand Rapids, MI: Eerdmans, 2020).

[11]Gal 2:11-14 and the crisis in Antioch present different interpretive challenges. For a discussion of the issues in Gal 2:11-14, see commentary and bibliography in A. Andrew Das, *Galatians* (St. Louis: Concordia, 2014), 196-231.

("Jewish manner of life") (Gal 2:14), and ἰουδαΐζειν ("to live a Jewish manner of life") (Gal 2:14) support both the Jew-Gentile binary and the ethnically specific reference to τὰ ἔθνη ("Gentiles") in Galatians 2:12.

Paul says Peter's act of separating from table fellowship with the ἐθνῶν ("Gentiles") led Barnabas (a Jew) and the rest of the Ἰουδαῖοι ("Jews/Judeans") to be complicit in Peter's ethnocentric hypocrisy (Gal 2:13), and their hypocrisy was out of step with the gospel (Gal 2:14). Paul, consequently, condemned Peter in the presence of "all" (in the presence of Jewish and Gentile Christ followers) (Gal 2:14) because of his behavior. Peter stood condemned by his actions (Gal 2:11) because he was out of step with Paul's gospel about God's saving action in Christ for Jews and Gentiles, a gospel that he received from God. God commissioned him to preach Jesus as good news to the τὰ ἔθνη (Gal 1:1, 6-12, 16-24; 2:11, 14; cf. Gal 1:16). This gospel, Paul says, in Galatians 3 gives Jews and Gentiles the blessing of Abraham by faith, which is realized in their reception of the Spirit by faith because of God's saving action in Christ for Jews and Gentiles.

For example, in Galatians 3:1-14 Paul argues the τὰ ἔθνη[12] do not need to be law-observant to receive the promises of Abraham (Gal 3:1-29). In Galatians 3:8, Paul uses τὰ ἔθνη to express that God's promise to bless the πάντα τὰ ἔθνη ("all the Gentiles") in Abraham is realized by the justification by faith of Jews and Gentiles in Christ apart from works of the law (cf. Gen 12:3; 18:18; 22:18; 26:4; 28:14). Paul's certainty that the Abrahamic blessing extends to Gentiles through a faith analogous to Abraham's is based on Christ's (Abraham's true offspring [Gal 3:16]) death and resurrection (Gal 1:4; 3:1, 13-14).[13] Paul uses τὰ ἔθνη alongside a conflation of multiple scriptural texts (cf. Gen 12:1-3; 15:6 with Gal 3:6-9, 16; Deut 21:23; 27:26; 28:58; 30:10 with Gal 3:10-14).[14]

---

[12]The word for Gentiles (τὰ ἔθνη) frequently appears in the first three chapters of Galatians. For a few examples, see Gal 1:16; 2:2, 8, 9, 12; 3:8, 14.

[13]On how faith justifies, see rightly Thomas R. Schreiner, *Galatians*, ZECNT (Grand Rapids, MI: Zondervan, 2010), 197-98.

[14]For primary texts, see Das, *Galatians*, 283. For a work on thematic narratives in Galatians, see A. Andrew Das, *Paul and the Stories of Israel: Grand Thematic Narratives in Galatians* (Minneapolis: Fortress, 2016). Das cautions readers of Paul's letters to avoid seeking "comprehensive stories" behind the letters of Paul, while he also offers a helpful path forward.

Paul quotes, for example, Genesis 15:6 in Galatians 3:6. Genesis 15:6 emphasizes that Abram (an uncircumcised non-Jew at that point in the biblical narrative) received right standing in the presence of God by faith apart from observance of the law before he was circumcised (cf. Gen 17). He applies these Jewish Scriptures to Jews and Gentiles with faith in Christ in the light of Jesus' death and resurrection (cf. Lev 18:5; Hab 2:4 with Gal 3:11-14).[15] God's universal work of justifying Jews and Gentiles by faith apart from works of the law fuels Paul's ensuing comments in Galatians 3:28 about the unity of Jews and Gentiles in Christ. The τὰ ἔθνη ("Gentiles") and the πάντα τὰ ἔθνη ("all the Gentiles") receive an equal distribution of the Spirit in Christ apart from works of the law (Gal 3:10-14). Jews and Gentiles by faith in Christ receive an equal portion of Abraham's inheritance and the Spirit by faith (Gal 3:29), even as their distinct ethnic and social markers remain apparent for all to see in the church and in society (esp. Gal 3:28). Therefore, they should use their freedom in Christ as an occasion to become slaves of one another in love (Gal 5:13-14), not as an occasion to gratify their sinful flesh, as they walk in the Spirit and by no means fulfill the lust of the flesh (Gal 5:16–6:10), since Jews and Gentile are all one in Christ (Gal 3:28). Because of God's saving action for Jews and Gentiles and for the world in Christ, Jews and Gentiles must rightly relate to one another horizontally in the church and in society (cf. Gal 3:28; 6:10).

The arguments put forth in this book about Paul's view of the Spirit, personal agency, ethical transformation, and eternal life in Galatians provide some important biblical and theological resources to help Christians develop a Christian social ethic (= doing what is right in society as we love God and neighbor as ourselves),[16] and this social ethic must not

---

[15]For work focusing on scriptural echoes, citations, and allusions in Paul, see Richard B. Hays, *Echoes of Scripture in the Letters of Paul* (New Haven: Yale University Press, 1993). For work focusing on Paul's hermeneutics of faith, see Francis Watson, *Paul and the Hermeneutics of Faith*, 2nd ed. (New York: T&T Clark, 2015).

[16]By Christian social ethic, I simply mean a commitment to doing what is right in the present evil age as we work out our faith in love for God and for our neighbors as ourselves. By the phrase *social ethic*, I do not refer to any ideological or political agenda pushed by those on the left, in the middle, or on the right.

THE SPIRIT, ETHICS, AND ETERNAL LIFE

be divorced from Paul's theology. Contrary to the vertical, horizontal, and cosmic vision of Paul's understanding of God's saving action in Christ for Jews and Gentiles and for the world, certain scholars and contemporary readers of Paul and Bible teachers may divorce his theology from his ethics. Divorcing Paul's ethics in Galatians from his theology is perhaps one of the unhelpful vestiges of modern critical New Testament scholarship from the early part of the twentieth century,[17] as critical scholars theorized about Paul's coherency as a thinker and as they fragmented his theology from his ethics.

As a result, there may be those within Christian contexts today who still may employ a hermeneutic that continues to divorce Paul's ethics from his theology in ways more akin to aspects of critical scholarship than the way Paul intended interpreters to read his theological ethics in Galatians, even as they claim to uphold the importance of the Scriptures for their faith and practice. Consequently, it should be no surprise to Christians today that more than one expression of Christianity in the modern and contemporary West either has a social ethic completely divorced from Paul's theology, while others have no consistent theological ethic for social engagement. This may explain in part why certain expressions of Christianity in the contemporary West lack the necessary biblical and theological resources to be helpful to racial and ethnic discourse in the public square or to be helpful in a Christian ethic of social engagement, even as some in the Christian West claim both to understand Paul's theology and to be defenders of it.[18]

---

[17]For the most comprehensive history of the discipline of New Testament scholarship, see William H. Baird, *History of New Testament Research: From Deism to Tubingen*, vol. 1 (Minneapolis: Fortress, 1992); *History of New Testament Research: From Jonathan Edwards to Rudolf Bultmann*, vol. 2 (Minneapolis: Fortress, 2002); *History of New Testament Research: From C. H. Dodd to Hans Dieter Betz*, vol. 3 (Minneapolis: Fortress, 2013).

[18]Bible readers who have historically read Scripture from a context of social oppression did not have the luxury of divorcing the Bible's theology from its social ethics. To the contrary, the readings of those who were part of oppressed communities came both from a hermeneutic of resistance against oppression and from a hermeneutic of hope for their liberation in this world and in the world to come. For a few examples of this in work on an African American reception history of the Bible in slave contexts, see Emerson B. Powery and Rodney S. Sadler Jr., eds., *The Genesis of Liberation: Biblical Interpretation in the Antebellum Narratives of the Enslaved* (Louisville: Westminster John Knox, 2016); Esau McCaulley, *Reading While Black: African American*

There are always exceptions, but when Christians without a carefully constructed biblically and theologically shaped social ethic, and without the necessary cultural awareness and critical self-reflection, engage in racial and ethnic discourse in the public square, we can speak in these dialogues in ways often void of wisdom, grace, truth, charity, and awareness. I know these things are certainly true in my own personal experience as I have unintentionally and with good intentions said things that have unfortunately offended and hurt people whom I dearly love because of my own lack of clarity, lack of nuance, lack of understanding, and imprecision in racial and ethnic discourse in the public square. We all sin and fall short in our words and deeds in many ways in public discourse. Thankfully, Paul's gospel in Galatians includes forgiveness and reconciliation because of God's saving action in Christ. Yet, thoughtful and patient reflection, transformed by the Spirit, on pressing issues of the day can help us as Christians be more effective and more helpful in contemporary conversations about race and ethnicity and in practicing a Christian ethic of social engagement on a host of other important ethical issues.

Too often contemporary dialogues about race, ethnicity, or any kind of social engagement in certain contexts have been guilty of hysteria and going to one of six extremes: (1) *ad hominem* personal attacks and character assassinations of faithful Christians who are simply trying to be faithful to Jesus and to love God and their neighbors as themselves; (2) a-theological discussions lacking a carefully constructed biblical and theological foundation that shapes the discourse, the methods, and the tone of public engagement; (3) symbolic conversations that do not directly confront the historical problems of categorizing the many diverse people created in the image God in the one human race into different races of people and the problem of the many ways ethnic minorities of color are also guilty of the sin of racism against Whites and against other

Biblical Interpretation as An Exercise in Hope (Downers Grove, IL: InterVarsity Press, 2020); Lisa M. Bowens, *African American Readings of Paul: Reception, Resistance and Transformation* (Grand Rapids, MI: Eerdmans, 2020).

ethnic minorities as they wrongly prejudge or mistreat entire groups of people based on the transgressions of some within those groups; (4) mere photo opportunities filled with hugs, handshakes, symbolic gestures, and the platforming of token ethnic minorities and token Whites who will uncritically parrot certain views of certain Whites or certain Blacks on race on the left, in the middle, or the right; (5) disrespectful critiques of Whites, Blacks, and other ethnicities,[19] and shaming those racialized into these groups without the participants (Black or White or other ethnicities) offering critical self-reflection and critical self-evaluation; and (6) too much unnecessary obsession on the Black and White divide in the US and too much of a focus on reducing everything down to race, while ignoring the global needs in many ethnically diverse communities, than offering a rigorous analysis of sin's individual and cosmic impact on human alienation, and how the Scriptures should shape our identities and discourse of these things. There is also too much obsession with race in the current contemporary discourse, and not enough focus on what it means to be fully human created in the image of God and recreated in Christ by the Spirit because of Jesus' death and resurrection.

Of course, it is important to be culturally aware and sensitive in ways consistent with Scripture and common sense that enable humans to honor the human dignity in each other. My point is without a vision of ethical transformation grounded in God's saving action in Christ, certain conversations about race and ethnicity in the public square could become more concerned with keeping people divided and creating more racial resentment among groups of people forced into a particular racial box because of the superficial and fictive social construct of race than the promotion of Spirit-empowered love for our neighbors created in the image of God. There are public discussions of race and ethnicity that often seem to place one group at the center of the conversation and attempt to reduce other groups to the status of children or silence them

---

[19]Any person, action, word, or group can be subject to critique. My point is that disrespectful and dehumanizing critique is in accordance with the flesh and contrary to God's saving action in Christ for Jews and Gentiles and for the world.

in public discourse while treating them as though they are at the mercy of the one group fixing themselves before further progress can be made. Instead God's vertical, horizontal, and cosmic saving action in Christ for Jews and Gentiles and for the world should be kept at the center of the discourse as Christians discuss the truth, the differences, and the complexity of racial and ethnic division and as we seek to offer real, tangible, and redemptive solutions and tradeoffs by the power of the Spirit to the problems created by these divisions. Thus, the result of wrong-headed dialogues from those with no good will or wrong-headed conversations among those with good intentions can be unhelpful conversations that play to one's base, build a brand, or make some feel good about themselves, but this kind of discourse does not lead to the kind of redemptive thinking, living, or transformation that impacts the lives of the many real people in the world affected by the many forms of racial and ethnic division in a broken world.

A goal of thoughtful Christian public discourse on race, ethnicity, or any other social matter is not perfect agreement with our interlocutors, but a goal within Christian communities should be to think, speak, act, and disagree redemptively on important matters related, for example, to racial and ethnic discourse, so that we can be part of redemptive and sustained change going forward in a rapidly changing contemporary world because of God's saving action in Christ. Paul's letter to the Galatians provides us with important theological resources to help us think theologically about Christian engagement in the public square on ethical matters related to race and ethnicity, for ethical matters are theological matters in Galatians.

More to the point, as I have argued elsewhere,[20] the Jew-Gentile ethnic and social problems in the first century were not and are not the same as the social problems throughout US history and today. Still, there are insights Christians can glean from Paul's message in Galatians of God's saving action in Christ for Jews and Gentiles and for the world.

---

[20]Williams, *Redemptive Kingdom Diversity*.

We can apply Paul's holistic, redemptive message of God's saving action in Christ for Jews and Gentiles and for the world to our contemporary social problems, not the least of which are our problems related to racial and ethnic division and social engagement.

Of course, Christians should work hard to know our contexts, to grow in a basic understanding of our history and the many differences between race and ethnicity, as well as our own complex racialized histories, and to grow in our understanding of the racialized histories of which we are part, that we did not create, and that are not fundamentally about us. However, most Christians are not social scientists, historians, scholars of race, or insightful social and cultural critics—nor should they be. Thus, I think most Christians would be more effective spending their energies and time thinking about what the Scriptures actually say about ethical transformation and how they should shape and impact the way Christians engage in ethical discourse in the public square than trying to be omnicompetent cultural critics.

God in Christ actually creates in Christ a transformed community of ethnically diverse people by the power of the Spirit so that they would live in pursuit of redemptive love for God and redemptive love for their ethnically diverse neighbors in their communities in society.[21] God's holistic vertical, horizontal, and cosmic saving action in Christ, as Paul sets it forth in Galatians, can contribute much to the Christian contribution to racial and ethnic discourse in the public square, Christian social engagement,[22] and to a biblical and theological development of a sustainable and consistent Christian social ethic in the contemporary world, especially when we consider the theological underpinning of Paul's exhortations to love our neighbors as ourselves in Galatians 5:13–6:10, because of God's saving action in Christ. Jesus Christ, the divine liberator (Gal 1:4; 3:13), models this selfless sacrificial love for us by his death for us (Gal 2:19-20).

---

[21]To see this point worked out more extensively, see Williams, *Redemptive Kingdom Diversity*.

[22]By Christian social engagement, I simply mean Christian involvement in speaking to and working toward the flourishing of humans in society in ways that are consistent with the message of God's saving action in Christ.

Thoughts for Further Study

As a result of my study in this monograph, I have several questions related to the relationship between Pauline ethics and Christian social engagement in the public square that others may be interested in developing in future work. These questions include, but should not be limited to, the following. How would Christians' contributions to current racial and ethnic discourse in the public square and to a redemptive pursuit of "social order" be helped by maintaining a close connection between Paul's theology and ethics in our discourse and in our social engagement? This connection is grounded in Paul's message of vertical, horizontal, and cosmic saving action in Christ for Jews and Gentiles and for the world in Galatians. How would conversations about anti-Asian racism be different if they were shaped by a Pauline theological ethic?

How would Christians and churches be better equipped by the Spirit, with the Scriptures, and with common grace and common sense to work to protect life in the womb and to care for those who are poor and the most vulnerable in their congregations, institutions, or society? How would the practical outworking of Paul's message of God's saving action in Christ by the power of the Spirit impact, inform, and shape the ways Christians redemptively live, redemptively love one another, redemptively think, and redemptively love all our neighbors as ourselves in a rapidly changing world? How would the ways Christians think about and help alleviate the injustices committed against and experienced by Whites in society, and committed against and experienced by poor Whites in rural communities, as well as Spirit-empowered and dignified ways to minister to disadvantaged poor Whites in rural communities, especially in Appalachian communities, be different if these conversations were shaped by Paul's view of the Spirit, personal agency, eternal life, and ethical transformation in Galatians?[23]

---

[23]In my native land of Southeastern Kentucky in Appalachia, poverty, for example, is complex. It is not simply Black and White. Yes, it is structural, but poverty also exists among poor Whites and others there for many reasons, and one reason is because of bad personal choices. There are poor Whites in Appalachia who have escaped poverty because of hard work and good choices. My point here, however, is while there are structural factors that keep people in poverty

How would the rhetoric in racial and ethnic discourse among Christians be more redemptive and respectful on social media and in other areas of the public square if grounded in a Pauline theological ethic that is grounded in his presentation of God's saving action in Christ? How would a holistic understanding of God's saving action in Christ for Jews and Gentiles impact the way certain American Christians view global Christianity, the suffering of global Christians, and how churches with religious liberties can work for the alleviation of the suffering of those without such liberties in this present evil age? How would Paul's message of God's saving action in Christ shape how Christians and Christian churches with an abundance of material goods use and steward their resources with Christians and churches who struggle to meet their basic needs? How would Christians be able to continue contributing to the flourishing[24] of people in society today when they lose everything for reasons that are no fault of their own (e.g., to natural disasters like flooding, tornadoes, etc.) if we simply refused to divorce Paul's ethics from his theology and from practical Christian living?

---

in Appalachia, these factors may have nothing to do with structural racism. In my view, whether it's Black poverty or White poverty, not all poverty exists because of racial discrimination, and not all disparities prove there is racial discrimination or other forms of discrimination. There are poor Blacks and poor Whites in certain parts of Eastern Kentucky who are a lot better off financially than poor Whites in other parts of Eastern Kentucky. There are also working-class Blacks in Eastern Kentucky who are economically in better situations than working-class or poor Whites in the same community in Eastern Kentucky. These economic divisions have absolutely nothing to do with race or racism. In Eastern Kentucky, there is certainly a racial history. Yet, poverty there is more times than not based on geographic location, class divisions, or bad personal choices. If the Christian's view of poverty were shaped by a careful analysis of Paul's view of the Spirit, personal agency, eternal life, and ethical transformation in Galatians, in addition to common sense and relevant verifiable data unique to each social demographic, then how much more inclined would we be to allow for complexity and nuance when discussing issues related to poverty. As a result, how much more helpful would we be in living redemptively in our efforts to help the many people trapped in poverty for a whole set of complex reasons that may or may not be due to any fault of their own, and how much more helpful could we be in complex conversations about the complexities of poverty.

[24]By flourishing, I mean Christians living and helping others to live in a transformed way in the power of the Spirit in love for God and neighbors as well as ourselves and doing good to all people inside and outside the household of faith as often as it is possible for Christians to do so. I use the term *flourish* in a redemptive sense, and I use the term in connection with the arguments I have made throughout this monograph regarding the Spirit, personal agency, ethical transformation, and eternal life in Galatians.

A FINAL WORD

These questions, and many more, matter for Christians living in a rapidly changing contemporary world under the curse of sin with real people. Paul's theology in Galatians does not give any space whatsoever for Christians to be apathetic about or disengaged from loving our neighbors as ourselves and to be disengaged from showing compassion about the suffering of real people in the real world. His theological discourse in Galatians was presented in specific theological and social contexts in intense theological and social conflict for the purpose of theological formation and ethical transformation of the Christian communities to which he wrote. Paul's remarks about the Spirit, personal agency, ethical transformation, and eternal life in Galatians have much to contribute to current Christian ethical discourse in the public square and on many related matters pertaining to "the Christian and the social order."[25] In Christ Jesus, God has in fact given Christians everything they need for eternal life and godliness. Christians would do well to carefully consider afresh Paul's soteriology in Galatians and how it speaks to these matters in a world enslaved to sin and its power, because what seems to be dominating the vernacular in public discourse on many ethical matters from those on the left, in the middle, and the right is (as one scholar has said) constant "gridlock."[26]

Christians ought to be healthy and helpful agents of reconciliation, helpful contributors to public discourse, and helpful agents of Christ as we engage in public discourse and in matters related to the Christian and the social order with wisdom and grace. This would be a welcome alternative to all forms of race hysteria, race shaming, and social anarchy on the internet or in the real world. However, to be helpful ambassadors of Christ in any form of public discourse and to contribute redemptively

---

[25]I get the language of the "Christian and the social order" from article XV in the Baptist Faith and Message 2000, my theological tradition's doctrinal statement.

[26]See George Yancey, *Beyond Racial Gridlock: Embracing Mutual Responsibility* (Downers Grove, IL: IVP, 2006); *Beyond Racial Division: A Unifying Alternative to Colorblindness and Antiracism* (Downers Grove, IL: InterVarsity, 2022). Yancey uses the phrase "racial gridlock" because he is specifically talking about the discourse regarding race.

to Christian engagement in the pursuit of social order in this present evil age, the first place Christians must start is with sacred Scripture. We must refocus our attention on what the Scriptures clearly teach us about God's saving action in Christ and Christian living in the present evil age. We must, for example, carefully consider Paul's holistic vertical, horizontal, and cosmic message of God's saving action in Christ for the world, and we must be informed on the ways in which sin works in society to enslave people to its power.

Christians must not imitate the world, retreat from being concerned about social order, or run to our ideological ghettos, which those on the left, in the middle, and on the right may create for themselves to insulate themselves from the suffering of real people in this present evil age and to have their own blind spots and ignorance reinforced. Ideological ghettos tend to echo and affirm our own worst thoughts and actions about a host of important issues and about people. Ideological ghettos also tend to make us think our own personal and narrow experiences are normative and universal for all people; they reinforce our own biases of and our own ignorance toward others with those who share the same ignorance of and the same biases about social contexts and experiences different from our own, and they cause us to vilify anyone who does not live within our particular ideological ghetto. This mindset can hinder Christians from being redemptive in our public discourse and in our public engagement. Instead, Christians should evaluate all public discourse by and engage in all public discourse with a firm grasp of God's saving action in Christ, with a firm grasp of the issues based on data and facts, and with a firm grasp of how to apply God's work in Christ to pressing issues in the real world.

Paul's message about God's saving action in Christ for Jews and Gentiles and for the world in Galatians is not a magic pill that will make all the world's ethical problems go away if digested. Yet, Paul's message of God's saving action in Christ for Jews and Gentiles and for the cosmos offers redemptive hope and important theological resources to help Christians create and live out a Spirit-saturated and sustainable Christian ethic in the public square. Paul's message of God's saving action in Christ in Galatians is vertical, horizontal, and cosmic. Paul commands those transformed by the gospel to live by the Spirit by faith because we have received life in Christ by the Spirit by faith. Paul reminds us in Galatians since we have eternal life by the Spirit, those who profess faith in Christ *can, must,* and *will* conduct our daily lives by the power of the Spirit, in obedience to the gospel, and in pursuit of love for God and for our neighbors as ourselves, or else we will not inherit the kingdom of God (Gal 5:16–6:10; esp. Gal 5:21; cf. also Gal 6:8-9).

Scripture Index